THE NAUGHTY BITS

THE NAUGHTY BITS

*What The Censors Wouldn't Let You See
in Hollywood's Most Famous Movies*

NAT SEGALOFF

Foreword by D.W. Griffith

Sticking Place Books
New York 2024

The Author wishes to acknowledge research by the Writers Guild of America for uncovering the names of uncredited writers; the Internet Movie Database (IMDb) for listing uncredited writers, producers, and directors; and the American Film Institute catalogue for their trade paper research. General citation: Motion Picture Association of America. Production Code Administration records, Margaret Herrick Library, Academy of Motion Picture Arts and Sciences.

Oscar®, Academy Award®, and AMPAS® are registered trademarks of the Academy of Motion Picture Arts and Sciences ©AMPAS. The Movie Ratings® G, M, R, GP, PG, PG-13, and NC-17 are registered trademarks of the Motion Picture Association.

Nothing in this book should imply endorsement by the Motion Picture Association, the Academy of Motion Picture Arts and Sciences, or their related organizations. Internet links were accurate as of the editing of this book. Neither the publisher nor the author condones the illegal posting of copyrighted material.

© Nat Segaloff 2024

www.stickingplacebooks.com

Cover Illustration by Thomas Warming
©2024 Thomas Warming

Designed by Goran Tovilovic

All rights reserved. No part of this book may be reproduced, stored in or introduced into a retrieval system, or transmitted, in any form or by any means (electronic, mechanical, photocopying, recording or otherwise) without the written permission of the publishers, except in the case of brief quotations embodied in critical articles or reviews.

ISBN 978-1-942782-65-0

To Barry Krost
Confidante, teacher, co-conspirator, friend

Contents

Foreword by D.W. Griffith — 1

Introduction — 5

The Adventures of Robin Hood — 13
All About Eve — 17
The Apartment — 21
Baby Face — 23
The Best Man — 27
The Best Years of Our Lives — 31
The Birth of a Nation — 35
Blow-Up — 39
The Bridge on the River Kwai — 43
Bringing Up Baby — 47
Casablanca — 49
Convention City — 53
Crossfire — 59
Design for Living — 63
East of Eden — 67
Ecstasy — 71
The Gay Divorcee — 77
Gentleman's Agreement — 81
Gone with the Wind — 85
The Grapes of Wrath — 91
His Girl Friday — 95
Hud — 99
In the Heat of the Night — 103
Irma La Douce — 105
Jezebel — 109
Kiss Me, Stupid — 111
Lawrence of Arabia — 115
The Lost Weekend — 119
Love Affair — 123
The Maltese Falcon — 127
Mr. Smith Goes to Washington — 129

Monsieur Verdoux	133
Mutiny on the Bounty	137
Ninotchka	139
Of Mice and Men	141
Pinky	145
A Place in the Sun	149
Psycho	153
Rebel Without a Cause	155
Rope	157
The Searchers	159
Some Like It Hot	163
The Sound of Music	165
Stagecoach	167
The Story of Temple Drake	169
A Streetcar Named Desire	173
Sunset Boulevard	179
The Ten Commandments	181
These Three	183
Tom Jones	187
Touch of Evil	189
Trouble in Paradise	193
Vertigo	195
Who's Afraid of Virginia Woolf?	197
Afterword	201
Appendix 1: Production Code Administration Employees	205
Appendix 2: The Production Code	207
Bibliography	221
Author biography	223
Personnel Index	225

Foreword by D.W. Griffith

Extracted from "The Rise and Fall of Free Speech in America"

D.W. Griffith published this essay in 1916, in reaction to the controversy generated by his 1915 film The Birth of a Nation. *While Griffith did not (could not?) recognize the film's racism as the trigger for editorials, boycotts and riots, his arguments against the suppression of ideas in general remain valid. Although he specifically cites his film's struggles in Chicago (which had a particularly rigid board of censors), his warnings applied then, and continue to apply, across the country. (This excerpt maintains Griffith's phrasing and punctuation.)*

Freedom of speech and publication is guaranteed in the Constitution of the United States, and in the constitution of practically all the states. Unjustifiable speech or publication may be punished, but cannot be forbidden in advance. Mayor Gaynor,[1] that great jurist who stood out from the ordinary gallery-playing, hypocritical type of politician as a white rose stands out from a field of sewer-fed weeds, said in vetoing a moving picture censorship ordinance in the city of New York:

> Ours is a government of free speech and a free press. That is the cornerstone of free government. The phrase "The Press," includes all methods of expression by writing or pictures... If this (moving picture) ordinance be legal, then a similar ordinance in respect to the newspapers and the theaters generally would be legal.[2]

Today the censorship of moving pictures, throughout the entire country, is seriously hampering the growth of the art. Had intelligent opposition to censorship been employed when it first made itself manifest it could easily have been overcome. But the pygmy child of that day has grown to be, not merely a man, but a giant, and I tell you who read this, whether you will or no, he is a giant whose forces of evil are so strong that he threatens that priceless heritage of our nation – freedom of expression.

The right of free speech has cost centuries upon centuries of untold sufferings and agonies; it has cost rivers of blood; it has taken as its toll uncounted fields littered with the carcasses of human beings – all this that there might come to live and survive that wonderful thing, the power of free speech. In our country it has taken some of the best blood of our forefathers. The Revolution itself was a fight in this direction – for the God-given beautiful idea of free speech.

[...]

The motion picture is a medium of expression as clean and decent as any mankind has ever discovered. A people that would allow the suppression of this form of speech would unquestionably submit to the suppression of that which we all consider so highly, the printing press.

And yet we find all through the country, among all classes of people, the idea that the motion picture should be censored.

When the first small board of censorship was established six years ago, we who took it seriously then, expected exactly what has come to pass – that a man of the mental caliber of the captain of police of Chicago can tell two million American people what they shall and shall not go to see in the way of a moving picture.

They tell us we must not show crime in motion picture. We cannot listen to such nonsense. These people would not have us show the glories and beauties of the most wonderful moral lesson the world has ever known – the life of Christ – because in that story we must show the vice of the traitor Judas Iscariot. Had the modern censors existed in past ages, and followed out their theories to a logical conclusion, there would have been written no Iliad of Homer; there would not have been written for the glory of the human race that grand cadence of uplift called the Bible; there would have been no Goethe. There would have been no thrilling, beautiful dramas given us as the grandest heritage of the English-speaking race – the plays of Shakespeare. And even today, none of the creations would these worthy censors leave in our possession, had they their way.

[…]

In other words, so long as censorship holds the motion picture under its thumb, it is in every way enslaved. It dares not speak the truth on any subject, and therefore must confine itself to ridiculous, injurious and childish slap-stick and absurd and weak dramatology. The moral reformers plead with us to put on pictures which speak editorially against certain evils of the day. How does any man dare to invest his money in any picture that speaks against any certain class or condition of people, however evil and open to condemnation their works may be, when he knows how easy it is for a few individuals to go to any one of the many hundreds of censorship boards in the country and influence them to destroy the property which the producer has gone to great pains and care to build up?

However alluring the theory of censorship may be to certain well-meaning people, in its practical working out, experience has taught us that whatever section or class of the people may feel offended by a particular production, their objection is found to have a vote value to the politicians, who in turn are very often influential in the actual work of the censors.

[…]

So long as this matter of censorship is allowed, so long as in a city the size of Chicago, for example, one or more men may tell two million persons what they shall or shall not see in a motion picture in the theaters of Chicago – so long as this is allowed – so long as even one man is given the privilege over another of deciding for him the thing he shall or shall not see in the way of even the simplest of motion pictures – then there is no such thing as entire freedom of speech in that community.

[...]

I thoroughly believe that the principal reason for the popularity of the motion picture is that it softens the hard life of the plain people with beauty and sweetness. It keeps men away from saloons and drink, because it gives them a place of recreation in pleasant surroundings, it brings to the poor who are unable to travel away from their own dingy surroundings, the beauty and poetry of living foreign scenes, of people, of flowers, and waving grasses.

[...]

According to the theory of the censors, the moving picture producers must slavishly avoid the truth, for fear of treading on the toes of races, politicians, and individuals. With a censorship board dictating what pictures are to be produced and displayed, truth is not to be pictured, but a sugarcoated, virtuously-garbed virgin alone can be presented, in order to satisfy the public mentors of our so-called morals.

[...]

It is said the motion picture tells its story more vividly than any other art. In other words, we are to be blamed for efficiency, for completeness. Is this justice? Is this common sense? We do not think so.

We have no wish to offend with indecencies or obscenities, but we do demand, as a right, the liberty to show the dark side of wrong, that we may illuminate the bright side of virtue – the same beauty that is conceded to the art of the written word – that art to which we owe the Bible and the words of Shakespeare.

---

1. William Jay Gaynor was mayor of New York City from 1910 to 1913.
2. Nevertheless, in 1921, New York established the New York State Motion Picture Commission, one of the most restrictive censorship boards in the country.

Introduction

Censorship in a free society may be odious, but some of it is legal. The First Amendment to the United States Constitution reads, "Congress shall make no law respecting an establishment of religion, or prohibiting the free exercise thereof; *or abridging the freedom of speech, or of the press* [emphasis added]; or the right of the people peaceably to assemble, and to petition the Government for a redress of grievances." Freedom of speech was so dear to the Founders that it was the first thing they put into their newly written Constitution in order to limit the powers of the government that they had just created. Then and now, the First Amendment means that the government may not curtail speech. This is why any government body that bans books, passes don't-say-gay, anti-Israel/BDS, or other such laws, has voted for a patently unconstitutional measure that the U.S. Supreme Court should be expected to overturn.

That's not what this book is about, because private institutions can ban, restrict, curtail, sanction and otherwise do as they wish with freedom of speech. This is why Twitter/X, YouTube, Facebook and other social media can censor or block users,[1] PayPal can refuse to allow business from adult entertainment accounts, colleges[2] can bar students from using Wikipedia, and even the ACLU can discipline its staff and Board members if they use speech that other Board members consider offensive.

The same holds true for movies.

In other words, Hollywood can censor itself and, for over forty years, it did. The film industry's censorship entity was the Production Code Administration, and from its founding in 1934 to its radical reorganizing in 1968, no motion picture could be released in America from a member film company that did not adhere to the letter of the Motion Picture Production Code of Self-Regulation and Censorship. Colloquially known as "the Code," the PCA held sway over its member film companies' features, shorts, serials, trailers, advertising, and titles. Their archive, currently housed at the Margaret Herrick Library of the Academy of Motion Picture Arts and Sciences in Beverly Hills, California, offers remarkable insight into the minds of the industry's censors.

It's easy to ridicule censors. The most common criticism of those who appoint themselves guardians of public morality is that they insist that they aren't affected by what they're censoring, they are only protecting others. When Lenny Bruce was busted for obscenity in the 1960s, it was never because anyone in his appreciative audience complained – it was because of the policemen who stood in the back of the nightclub (having been admitted for free with their badges, no doubt) waiting for him to say something blue. How policemen, who fought murderers, thieves and wife-beaters, and who probably used the same language among each other, could be offended by a comedian's language on stage is a hypocrisy beyond discussion. But that's what censorship is.

Movie censorship was born out of pragmatism, a pragmatism which, on inspection, reveals a deep cynicism in the American character: how can we boast that we're the best country on earth when our actions say our democracy is so fragile that it can be destroyed by words and thinking? Just as a movie hero is no stronger than the villain with whom he must do battle, the necessity for the Production Code is proof that community leaders deem the public too weak to face reality. The examples that follow are not only about sex; they address race, national origin, sexism, stereotypes, language and attitudes – any of which, even seen within the context of their times, offends somebody, somewhere.

In a bizarre way, the Production Code Administration was "woke" a century before snowflakes. It was created by social and religious conservatives to enshrine ideals that were, for the most part, understandable: not exposing people to new ideas before they were ready for them – except in doing so, they also restricted artistic expression and suppressed progressive thought.

But the Code was not cut-and-dried, nor were the people who administered it, and this is something this book quite surprisingly reveals.

In an old Friar's Club roast of Humphrey Bogart from the 1950s that has circulated for decades on bootleg audio recordings, actor Charles Coburn tells a joke that he says perfectly describes the mind of a censor, a way of thinking that has to see the dirty side of everything, just in case:

A traveling troupe of entertainers arrives in a small town and announces their presence. Almost immediately a man introduces himself to the company manager as the local censor. "If you say anything vulgar," the man says, "I'll close your show."

"That's strange," the company manager says, "because we pride ourselves in having a very clean show."

"Never you mind that," the self-appointed censor says, "I'll be in the front row for your first performance and if you say anything dirty, I'll close you down."

Sure enough, the show begins and this man is in the first row all primed. There are two comics on stage and the first comic says, "What's the best thing about a woman?"

The second comic says, "I don't know, Mr. Bones, what is the best thing about a woman?"

With this, the censor stands up and shouts, "If you say *pussy*, I'm closing the show!"

*

When did movie censorship begin? It may have started with Fatima, also known as "Little Egypt," a belly dancer who shook her booty and anything else that shimmied in the "A Street in Cairo" number at Chicago's 1893 World Columbian Exposition. Her real name was Fahreda Mazar Spyropoulos and she was twenty-two at the time, having gained a modicum of fame at the

Bird Cage Theater in Tombstone, Arizona just prior to being engaged by showman Sol Bloom and producer Gaston Akoum to appear with his Raqs dance troupe at the Chicago fair.[3] Performing what became known as the "hoochie koochie" dance, she gyrated – fully clothed, mind you – not only to thrilled live audiences but, three years later, before the camera of the Thomas A. Edison company. Directed by James H. White and exhibited in both peepshow machines[4] and a growing number of nickelodeon theaters, she became a sensation. She also became a target for early forces of censorship who demanded that certain parts of her body be obscured if she were to be shown in public.[5]

That same year saw the release of *The Kiss*, a scandalous moment from the 1895 play *The Widow Jones* enacted before Edison's camera by its stars May Irwin and John C. Rice. Lasting less than one minute, its close-up smooch caused the Catholic church to call for its suppression (kissing in public was illegal at the time). But the public loved it, and prints of the sixty-foot, 35mm film were sold to exhibitors for the agreeable sum of $7.50 (about $250 now) and shown promiscuously at the end of almost every show as an audience lagniappe.

Censors soon locked horns with what people then called the "flickers."[6] Cheap to see, presented in spartan venues, and silent (no language barriers) – except perhaps for a piano – they quickly became a favorite of lower classes and immigrants who flocked to them as affordable entertainment. This made movies a perfect target for self-righteous citizens who wanted to protect the masses from moral corruption (ignoring that jobs, education and affordable housing might be a better savior). Thus the stage was set early on for a showdown between moralists and movies.

Yet for the next two decades the skirmishes were carried out at the local level; that is, some church committee or women's group here or there would lean on a neighborhood movie house to shutter a film, or pressure a distributor to make cuts before a picture could be shown in their municipality. This was inconvenient for film companies, which had to create different versions of every release for different locations and then restore the deleted footage when the prints were shipped to another territory that might have different mores. There was no codified set of rules.

Throughout all this there was the omnipresent threat that Congress would step in and become America's official censorship board. Two things made this a real possibility. One, the First Amendment, which, although it had been in the U.S. Constitution since the Bill of Rights was passed in 1791, had not been fully upheld until the American Civil Liberties Union was formed in 1920 and began litigating it. Two, motion pictures were not protected by the First Amendment until 1952.[7]

Then, as now, picking a fight with the movies was good publicity. Chicago holds the distinction of having America's first movie censorship board, created in 1907. In 1909, the idea went national when Protestant leaders in New York City formed the National Board of Censorship. In 1914, the Women's Christian Temperance Union declared movies to be addictive, as they had already declared alcohol to be.[8] What's revelatory is that none of these or similar organizations were in the least embarrassed to call themselves censors.

With the rise of the studio system, adventurous movie content might have become an audience draw, like fights at hockey games or pile-ups at the Indy 500, had it not been for a series of public scandals emanating from Hollywood, which is where the American film industry became centered by the late 1910s. It's not necessary to rehash the details here, only the docket: the murder of director William Desmond Taylor (1922), the drug death of top star Wallace Reid (1923), the unexplained shooting death of director Thomas Ince (1924), revelations of comedienne Mabel Normand's involvement in the William Desmond Taylor affair (1924), and, of course, the three 1921-22 rape/murder trials and the ineffectual exoneration of Roscoe "Fatty" Arbuckle. All these fed the headlines about the film community's vice sans shame.

Hollywood censorship was an outgrowth of crisis management. In 1922, to mollify public revulsion over Tinseltown scandals as well as to consolidate their lobbying strength in Congress, the major film companies formed the Motion Picture Producers and Distributors of America (MPPDA) and hired former U.S. Postmaster General Will H. Hays to run it. While the '20s roared, in 1924 Hays asked his member studios to submit to him in advance the plots of films they intended to produce, and he would then apply what he called "The Formula" to determine if there might be problems down the road with local censors. This was met with indifference by studios, and so, in 1927, Hays assembled a committee that included Irving G. Thalberg of newly formed Metro-Goldwyn-Mayer, Fox Film Corporation's Sol Wurtzel, and E.H. Allen of Paramount. These men devised a list of "Don'ts and Be Carefuls" that producers should avoid, got the Federal Trade Commission to approve it, and created the Studio Relations Committee to enforce it. Still, nobody cared.

In 1929, Hays got tired of the SRC's torpor and the next year introduced "A Code to Maintain Social and Community Values in the Production of Silent, Synchronized, and Talking Motion Pictures." Published in a pamphlet titled "A Code to Govern the Making of Motion Pictures," it quickly came to be called The Production Code. Hays administered it himself (it was dubbed "The Hays Office," and Hays himself was nicknamed "the czar of all the rushes") until he had to face the fact that he was still toothless and needed to bring in some muscle. This is when he promoted Joe Breen.

Joseph Ignatius Breen, a Catholic layman and former journalist, became head of the Production Code Administration in spring 1934, though he had joined the organization earlier as its public relations director.[9] History has tended to misrepresent him because of what he did for a living. Breen was a remarkable man. He used a combination of an iron fist and Irish charm to run the PCA, assembling a staff of readers whose endless task was to examine all material submitted by member studios that were considering them as film projects. Code staffers tracked every picture from script to release print to ensure that it adhered to Code standards.

When Breen took charge, he declared that all films released after July 1, 1934 would require a numbered Code "seal of approval," indicating that they met the moral and political demands of the Production Code Administration. The first film thus anointed was John Ford's *The World Moves On*, which went into release on June 28, 1934. All films prior to that date can be considered "pre-Code *seal*," although they were still subjected to scrutiny and censorship of the Code, however perfunctory. Many are celebrated today as having somehow escaped inspection, which is not the case, and have benefited from having had censored footage restored.

With the Big Five studios (MGM, Paramount, 20th Century Fox, RKO and Warner Bros.) and the smaller ones (Universal, Columbia, United Artists) and others turning out an average of fifty titles apiece each year, the Breen Office had its eyes, ears, and blue pencils busy. Even considering that their job was to impose restrictions on artistic expression, they were diplomatic and intelligent in their written correspondence. They were extremely well-read, articulate letter writers. At the same time, it was the filmmakers' sworn duty to get around the Code whenever possible. This made for a lively symbiosis and an astonishing level of creativity when forbidden ideas had to be implied but not shown and suggested but never spoken. Audiences who were intelligent enough to catch the innuendos could do so while they flew over the heads of less worldly audiences. Looking at the best of the movies released between 1934 and 1968 (when the Code was eliminated), it's astonishing how many quality films were turned out despite moments of enforced innocence.

How did the Production Code impose its morality? What did they demand to be cut, and how did such cuts affect the films that survived to tell the tale? That's what this book is about. Were there lost opportunities? Yes. Were there downright stupid decisions? Yes. Did the Breen office miss things? Sure. Would the films have been better if the Breen Office hadn't stepped in? Ah, that's the question.

It must also be noted that there was a religious element to the Production Code. Hollywood in those days was largely Jewish. Speculation has persisted for a century that Will Hays was hired because he wasn't. The 1920s were an era when anti-Semitism was on the rise. The Palmer Raids in 1920, led by attorney general A. Mitchel Palmer and his new assistant J. Edgar Hoover, rounded up and deported – questionably applying the 1917 Espionage Act – scores of people, including American citizens, whom they considered to be communists, anarchists, and insurrectionists. Most were Eastern European Jews like Hollywood's founding moguls. In 1925, the Ku Klux Klan marched massively and openly down Pennsylvania Avenue in Washington, D.C. Who better to represent Hollywood than a Protestant who looked like he just fell off a turnip truck?

Then there was the writing of the Code itself. Although Thalberg, Wurtzel and Allen brought it forward, it was, in actuality, composed by trade paper publisher Martin J. Quigley and Reverend Daniel A. Lord. These men were also involved in the formation of the Catholic Legion of Decency in 1933 out of frustration that the Code was not being strictly enforced. Like the present composition of the U.S. Supreme Court, of which six out of nine justices are Catholic, a ratio far in excess of Catholic population in the United States, the Production Code reflected the morality and philosophy of the Catholic church. This was apparently encouraged by Hollywood's Jewish founders. In an age of rising anti-Semitism, avoiding Jewish content – changing actors' names, removing Yiddish words, excluding Jewish themes – provided cover, however tenuous. Given the abundance of clergy in so many films from *Going My Way* to *The Exorcist*, it might be said that movies were all about Jewish Hollywood telling Protestant America how to be more Catholic. The Production Code enforced it.[10]

This book is not a history of the Production Code. There are plenty of those, some of them self-righteous, some of them evenhanded. This book is more of a "greatest hits." It is concerned with films that had to earn Production Code seals, although a few significant pre-Code titles appear as reference. Cognoscenti searching these pages for the infamous Code battles over *The Moon is Blue* and other Otto Preminger productions won't find them here for the exhilarating reason that Preminger refused to yield to the Code and threatened to release his uncensored movies without a Code seal. In so doing, he speeded the erosion of the Code's power (and, not by accident, gained free publicity that helped at the box office). Readers wishing a detailed account of the Preminger-Code pageant should consult this author's earlier book, *Breaking the Code: Otto Preminger vs. Hollywood's Censors*, which also contains *Code Blue,* a play by Arnie Reisman & Nat Segaloff.[11] The entries that follow are the author's selection of films that represent a series of mini-adventures within the panoply of contests confronted by the Code, from notorious pre-code titles like *Baby Face* and *Convention City* to benign entries like *The Sound of Music* and *The Ten Commandments*, and dozens of great and memorable motion pictures in between.

My great thanks to the indefatigable staff of the Margaret Herrick Library who facilitated access to Code records, particularly Genevieve Maxwell and Elizabeth Youle. Thanks also to my literary agent Lee Sobel. Profound thanks to editor-publisher Paul Cronin for shepherding this entry through Sticking Place Books and for many years of stimulating friendship.

Throughout the research and writing process the author gained a certain respect for the people who had to implement the Code, sometimes in opposition to their personal beliefs. As to whether Hollywood made better movies under censorship, that's a judgment best left to the readers and viewers.

Note: The material in this book was written in a more elegant time. Grammar and punctuation of the period have been preserved, as have some labels and language.

Another note: This book is a minefield of spoilers. If you haven't seen these films by now, what are you waiting for?

---

1. There is, however, a growing awareness that these platforms are acting with government complicity, often by data-mining their users, a reality that may at some point inspire legislation.
2. If a school receives federal funding, however, it must adhere to the Constitution, not only as to speech but also religion and free assembly.
3. Donna Carlton, "Looking for Little Egypt," *International Dance Discovery*, June 1995.
4. These were single-person viewing devices, not the kind of X-rated peep show parlors that once littered Times Square.
5. Film clip: https://www.youtube.com/watch?v=3-g13hJ8NdI.
6. Shutter synchronization and bulb illumination problems often caused flickering in very early movies and the pejorative nickname stuck.
7. *Joseph Burstyn, Inc. v. Wilson*, 343 U.S. 495 (1952), reversing *Mutual Film Corporation v. Industrial Commission of Ohio*, 236 U.S. 230 (1915), which said that motion pictures were not protected by the First Amendment and local censor boards were free to operate.
8. National Coalition Against Censorship (http://ncas.org).
9. There is ample evidence that Hays hired Breen and cleverly assigned him to the MPPDA's Hollywood office to keep a close eye on the studios and learn their ways.
10. Fascinating article about religion and the Code: John Wranovics, "Uncommon Ground: Anthony Mann, Geoffrey Shurlock, and the Cult of Theosophy," *Noir City* #1, Filmfoundation.org.
11. Applause Theatre & Cinema Books, 2023.

The Adventures of Robin Hood

Warner Bros., 1938
Written by Norman Reilly Raine and Seton I. Miller "based on ancient Robin Hood legends" and Rowland Leigh (uncredited contributor to treatment).
Produced by Jack L. Warner, Hal B. Wallis, Henry Blanke (no producer credits)
Directed by Michael Curtiz and William Keighley
Code seal #3790

Synopsis
In 1190s England, a rogue knight, Sir Robin of Loxley (called Robin Hood), fights a guerilla battle against the pretender to the throne, Prince John, while King Richard the Lionheart is off fighting the Crusades. Living in Sherwood Forest with his band of Merrie Men, Robin romances Richard's ward, Maid Marian, while being sought by the Sheriff of Nottingham for stealing from wealthy people and using the loot to feed the poor vassals whom Prince John is oppressing.

Background
Filmed innumerable times over the decades, including a notable 1922 silent version with Douglas Fairbanks, the legend of Robin Hood is a ripping good swashbuckler with sword fights, horse chases, romance, archery contests, pageantry, blackguards and a veneer of political commentary. This version is recognized as the best of all that followed it thanks to seamless direction by two filmmakers, a rousing symphonic score by Erich Wolfgang Korngold, colorful (if inventive) costumes by Milo Anderson, sumptuous Technicolor photography by Sol Polito and Tony Gaudio, and perfection in casting led by Errol Flynn as the charismatic Robin, Olivia de Havilland as a spirited Maid Marian, Basil Rathbone as the dastardly Sir Guy of Gisborne, Claude Rains as a lubricious Prince John and distinctive portrayals by Eugene Pallette, Alan Hale, Melville Cooper and Una O'Connor. Despite this, it was not clear sailing past the Production Code.

Everyone knows that Robin Hood stole from the rich and gave to the poor, but when Warner Bros. fleshed out the story for a feature-length motion picture, they discovered to their horror that their swashbuckling hero was a twelfth-century socialist. Jack L. Warner – who in 1947 would promise the House Un-American Activities Committee that he would finance "a pest-removal fund" to send Reds back to Russia – found himself in political poo after sending the screenplay to Joseph Breen in September 1937. Breen wasted no time writing back to tell J.L. that "the story seems to meet the requirements of the Code," but went into great detail here and in subsequent letters about "political censor boards" as opposed to censor boards that were on the lookout for sex and vulgarity.[1]

"Political censor boards will probably delete the scene of the gallows and the dangling feet and legs, as they have regularly in the past," the PCA head warned in a follow-up September 21 letter. "The same applies to the scene of the serf being flogged. We recommend that you get it over by suggestion and not show it in detail." Here and elsewhere, Breen objected to shots of rats, shots of people being shot by arrows, shot in the neck, feet twitching on a hanged man, and the hangman's gibbet. He also wanted the word *outhouse* removed "on account of its present toilet connotation."[2]

By October 21 the "gruesomeness" that ran throughout the earlier scripts had been removed or toned down[3] (subject, of course, to the final film) but on November 1 a more crucial matter had been brought to the attention of the Production Code Administration. "Your company, on location at Chico," Breen wrote studio operations chief Walter MacEwen, "had secured from [stables] near your studios some 38 horses which... were to be destroyed in shooting certain scenes of ROBIN HOOD." The report came from the Los Angeles branch of the S.P.C.A. "I tried to assure him that no such plan was in mind," MacEwen continued. "I called the head of the Society and told him, quite definitely, that the story was pure fabrication and that you had no such plan, nor would you entertain any such plan for an instant." He then urged that the studio keep an S.P.C.A. representative on location at all times to prevent stories like this from being circulated.[4]

By January 3, 1938, Breen was again urging trims to prevent political censorship, notably a farmer with an arrow in his back as part of the film's opening montage showing Prince John's campaign of cruelty in Richard's absence.[5] Film scholars might want to note that not only does this reveal the meticulousness of the Breen Office, it also shows how precisely the Warner Bros. shooting screenplay was laid out so that directors Curtiz and Keighley would know what to shoot.

The Adventures of Robin Hood received its Code seal on February 3, 1938 and went into general domestic release on May 14, but that wasn't the end of its troubles. A September 2 confidential memo from Breen to the Code's files reports that Singapore had banned the film in its entirety because "the Film Censor... cannot pass the film which has for its theme robbing the rich to feed the poor as at the present time gangsterisms (sic) with violence are rampant in up country."[6]

At least Sweden, in Breen's September 27 confidential memo, was more concerned with violence than philosophy. That country had censored, from reels three and four, "the whole scene of young soldiers kissing [a] young girl," from reels seven and eight the gallows scene, and from reels eleven and twelve "the scene of Sir Guy falling down dead and close-up of his dead body."[7]

None of this mattered. On a budget of just over $2 million, *The Adventures of Robin Hood* grossed just under $4 million.[8] Its success, however, was not felt by the artisans who had worked on the film, nor any other studio employees. At the outset of the Great Depression Warner Bros., like their studio brethren, cut salaries by as much as fifty percent in order to survive, and their loyal employees agreed to the measure as a means to keep the company open. When the Depression lifted, however, the executive salaries were restored but not those of the rank and file. Labor unrest and rise in union organizing resulted from this trickery.[9] Unlike the successful film they had just produced, Warner Bros. might be said to have stolen from the poor and given to the rich, not only predicting American capitalism for the second half of the century but absolving themselves forever of any taint of socialism.

---

1. Breen to Warner, September 13, 1937 (AMPAS).
2. Breen to Warner, September 21, 1937 (AMPAS).
3. Breen to Warner, October 21, 1937 (AMPAS).
4. Breen to MacEwen, November 1, 1937 (AMPAS).
5. Breen to Warner, January 3, 1938 (AMPAS).
6. Breen to file, September 3, 1938 (AMPAS).
7. Breen to file, September 27, 1938 (AMPAS).
8. Glancy, H. Mark. "Warner Bros film grosses, 1921–51," *Historical Journal of Film, Radio and Television*, March 1995
9. Eric Hoyt, "How the Great Depression Reshaped Hollywood Studios' Ties with Workers," *The Hollywood Reporter*, March 19, 2022.

All About Eve

20th Century Fox, 1950
Written by Joseph L. Mankiewicz, from a story by Mary Or (uncredited)
Produced by Darryl F. Zanuck
Directed by Joseph L. Mankiewicz
Code seal #14544

Synopsis
Margo Channing (Bette Davis), an ageing Broadway actress, allows a devoted fan, Eve Harrington (Anne Baxter), to become her assistant, not able – or perhaps unwilling – to see that Eve wants not only to serve her but to replace her. Blinded by the adoration, Margo alienates her husband, Bill Simpson (Gary Merrill), her playwright, Lloyd Richards (Hugh Marlowe), her best friend, Karen Richards (Celeste Holm), and her dresser (Thelma Ritter). Only the droll theatre critic Addison DeWitt (George Saunders) sees through Eve's scheme and claims her for himself.

Background
Joseph L. Mankiewicz's pointed, bitchy meditation on backstabbing in the theatre won multiple Academy Awards in 1951, no doubt because Oscar voters were relieved that the picture was set three thousand miles away from a Hollywood where they were guilty of the same ego sins. Mankiewicz was a house producer at MGM before coming to Fox with the promise of making his own films, which he did to enormous success, sometimes running against studio chief Darryl F. Zanuck, who demanded producing credit. *All About Eve* won ten Academy Awards (including best picture, screenplay and director) even against *Sunset Boulevard* which, in a sense, espouses many of the same themes.

Over the years, *All About Eve* has become celebrated not only by fans who lament the paucity of witty dialogue in modern cinema but who appreciate the sheer power of its star, Bette Davis, whose Margo Channing eviscerates not only her foes but her friends. The visual style, or lack of it, no doubt accounts for its popularity; it could easily be a television movie, and its adaptation to the Broadway stage as the 1970 musical *Applause* speaks to its theatricality and remarkable array of roles for women.

And it was women who were on the mind of the Production Code Administration when Jason S. Joy of 20th Century Fox sent, not the script, but wardrobe photos to Joseph I. Breen in March 1950. (Although titled Director of Public Relations, Joy was more properly liaison between Fox and the Code, where he had worked before joining Fox.) Of concern was that the costumes, particularly the decolletage of actresses Anne Baxter (Eve), Celeste Holm (Karen) and Barbara Bates (Phoebe), hold to the Code's demand for modesty. A March 30, 1950 letter to Joy specified,

"We direct your attention to the need for the greatest possible care in the selection and photographing of the dresses and costumes of your women. The Production Code makes it mandatory that the intimate parts of the body – specifically, the breasts of women – be covered at all times. Any compromise with this regulation will compel us to withhold approval of your picture."[1] Breen's comments on the script itself reflect his reaction to its adult talk. About the early scene in which Eve is introduced to Margo after a performance and Margo is running on about the South, he writes:

> Page 15: We ask that the use of the word "sex" be changed to something less blunt in the circumstances; some such phrase as "love" starved might be satisfactory. The present film has Margo saying, "That's why I don't understand all these plays about love-starved Southern women. Love is one thing we were never starved for in the South." The original script said, "'an that's what I don't unnerstand about all these plays about sex-starved Suth'n women – sex is one thing we were nevah stahved for in the South!"
>
> Page 16: The dialogue, "where it never even occurred to them whether they wanted to marry their fathers more than their brothers," seems unacceptable.

The final film cuts the line entirely.

The original script reads: "Honey chile had a point. You know, I can remember plays about women – even from the South – where it never even occurred to them whether they wanted to marry their fathers more than their brothers." In an interview, Mankiewicz elaborated by explaining that, in any event, the word wasn't *marry*, it was *screw*.[2] Not surprisingly, that was a non-starter.

Breen raised other issues with the script, such as reminding the studio not to show a toilet in the bathroom, changing the name *Ladies Room* to *Lounge Room* or *Powder Room* "or something similar," cutting the word *tart* where it appears, removing the word *brassiere*, not allowing a face slap to happen, and ensuring that "there will be nothing coarse about the burp" on page 83.

As always, Breen ended his cordial cautions with the verbal sword of Damocles, "You understand, of course, that our final judgment will be based upon the finished picture." It was a positive judgment, of course, as history and the existence of an appreciative cult audience have enjoyed for years. But just think of what might have lengthened *All About Eve* into *More About Eve*.

---

1. Breen to Joy, March 30, 1950. AMPAS. If this concern seems undue, it might be the Breen Office's awareness of Fox chief Darryl F. Zanuck's penchant for auditioning actresses (not stars) in the privacy of his office and that perhaps this permissiveness

would pervade the studio's films. DFZ's secretaries were told to hold calls every afternoon at 4 p.m. for what became known as Zanuck's "four o'clock girls." (Source: author researched and co-produced the Zanuck *Biography* episode for A&E Networks.)

2. Joseph L. Mankiewicz and Gary Carey, *More About All About Eve: A Colloquy by Gary Carey with Joseph L. Mankiewicz*, New York: Random House, 1972

The Apartment

United Artists, 1960
Written by Billy Wilder and I.A.L. Diamond
Produced and Directed by Billy Wilder
Code seal #19647

Synopsis
An ambitious young insurance company clerk (Jack Lemmon) rises up the corporate ladder by allowing his adulterous superiors to use his apartment for their trysts, then becomes involved with the building's elevator operator (Shirley MacLaine), who is being two-timed by his boss (Fred MacMurray).

Background
The winner of numerous Academy Awards, *The Apartment* grew from a Hollywood scandal in which a major talent agent was caught cheating and Wilder and Diamond wondered what it must have been like to be the low-level employee who had let his boss use his apartment – coming home, having to clean up someone else's mess, and slip into still-warm bedsheets.

The Apartment was a film about adultery, a subject that was normally wholly unacceptable under the Code, but here the Breen Office was unusually silent. Under the Code, adultery had to be punished, and so adultery was accepted in *The Apartment* because the chief adulterer, MacMurray, presumably has to get divorced when his affair is reported to his wife by his secretary (a former mistress). The other executives involved receive no stated comeuppance for their dalliances. MacLaine's character is not punished, although she does attempt suicide (also forbidden under the Code) at being ill-treated by MacMurray.

In the scene where Sheldrake (MacMurray) gives Fran (MacLaine) $100 as a Christmas present because he has to cancel their date to be with his family, the Code wanted all of the following dialogue removed. Wilder kept most of it in and got a Code seal anyway, although the film was classified as adult entertainment (which was a meaningless category at the time):

Fran
Okay, I just thought as long as it was paid for...

Sheldrake
Don't ever talk like that, Fran. Don't make yourself out to be cheap.

Fran
A hundred dollars? I don't call that cheap. And you must be paying somebody something for the use of the apartment.

Sheldrake

Stop it, Fran.

Using a form called Analysis of Film Content, an unidentified Code staffer screened the completed film and noted, among other things, that a doctor character was portrayed sympathetically; that Jewish, Chinese and Negro characters, though incidental, were portrayed sympathetically and were American citizens; that there was drinking but nobody gets drunk; that no crime was portrayed; and that adultery, while present, was not presented as illicit. On this last incongruous point there is no further explanation except to note that the Code seal was awarded without further comment on May 6, 1960.

When the 1960 Oscars were handed out, *The Apartment* won best picture (beating *The Alamo, Elmer Gantry, Sons and Lovers* and *The Sundowners*) as well as best director and best original screenplay, among other honors. In 1968 it became a Broadway musical called *Promises, Promises*, adapted from the Wilder-Diamond script by Neil Simon. It has music and lyrics by Burt Bacharach and Hal David, respectively, and was nominated for a Tony award.

Baby Face

Warner Bros., 1933
Written by Gene Markey and Kathryn Scola, from a story by Mark Canfield (a.k.a. Darryl F. Zanuck)
Produced by Raymond Griffith and William LeBaron
Directed by Alfred E. Green
Pre-Code

Synopsis
An ambitious young woman (Barbara Stanwyck), angry at being exploited by men, sleeps her way up the corporate ladder.

Background
Years before the glass ceiling got its name (it had always been there, of course), Warner Bros. challenged the power of the pre-Code seal Hays Office with this male fantasy that has, over the years, become one of the most beloved movie middle fingers to a sexist America.

Keep in mind that, although the Production Code was established to head off local censorship boards, it took a while for the Production Code Administration to get its own house in order. Before Joseph Breen arrived to actually enforce it, all the Code could do when it saw a difference between its standards and those of the rest of the country was huff and puff. A clear statement of this powerlessness appears in a memo from James Wingate to Will Hays on December 30, 1932:

> Under sex pictures, one new script was submitted during the week: *Baby Face* – Warner Brothers. It is the chronicle of a woman who uses her beauty to get along. Naturally, it presents a problem, and rather a serious one from the censorship standpoint. With regard to the Code there is nothing we can find in it which is a violation, despite the fact that the theme is sordid and of a troublesome nature. However, we will do our best to clean it up as much as possible. The fact that Barbara Stanwyck is destined for the leading role will probably mitigate some of the dangers in view of her sincere and restrained acting.[1]

Wingate elaborated on this dichotomy in a letter[2] to Darryl F. Zanuck, then the head of production at Warner Bros. (and who, under the pseudonym Mark Canfield, had written the film's story), advising that "it contains elements that will make it satisfactory from the standpoint of the Code" but which will draw local censors' scissors once it goes into release. The three-page letter contains two pages of notes cautioning against such words as *fanny, tramp, bitch, son-of-a, good lord* and other specifically prohibited expressions as well as a man's hand touching a woman's rear end or brushing against her breast. Overall, the letter recommended restraint in staging all the suggestive scenes. Wingate drove home his point by citing an MGM film (not named) with similar plotting that suffered censorship in Australia, Ontario, Quebec and British Columbia as well as stateside in Pennsylvania, Ohio and Massachusetts.

Zanuck proceeded with production and *Baby Face* was shot over a remarkably short eighteen-day schedule on a frugal $187,000 budget.[3] After screening the finished picture, Dr. Wingate wrote Zanuck that, although the picture technically satisfied the requirements of the Code, there were still public objections to films with such themes. To forestall any complaints, he suggested removing the passing of money from a sequence in which Lily's (Stanwick's) father sells his daughter to a politician; omitting the moment where the politician locks the door behind them; fading out on a scene in which Lily suggestively asks a railroad brakeman who is about to throw her off a boxcar "can't we talk this over?"; and a time-saving montage of Lily's numerous indiscretions.[4]

Although Zanuck and Wingate exchanged cordial missives about their successful collaboration, the trade press in April 1933 sounded alarms and several Warner and Code people – among them Jack Warner, Al Green (the film's director), William Koenig (production manager), Hal Wallis, James Wingate, Code staffer Geoffrey Shurlock, Harry Warner, Will Hays and Joe Breen – met to decide what to do.[5] There had been ongoing discussions about what Hays called the film's "Nietzschean" philosophy of Lily being told by cobbler Adolf Cragg (Alphonse Ethier) to use her charms to get ahead.[6] It's a riveting scene, and no wonder it raised Hays' hackles when Lily asks, "What chance has a woman got?"

> *Adolf*
> More chance than men. A woman young, beautiful like you can get anything she wants in the world because you have power over men. But you must use men, not let them use you. You must be a master, not a slave. Look, here. [*takes a book*] Nietzsche says, "All life, no matter how we idealize it, is nothing more or less than exploitation." That's what I'm telling you. Exploit yourself! Go to some big city where you will find opportunities. Use men. Be strong! Defiant! Use men to get the things you want!

This was followed by a scene in which Lily and her friend Chico (Teresa Harris) try stowing away in a boxcar to New York. When the brakeman finds them, Lily buys their passage with her personal favors while Chico looks away singing "St. Louis Woman."

Wingate was adamant about constructing an ending "to indicate that Lily disregarded the cobbler's advice, and in the end show her stripped of wealth and social standing, and thus drive home the point that the philosophy now in the picture (even though Nietzsche has been deleted) namely, 'use your body for material advancement,' has been entirely defeated and discredited."[7]

With a July 13, 1933 release date staring the studio in the face, the Warner editorial department went to work sculpting an acceptable picture. On May 19, the department sent a meticulous eight-page document to Wingate with the offensive language on the left-hand side of the page and the eliminations on the right-hand side. For instance:

OLD DIALOGUE	ELIMINATIONS
You've got to think of your wife and kids. I can't see you any more.	You've got to think of your wife and kids.
Stick around after five. Yes, this is a very serious case. I'm afraid I'll have to foreclose.	Stick around after five.
But are you sure of that?	– are you sure of that?
We've done all we can, lady. He has a good chance.	He has a good chance.

The deletions shortened the film by 1,000 feet, or just over ten minutes. There was also a new moralizing scene at the end, as requested, in which both Lily and her eventual husband, Trenholm (George Brent), wind up with nothing after everything they have been through.[8] By May, *Baby Face* had had so much surgery that Hays and Wingate were in cahoots to hold up approval until they saw a final print.[9] A copy was sent to Jack Warner himself, and Warner, either in a misunderstanding or as a ploy, thanked them for their cooperation, making it sound as if they had given their approval.[10] Nevertheless, Wingate sent Warner a copy of a memo from Joe Breen to Hays dated June 8 in which Breen, based in New York, screened the recut picture with other Code employees. He congratulated Warner Bros. for fixing the film so that it met the responsibilities of the Code, and closed:

> Of course, this picture, even as it is now, ought not to suggest any jubilation on our part. Its theme is still a questionable one and suggests the kind, or type, of picture which ought not to be encouraged. My enthusiasm in the matter is prompted by the splendid spirit of helpfulness which the Warners have displayed

in this matter and the promptness with which they set about to clean up a very bad picture – and succeeded very well.[11]

Needless to say, the cuts destroyed the very theme of the picture, but that didn't help it in Ohio, Pennsylvania, Virginia, British Columbia, Alberta, Quebec, Australia, Geneva and Nationalist Spain, all of whom banned it in their territories. Despite this, *Baby Face* – in its restored, original cut – has survived to become one of the touchstones of pre-Code Hollywood. Time passes.

---

1. Wingate to Hays, December 30, 1932 (AMPAS).
2. Wingate to Zanuck, January 3, 1933 (AMPAS).
3. American Film Institute catalogue.
4. Wingate to Zanuck, February 28, 1933 (AMPAS).
5. This April 1933 mention of Breen predates his appointment as head of the Production Code in 1934. Before that time, he was press liaison (AMPAS).
6. Hays to file, April 20, 1933 (AMPAS).
7. Wingate to Warner, April 26, 1933 (AMPAS). These scenes have been restored in recent Blu-ray editions of the film.
8. Warner Bros. editorial dept. (indistinct signature) to Wingate, July 13, 1933 (AMPAS).
9. Hays to Wingate, May 22, 1933 (AMPAS).
10. Warner to Wingate, May 26, 1933 (AMPAS).
11. Breen to Hays, June 8, 1933 (AMPAS).

The Best Man

United Artists, 1964
Written by Gore Vidal, from his play
Produced by Stuart Millar and Lawrence Turman
Directed by Franklin J. Schaffner
Code seal #20641

Synopsis
A political party whose nominee is almost certain to be elected the next United States President is deadlocked at its convention between William Russell (Henry Fonda), a liberal candidate with a past, and Joe Cantwell (Cliff Robertson), a conservative candidate whose past would eliminate him if William Russell, who learns about it, were to make it public. While Russell is weighing the moral issues of exposing Cantwell and Cantwell is ready to destroy Russell, ex-president Art Hockstader (Lee Tracy) is dying, Russell's marriage is on the rocks, and the party is desperate for a leader.

Background
Gore Vidal's hit 1960 play made it to the screen in a dynamic rendering whose characterizations were based on actual political figures, some more recognizable than others. Vidal, a political gadfly, took jabs at everybody in this serious but frequently funny drama that ventured into some of the same sexual controversy of its contemporaries, *The Children's Hour* and *Advise and Consent*.

Line for line there is more political wisdom in *The Best Man* than in most newspaper columns by any given opinion maker. "No mention of Darwin; before the garden of Eden was The Word," a Southern senator "has all the characteristics of a dog except loyalty," and "you can talk like a liberal but at heart you're an American" still ring true. Vidal, the prolific novelist, memoirist and scriptwriter, based the contemplative William Russell on former U.N. ambassador and failed presidential candidate Adlai Stevenson and the reactionary hypocrite Joe Cantwell on Bobby Kennedy, whom Vidal loathed, and Richard Nixon, whom everybody else despised. Art Hockstader was a blend of presidents Harry S Truman and Dwight D. Eisenhower, southern Governor T. T. Claypoole (John Henry Faulk) was clearly the racist Alabama governor George C. Wallace, and the satire flowed.

The first director to take up *The Best Man* was Frank Capra, no stranger to political cinema, having made *Mr. Smith Goes to Washington* (1939) and *State of the Union* (1948). Moreover, his best works (*It's a Wonderful Life*, 1947; *American Madness*, 1932; *Meet John Doe*, 1941, etc.) stressed the struggle of the little guy against the big guy, so much so that he was, at times, suspected of being a Leftie. By the early 1960s, however, his directorial star was fading. Although *A Hole in the Head* (1959) was well received and *Pocketful of Miracles* was in post-production in late 1961, Capra's disenchantment with filmmaking was growing, largely because the industry was becoming more corporatized.[1] Nevertheless, he attached himself to *The Best Man* and hired playwright Myles Connelly (with whom he had made *State of the Union*), not Vidal, to adapt it.

The urbane Geoffrey Shurlock, who had replaced Joseph Breen as director of the PCA in February 1954, wasn't bothered by the play's politics, but he was concerned with the script's salty language. In his November 7, 1961 letter to Capra he remarked on "an over-abundance of 'hell's and 'damn's" and suggested that "you delete as many of them as possible," a refreshing change from when a single damn in *Gone with the Wind* brought on the apocalypse (q.v.). He also wanted several lines removed ("A lot of men need a lot of women" as a justification of promiscuity; the elimination of *bitch*, *bastard*, *contraceptive* and *sleeping around*) and the word *homosexual* changed to *degenerate*.

The script was not changed. Instead, the director was, and then the script. As Joseph McBride discovered when he wrote *Frank Capra: The Catastrophe of Success* (correcting Capra's earlier memoir, *The Name Above the Title*), Capra was taken off *The Best Man* by United Artists chief Max Youngstein, who didn't like where the famed filmmaker was going with the rewrite ("[You're] laying it on too thick to make the point," he wrote Capra[2]). Capra also objected to Vidal's atheism, a belief (or, rather, non-belief) with which he imbued all of his play's characters, even the supposedly Christian Cantwell.[3] Vidal's homosexuality may also have bothered Capra, who referred to him in his book as a "gay blade." Not only were Capra and Connolly turning Vidal's hit play into an anti-Communist screed to please Capra's friend Richard Nixon, they also invented a mixed-race character, a governor of Hawaii, who emerges from the shadows reciting patriotic phrases to become the nominee. McBride quotes Vidal as saying, "I was brought up on Frank Capra, so at first I thought, 'Well, yeah, Frank Capra – interesting idea.'"[4] Then he saw the rewrite.

Capra explained his departure from *The Best Man* as the consequence of *Pocketful of Miracle*'s "unmiraculous box office performance." In fact, his kind of film was over and his political naïveté made him unprepared for the complexities of the project. Instead, United Artists handed it to young producers Stuart Millar and Lawrence Turman, who engaged Vidal to start over, or, rather, return to the source. In June 1963, they submitted this new version to the Shurlock Office and were told, on June 17, to make three interesting changes which can be tracked in the finished film:

> Page 23: There are several uses of the word "bastard" in this story. Some uses seem valid, but the one spoken by Hockstader on this page should be omitted. The film now carries the dialogue in which Hockstader berates Cantwell, "I don't mind your being a bastard, it's your being such a stupid bastard that I object to."

Page 26: Hockstader's expression, "...you sons of bitches...", is unacceptable. The line, which Hockstader delivers to Russell after he has told Russell that he is dying, is, "The only thing I find is that the rest of you bastards are going to join me." The film now has Hockstader saying, "the rest of you so-and-sos are going to join me."

Page 81: Hockstader's line, "...if Joe Cantwell enjoys deflowering sheep by the light of the full moon," is unacceptably vulgar. The film changes the line to, "I, too, am a tolerant man. I do not care if Joe Cantwell enjoys carnal knowledge of a McCormick reaper."[5]

The McCormick reaper line was still held to be vulgar by "unanimous consensus," Shurlock wrote Millar on July 9, 1963 in response to Millar's June 28 insistence that the line was in keeping with Hockstader's folksy character. Shurlock suggested that Millar appeal to the full Code board, but there is no indication that he did. Instead, Millar agreed to double-shoot the line when they made the film – that is, try something else in an alternate take and see which works better in the final picture. Clearly the McCormick reaper line worked because it's in the movie.

Vidal posed an interesting contrast in his play that the film subtly changes. He wrote that he wanted to compare a figure who led a virtuous private life but whose public life was monstrous with a man whose private life was a mess but whose public life was commendable. William Russell is an honorable public figure but his married life is one of philandering; Joe Cantwell, on the other hand, has a normal private life (deems Russell, "any man with that awful wife and those ugly children can't be anything but normal") but in public is an ignorant, right-wing zealot.

The film shows Cantwell as more sanctimonious, a trait that Vidal readily ascribed to Bobby Kennedy. Where the younger Kennedy also served on Joseph R. McCarthy's Permanent Subcommittee on Investigations of the U.S. Senate, his opportunistic politics, combined with Nixon's, gave Cliff Robertson, who played Cantwell, a lot to work with.[6]

Cantwell is ready to reveal that Russell once had a nervous breakdown, and the smear that Russell debates using against Cantwell is that he was discharged from military service following a homosexual incident. ("No, I have not read *Advise and Consent*," Vidal famously held.[7]) In the story's climax, Cantwell tells Russell that, when he found out about a friend's homosexuality, he turned him in, after which his ex-friend smeared him. It's a bluff and Russell falls for it, revealing an act of human decency that marks him as unfit to be president.

The Best Man remains one of the most telling, prescient films about American politics. In avoiding politics and focusing on the dirty words, the Code allowed greatness to slip through. Or perhaps it was no accident.

1. Frank Capra, *The Name Above the Title*, New York: MacMillan and Company, 1971.
2. Youngstein to Capra, January 24, 1961, quoted in McBride, op cit.
3. Capra, *The Name Above the Title*.
4. Joseph McBride, *Frank Capra: The Catastrophe of Success*, New York: Simon & Schuster, 1992.
5. Gore Vidal, *The Best Man* screenplay New York: Appleton-Century-Crofts, 1960.
6. Author conversation with Cliff Robertson.
7. Gore Vidal, introduction to *The Best Man*, New York: Signet Books, 1964.

The Best Years of Our Lives

RKO Radio Pictures, 1946
Screenplay by Robert E. Sherwood, from the novel *Glory for Me* by MacKinlay Kantor
Produced by Samuel Goldwyn and Lester Koenig (uncredited)
Directed by William Wyler
Code seal #11972[1]

Synopsis
Three servicemen – a middle-aged banker (Fredric March), a sailor who lost his hands (Harold Russell) and a former lunch counter worker (Dana Andrews) – return to their homes after World War II and have trouble resuming their peacetime lives. The banker realizes the futility of his profession; the sailor must deal with the discomfort he creates in others, including his girlfriend; and the lunch counter worker misses the respect he earned as an aerial gunner. All they have is their friendship with each other as so many veterans painfully discovered when they tried to pick up where they left off before the war.

Background
The Best Years of Our Lives challenged the Production Code to grow up just as America had been challenged to grow up during World War II, but, unlike America, the Code refused to face the reality that America had matured between 1941 and 1945.

Samuel Goldwyn loved to fight. He believed that "pleasant shoots make pleasant pictures" but he didn't want his pictures to be merely pleasant – he wanted them to engage audiences and arouse emotions. It was his management technique to set creative people against each other, and if he couldn't set them against each other, he would set them against himself. From that friction emerged a filmography of taste and substance that no other single producer has yet achieved, and he did it with his own money.

For *The Best Years of Our Lives*, Goldwyn decided to fight the Production Code.

Perhaps the Code needed to be fought. America had reached a new, if unwilling, maturity during World War II, but the Code was still mired in 1934. When he bought journalist MacKinlay Kantor's free-verse 1945 novel *Glory for Me* and hired Robert E. Sherwood to adapt it – going so far as to have Sherwood and Sherwood's wife Irene lodge with Goldwyn and his wife, Frances, while working on it – he promised the screenwriter that he wouldn't change a word when he made the film. He even came down on director William Wyler when he cut speeches. Then he ran up against the Breen Office.

He could have seen it coming. After Goldwyn's Pat Duggan sent the book to the Code offices on July 30, 1945 asking for a quick response as it was to be their next picture, Breen sent a letter two days later withholding approval as a film for the usual reasons of the presence of drinking and sex. In particular, the latter: do not be too intimate showing the reunion night of the Sergeant (March) and his wife (Myrna Loy); don't let on that the lieutenant fooled around overseas; and be sure to inject "compensating moral values" when it comes time for the marital break-up (Andrews and Virginia Mayo).[2] Breen offered to meet personally with Goldwyn to discuss it. Meanwhile, Sherwood, after a false start, finished a screenplay seven months later that was sent to the Code office for inspection.

On March 30, Breen did have that meeting with Sherwood and Wyler at Wyler's home to discuss the script and, on April 1, Breen confirmed in writing to Goldwyn the substance of their talk.[3] The chief cautions were excessive drinking and drunkenness. This mainly affected the Fredric March character and any scenes set in the bar owned by Russell's uncle Butch, played by Hoagy Carmichael. The divorce subplot of Andrews and Mayo should not be written "as a condonation of this tragedy" (it is now played that time and distance eroded their mutual love) and, in general, he wanted to reduce the passion of people kissing. The eight pages of line-item notes that followed ranged from erasing the word "lousy" to eliminating "God" from dialogue to cutting Peggy's (March's and Loy's daughter played by Teresa Wright) eagerness for Andrews' marriage to break up and not showing an actor in his shirtsleeves.[4]

Several back-and-forth exchanges of revised pages and Breen okays continued until April 19 when Pat Duggan assured Breen in a three-page letter that certain delicate scenes in which the Code urged caution would not be filmed in an offensive manner, while insisting that there were some scenes that they intended to leave as they were in the script.[5] Breen knew this was a shot across his bow and told Duggan on April 24 that he was free to do as the script said but that the Code would withhold their final judgment until they saw the completed film.[6] This was more than a veiled threat – it was a challenge.

A few script changes later, it was "Pat" writing "Joe" grousing that he, Breen, was being overly critical of certain dialogue but that, more importantly, "We cannot find another ending since we believe this ending is honest, true, and within the bounds of decency and good behavior. Peggy was reprimanded by her father and mother for stating that she would break up the marriage. Peggy had nothing further to do with the breaking up of the marriage. If… Peggy and Fred get together, we cannot see how you can consider this a breach of the Code regarding the sanctity of marriage."[7]

According to Goldwyn's biographer, A. Scott Berg, Goldwyn's intransigence cost him a $25,000 fine from the Production Code Administration, although there is no indication of this in Code files for the picture.[8]

Reviews acclaimed the film's maturity, and *The Best Years of Our Lives* went on to win Academy Awards for Fredric March (best actor), William Wyler (best director), Harold Russell (best supporting actor plus a special Oscar), Robert E. Sherwood (best adapted screenplay), Daniel Mandell (best film editing), Hugo Friedhofer (best musical scoring) and best picture.

Russell, an actual amputee from a wartime demolition accident, won his special Oscar "for bringing hope and courage to his fellow veterans through his appearance in *The Best Years of Our Lives.*" The film was embraced by audiences for its realistic look at how the nation was coming to terms with its new place as world leader. It would take the Production Code more than twenty years to do the same.

---

1. Certificate issued with Breen's stipulation that "you have deleted from all prints the broken line, 'We'll nail Old Glory to the top of the pole, and we'll all re-enlist…' and also the line, 'I feel just like a bride.'"
2. Breen to Goldwyn, August 1, 1945 (AMPAS).
3. Breen to Goldwyn, April 1, 1946 (AMPAS).
4. Duggan to Breen, March 28, 1946 (AMPAS). This referred to the handless Russell.
5. Duggan to Breen, April 19, 1945 (AMPAS).
6. Breen to Duggan, April 24, 1946 (AMPAS).
7. Duggan to Breen, June 24, 1945 (AMPAS). In the film, Al (March) asks Fred (Andrews) not to see Peggy (Wright) again, and he breaks it off. After Fred and Marie divorce, Fred sees Peggy at the wedding of Homer (Russell) and Wilma (Cathy O'Donnell) and their love is rekindled, with Code permission.
8. A. Scott Berg, *Goldwyn: A Biography*, New York: Alfred A. Knopf, 1989.

The Birth of a Nation

David W. Griffith Corporation, 1915 (1930 & 1938 reissues)
Written by Thomas Dixon, Jr., from his novel and play *The Clansmen*, D.W. Griffith, and Frank E. Woods
Produced by D.W. Griffith and H. E. Aitken (uncredited)
Directed by D.W. Griffith
Pre-Code

Synopsis
The sprawling story of the Stoneman family of the North and the Cameron family of the South as they live through the Civil War and Reconstruction.

Background
No American film is more respected or more damned than *The Birth of a Nation*. Director D.W. Griffith used his mastery of the still-developing medium of motion pictures to tell a story with such exquisite skill that it roused audiences in support of a defeated Confederacy and to cheer the South's rescue by the Ku Klux Klan from the imposition of Reconstruction. Its blatant racism, criticized at the time of its 1915 release, still draws fire on those rare occasions when anyone dares announce it for public screening today. This essay addresses only the involvement of the Production Code with this film.

When the Triangle Film Corporation, the new rights-holders to *The Birth of a Nation*, sought to re-release it with added music and sound effects in 1930,[1] they arranged for its director, D.W. Griffith, to sit for a prologue interview with Walter Huston, the star of his recent 1930 film, *Abraham Lincoln*.[2] The sound reissue was not, strictly speaking, the original version. Griffith himself was directing the sound effects, captured live at the Lasky ranch as horsemen rode past the sound recording units, a one-hundred-piece orchestra under Louis Gottschalk was warming up to play, and premieres were being arranged in New York and Los Angeles. Griffith also edited an hour out of its running time.

Not everyone was primed for the film's re-release in any version, let alone one with music and sound effects. Will W. Alexander of the Commission on Interracial Cooperation got the false impression that the film was being remade and wrote Will Hays that "it would be particularly unfortunate to give this film to a new lease on life at the present time," recalling that it "has undoubtedly helped to keep alive sectional bitterness" and "has helped to intensify the feelings out of which [lynchings] grow and that it has also been very useful in promoting the Klan in the South."[3] Hays' secretary answered instead of Hays, sending Alexander the MPPDA's Advertising Code that had nothing whatsoever to do with the matter-at-hand, which was mistaking a re-release for a remake.⁴ A month later, David D. Jones, president of Bennett College for Women in North Carolina, followed up Dr. Alexander's letter, writing to Jason Joy, who was then with the Studio Relations Committee, imploring him to use "careful consideration" and explaining that "all of us who have the best interest of the South at heart, whether Negro or White, would sorely deplore seeing *The Birth of a Nation* revived at this time."⁵ Joy responded on August 12 that he and the Code were not connected with the film or its distributors and thus had no way of knowing if the quality of the picture had changed in any way.⁶

In spring 1938 there was a renewed attempt by a new company called the Royal Film Exchange to re-release *Birth*. It was a cause of concern for Hays and Francis S. Harmon, a Code staffer, when M.L. Mayer of the Royal Film Exchange asked to submit the film for review. Harmon wrote Mayer a studiously vague letter, explaining, "This motion picture, produced 16 years before the Production Code was adopted, has been continuously in the stream of public motion picture exhibition since 1915 and is an important part of the documentary history of the motion picture industry, and as such should be preserved intact. You understand, of course, that extremely few film masterpieces are in this special category, and then only in the original versions."⁷ In other words, the Hays Office would take no position. This was a utilitarian answer. After all, how could Hays order cuts on a film for which, at this point in time, no definitive version existed? Because of the many local censorship boards throughout the country when *The Birth of a Nation* was released in 1915, the myriad silent circulation prints were repeatedly cut and recut to suit local community standards. How could they suggest cuts on one print that might have less, more, or different footage than another?

Things changed after Joseph Breen's arrival in 1934 and his creation of Code seals to verify adherence. At the same time, he declared that any pre-Code film that was to be reissued needed a retroactive Code seal, and if cuts were needed to meet enforcement, so be it. For this reason, for example, *Little Caesar* was approved for a Code seal because it was considered a "period piece," while its spiritual companion *The Public Enemy* was not because it included sex and also misrepresented American values in a world threatened by Communism.⁸ Thus when Louis S. Sunny of the Sunny Amusement Corporation, which had acquired *The Birth of a Nation*, duly submitted it for a Code seal, Breen responded with a virtual copy of Harmon's letter to Mayer from ten years earlier ducking the issue.⁹

An announced 1954 re-issue drew an urgent letter from Walter White, executive secretary of the National Association for the Advancement of Colored People, informing the PCA that businessman Ted Thal of Owens-Corning Fiberglass Corporation had purchased the rights to *The Birth of a Nation* for $750,000 and was planning both to distribute the original film and remake it. "We are writing to enlist your interest and support," White wrote Eric Johnston, who had taken over as head of the PCA from Hays. "But aside from its distortion both of history and its maligning of the Negro," White wrote passionately, "we wish to further point out that the original film made by D.W. Griffith and released in 1915 was one of the major factors in the revival of the infamous Ku Klux Klan who, following World War I, resulted in the spreading of anti-Negro, anti-Jewish, anti-Catholic, and other hatreds. Many persons were killed or maimed by mobs inflamed by the picture, and one of the darkest periods of American history was to be written."[10]

The Birth of a Nation has, of course, remained available in some version or another for over a hundred years. First-rate 8mm and 16mm copies were sold for decades by Blackhawk Films of Davenport, Iowa under license from the then-rights holder. When its copyright lapsed in 1973 it fell into public domain and anybody can now own a copy in any home video medium or watch it on YouTube. Showing it publicly, however, is a moral and political matter outside the scope of this book.

---

1. The feature (mistakenly identified as 1933 from Mutual Film Corporation): https://www.youtube.com/watch?v=UmBEA12R-9.
2. Interview: https://www.youtube.com/watch?v=x8UUl1mhsrw.
3. Alexander to Hays, July 3, 1930 (AMPAS).
4. Secretary (unnamed) to Alexander, July 28, 1930 (AMPAS).
5. Jones to Joy, August 2, 1930 (AMPAS).
6. Joy to Jones, August 12, 1930 (AMPAS).
7. Francis S. Harmon to Mayer, May 12, 1938 (AMPAS).
8. Jack Vizzard to file, August 13, 1953 (AMPAS).
9. Breen to Sunny, October 12, 1948 (AMPAS).
10. White to Johnston, December 9, 1954 (AMPAS).

Blow-Up

Premier Productions, 1966
Written by Michelangelo Antonioni and Tonino Guerra; story by Michelangelo Antonioni, from a short story by Julio Cortazar; English dialogue by Edward Bond
Produced by Carlo Ponti and Pierre Rouve
Directed by Michelangelo Antonioni
Code seal denied

Synopsis
Thomas (David Hemmings), a freelance British photographer, casually takes a picture of a placid park but later, when he enlarges it in his darkroom, he begins to think that he has accidentally photographed a murder. The more he enlarges the image, however, the less distinct it becomes, yet a series of events involving him begin to make him think he has stumbled into a crime. Then it all goes away as if it never happened.

Background
Blow-Up may well be the motion picture that inspired the wisecrack, "A *film* is a *movie* you don't quite understand."[1] It is easily one of the most demanding films ever to entrance the public. It is also a deeply unsettling articulation of the existential dilemma – that is, the more you know, the less you know. Its visual storytelling found an audio counterpart in Brian De Palma's 1981 homage, *Blow Out*. Both films brilliantly address the ultimate philosophical question, "what is truth?"

Foreign language films have had a mixed history in America. In the silent days, of course, a movie's country of origin wasn't important since English intertitles could be translated and spliced in. With sound, movies had to be either subtitled (restricting their appeal to mass audiences) or dubbed (often restricting the quality of performance). At the same time, motion pictures from other countries became noted for their sophistication, at least those that reached American theaters. In other words, they were known for their sexual content, which is why many of them played in "adult" rather than mainstream theaters. (One wonders what the raincoat crowd thought of Bergman's *Summer with Monika*, 1953).

Foreign language films, although honored by the motion picture Academy starting in 1956, still took a while to catch on. On *Sunset Boulevard*, for instance, Billy Wilder supposedly told his cinematographer, John Seitz, "Keep a few scenes out of focus. I want to win the foreign film award."[2] Projectionists were rumored to mix up the order of reels to see if audiences noticed. Gene Hackman in Arthur Penn's 1975 *Night Moves* famously referred to a French film as "like watching paint dry."[3] And bilingual viewers were often frustrated by a movie's inexact subtitles.

Thus when the venerable, respectable, traditional Metro-Goldwyn-Mayer offered Italian director Michelangelo Antonioni a two-picture deal when they saw the grosses of his quartet of successful Italian pictures (*L'Avventura*, 1960; *La Notte*, 1961; *L'Eclisse*, 1962; *Red Desert*, 1964), they effectively handed him the keys to the studio hoping that lightning would strike a fifth and sixth time. When he delivered them *Blow-Up* in 1966 it came with the expected bolt of lightning, all right, but it also ignited an unexpected firestorm with the Production Code.

At issue was what became known as "the purple paper sequence" and the presence of Vanessa Redgrave's uncovered breasts. But in the way censors have of seeing pieces instead of context, Geoffrey Shurlock, who then ran the Production Code Administration, raised the flag of mixed signals after reading only a treatment for what was then titled *The Shot*.[4] In a letter to MGM producer Robert Vogel, Shurlock, on the one hand, deemed that the material "seems acceptable under the provisions of the production Code." But he then forbade the studio from showing nudity "in various forms and stages," a sex relationship between two teenagers that "would not be approvable under the code," and "a scene in which Bill and his wife are making love and she looks invitingly at him. That, he said, "seems to us to verge on the pornographic."[5]

By April 27, Shurlock had seen a screenplay for what was next titled *The Antonioni Picture*. He repeated that it was basically acceptable but that the scene of Thomas having sex with teenagers was not, and that another scene in which he tries to bring a woman to orgasm with the phrase, "Make it come..." was crude. He also objected to the expression, "Thank Christ" on page 17.[6] A letter on July 19 from Shurlock to Vogel expresses relief that everything but "Make it come..." had been fixed for the film now titled *The Antonioni Picture (The Blowup)*.[7] But it hardly mattered, as Antonioni considered the script only a starting place, not a finishing point, and, besides, he was shooting 5,500 miles away in London.

Some time between July 19 and November 9 – in other words, when Antonioni delivered his cut to MGM – the venerable, respectable, traditional studio had a seizure. The Production Code Administration, having seen *Blow-Up*, refused to accord it a Code seal. With the $1.8 million film's New York opening slated for December 18, and with MGM obligated not to release a film sans seal, the company looked for a solution.[8] They found it in Ben Melniker, the company's longtime negotiator nicknamed The MGM Lion when he was spoken of out loud, but more often called the studio's hatchet man.

Melniker, in telephone and informal meetings with Sidney Schreiber of the Production Code Administration and in conference with Robert O'Brien, who then headed MGM, settled on forming a new company, Premiere Productions, that would not be a Code signatory and could therefore distribute *The Blow Up* (sic). MGM's name would appear nowhere, only producer Carlo Ponti's. Advertising would indicate that the film was "Suggested for Mature Audiences" (SMA) and MGM's advertising chief Dan S. Terrell would clear the ads with Michael Linden of the MPAA's Advertising

Code office.[9] Linden confirmed this agreement to Shurlock with copies to, among other people, Jack Valenti, the new president of the MPAA.[10]

Antonioni rejected MGM's proposed cuts that would earn the film a Code seal. He added that the only cuts he was obligated to accept were those made by a government. An unnamed MGM source responded that this was not the case but deferred to Antonioni's wishes.[11] The SMA chicanery avoided a messy conflict with Antonioni who, although he did not have final cut, held sway as a major figure in international cinema whom MGM did not want to aggrieve. What's noteworthy is that everybody on the street knew that *Blow-Up* was an MGM picture regardless of what the posters, advertising, and opening credits of the film insisted.

Yet the Code files reveal something never brought to light about those proceedings. On November 14, 1966 Shurlock and his assistant Jack Vizzard flew to New York to screen the film and asked for cuts in two sequences. MGM approved them and resubmitted the film for a Code seal and were told that one would be issued. Only then did the studio bring Antonioni into the discussion, as he would have to approve the cuts. The studio then asked to delay in issuing a certificate. In early December, Vizzard flew to MGM and explained to Antonioni why the cuts were necessary. Antonioni again rejected them.[12] But then, curiously, he quietly made the requested edits anyway (trimming the sex scene between Bill and his wife), as *Variety* reported on January 26, 1967 after its astute reporter compared what he had seen at the trade screening with what was then playing.[13] The next day producer Robert Vogel wrote Shurlock asking to reapply for a Code seal.[14] Suddenly, on January 27, 1967, the request was withdrawn.[15] No clarification is noted.

The film's opening on December 18, 1966 had drawn the expected range of opinion from critics, some embracing its obscurity and others yearning (and yawning) for answers. Among the college crowd – that is, young mature audiences whom the SMA rating suggested should see the film – the results were more positive, at least surrounding the "purple paper" sequence. This was a scene (at 1:11:00) in which fashion photographer David Hemmings picks up and has a fling with two young women and together they romp on a purple-colored paper studio backdrop which tumbles with them to the floor and enwraps them all. Rumors at the time were that the actresses, who were topless, also expose themselves in the course of the tussle.[16] The advent of home video with single-frame capability yielded the answer: Yes.

The MPAA never officially rated *Blow-Up*, but history has.

---

1. Attributed to cartoonist Johnny Hart in "B.C."
2. Ezra Goodman, *The Fifty-Year Decline and Fall of Hollywood*, New York: Simon and Schuster, 1961.
3. Screenplay by Alan Sharp.
4. A treatment is a detailed prose rendering of a proposed film.
5. Shurlock to Vogel, March 30, 1966 (AMPAS).
6. Shurlock to Vogel, April 27, 1966 (AMPAS).

7. Shurlock to Vogel, July 19, 1966 (AMPAS).
8. Schreiber to file, November 9, 1966 (AMPAS).
9. Terrell to Linden, November 28, 1966. (AMAPS).
10. Valenti was hired June 1, 1966 at the urging of Lew Wasserman of Universal Studios and with the consent of President Lyndon Johnson, for whom Valenti had previously served as Special Assistant
11. Unsigned, "*Blow-Up* Director Puts MGM in Code Hang-Up; Catholics' Views Pend," *Variety*, December 14, 1966; addendum, December 13, 1966 (AMPAS).
12. Unsigned report-to-file (AMPAS).
13. Unsigned, "MGM Prunes Print on QT," *Variety*, January 26, 1966 (AMPAS).
14. Vogel to Shurlock, January 27, 1967 (AMPAS).
15. Unsigned report-to-file (AMPAS).
16. See for yourself: https://www.youtube.com/watch?v=nFJg3bsRJm4.

The Bridge on the River Kwai

Columbia Pictures, 1957
Written by Carl Foreman and Michael Wilson (both initially uncredited), from the book by Pierre Boulle (who was initially credited)
Produced by Sam Spiegel
Directed by David Lean
Code seal #18737

Synopsis
British troops in a Japanese prison-of-war camp in occupied Burma during World War II are ordered to build a railroad bridge under the direction of their own Colonel Nicholson (Alec Guinness), who is engaged in a test of wills with the Japanese Colonel Saito (Sessue Hayakawa), who both men realize is in over his head. At the same time, a team of British commandos (Jack Hawkins, Geoffrey Horne) and an American escapee from the POW camp (William Holden) make their way to the Kwai bridge to destroy it, which they do – but at what cost?

Background
Written by two blacklisted screenwriters (Carl Foreman and Michael Wilson, sequentially) whose credit was wrongly accorded to the French book author who spoke no English, *The Bridge on the River Kwai* was the film that brought director David Lean to international attention and mercurial producer Sam Spiegel to international notoriety. It was among the first Hollywood super-productions to be shot on a distant location, beginning a wave of so-called runaway productions that – for good or ill – spread Hollywood influence worldwide.

The name David Lean is inescapably associated with quality, but he was not an internationally known director when he embarked on *The Bridge on the River Kwai*, and Geoffrey Shurlock of the Code office was not impressed. He wrote Duncan Cassell of Columbia Pictures on October 12, 1956 of "important items which will require your careful consideration."[1] The violence in what was clearly a war film was minimal but nevertheless worrisome:

> Page 74: The manner in which the last surviving Japanese is killed seems unduly brutal and we ask that it be altered. We suggest that the wounded soldier still be capable of some sort of resistance when Shears (Holden) goes after him.

In the final film: he's killed and that's that.

> Page 148: The killing of Joyce (Horne) and Warden (Hawkins) should not be excessively brutal.

In the final film: Joyce is shot without apparent damage and the reaction is played on the female bearer, who has become fond of him. Warden is not killed.

It may be noted that the Code office had no problem with Colonel Nicholson's torturous but bloodless confinement in the "sweat box" designed to make him capitulate to Colonel Saito's demand that officers work alongside the men.

David Lean's films are known for their elegance and classicism, not violence. Even *Lawrence of Arabia* (q.v.), with its "no prisoners" slaughter sequence, shows the killings only by suggestion, and then just their horrifying aftermath. Sex, however, was something from which Lean never shied, though he generally kept it as a simmering subtext (the Sarah Miles-Christopher Jones idyll in *Ryan's Daughter* is an exception). The Code was concerned about that, too, in the otherwise all-male cast of *Kwai*. In the film, women are villagers who rescue Shears after he escapes from the POW camp and play a selection of guides who bring the commandos back to the camp.

The women, needless to say, were added to the story for commercial reasons. Says Stephen M. Silverman, David Lean's biographer, "Harry Cohn himself, and then the studio execs, were concerned there were no white women in the picture, and given that they had a romantic lead in William Holden, Columbia insisted that the small role of the nurse, played by Ann Sears, be inserted. David thought that 'ridiculous' but went along. Beyond that, he never mentioned to me any deletion or alteration of language or action."[2]

Shurlock was concerned about the native women, writing:

> Page 71 and 72: We could not approve the indication that the women had stripped themselves naked as indicated in scene 323. In addition, the men must be adequately clothed throughout this sequence in order to avoid anything of an objectionably suggestive nature when the women help them remove the leaches.

In the final film, the women remain fully clothed and the men remove, if anything, their shirts. There is one leach.

> Page 73: In order to prove acceptable, the women should not be bathing nude throughout the scene on this page.

In the final film, Only the men bathe, although a topless Shears does get a bath from one of the women.

> Page 75: We assume careful discretion will be exercised when Barnet almost loses all of his clothing.[3]

In the final film, there is no character named Barnet, nor is he in the studio synopsis.

Given the call for rewrites, the authorship of the script is of interest, although the Code files give no indication that blacklistees were involved. Sam Spiegel initially hired Carl Foreman, who was at the time blacklisted, to adapt the Boulle book. When David Lean read Foreman's take, he believed that Foreman was only using the book to articulate his own political feelings, not those of the story that Lean wanted to tell.[4] After some weeks of collaboration, Lean asked Spiegel to replace Foreman and hire Michael Wilson. Wilson, another blacklisted writer (who would go on to write *Lawrence of Arabia*, also initially without credit), focused on Shears, the American. Nevertheless, Lean always maintained that Wilson was the principal writer of *Kwai*.[5]

One instance of censorship, however, was volunteered by Lean himself. At the beginning of the film, Colonel Nicholson's men, who have been ordered by their British higher-ups to surrender, march haughtily into the POW camp to show that they are unbroken (even though, of course, they are). As a way to take the mickey out of the Japanese, Lean had them whistle the "Colonel Bogey March," which few audiences outside of Britain knew at the time but, with *Kwai*'s popularity, everybody since then does. Lean could not allow them to sing the lyrics, however, which are enthusiastically vulgar:

> Hitler has only got one ball;
> Göring has two but they are small;
> Himmler
> Has something sim'lar;
> And poor old Göbbels
> Has no balls at all.

The Code files reveal something else that has baffled film scholars for decades: the ending in which the mortally wounded Colonel Nicholson falls on the plunger to detonate the bridge explosives. Does he do so purposely or fortuitously? The official synopsis from Colombia Pictures reads:

> Warden (Jack Hawkins) aims his mortar. The train is starting across the bridge. Nicholson (Alec Guinness) looks down at Shears (William Holden), murmuring, "What have I done?" Warden's mortar shell explodes near Nicholson, who, fatally wounded, now tries to reach the detonator himself. As he collapses, his body falls on the plunger.[6]

It would seem to end the debate. But as anyone who has ever seen a David Lean film should gather, there are no easy answers, and even a character's dying determination may not be predictable. In the book, for example, the bridge is not destroyed, it is only damaged, and can be easily rebuilt; such is Pierre Boulle's comment on the futility of war. Of course, a $2.8 million film could never end with such ambiguity, so the river Kwai had to be strewn with the detritus of the hard-fought bridge – a bridge which was the obvious symbol for the hope of uniting world cultures.[7]

John Milius, who is both a filmmaker and military historian, disputes the official explanation. "My interpretation of the ending," he says, "is that he doesn't fall on [the plunger] deliberately, that he just dies and falls on it, and it just happens to be there and it goes off at just the right time. Because he would never blow up his bridge. He's been doing everything he can to stop it and he's not going to realize all of a sudden, 'My god, I've got to blow this up and blow this train up.' I mean, that's not in his character. He just happens to fall over on the charging handle and it goes up. That's probably a bit of a Hollywood stretch, but it's okay because everything else is so wonderfully crazy in the end."[8]

"But," adds Norman Spencer, David Lean's assistant, "on the day of shooting it was never really decided or clearly defined as to the motivation. Did he do it in a moment of repentance or did he just fall on it? And it was never, ever really resolved. Never... and David said, 'well, maybe be stunned by the bomb blast that's gone off, look toward the heavens, spin around, and then fall on the detonator, and that way it really doesn't matter. The motivation can be enigmatic.'"[9]

Kwai and its Oscars conferred world-class status upon David Lean, and the Code correspondence showed how diligent the Hays/Breen/Shurlock Office was, even when it seemed there should be nothing to criticize. Considering that all the member film companies tithed to support the MPAA and Code, this tempest in a cinematic teapot seems more like busywork intended to show Columbia Pictures that the Code office was earning its keep rather than that there was anything with *Kwai* worth complaining about.

---

1. Shurlock to Cassell, October 12, 1956.
2. E-mail interview with Stephen M. Silverman.
3. This refers to an October 5, 1956 draft script that was sent to the Code office in error and corrected with an apparently later script submitted with a November 14, 1956 letter to Shurlock from Sam Rheiner of Horizon-American Pictures, Inc., Sam Spiegel's company.
4. Kevin Brownlow, *David Lean: A Biography*, New York: St. Martin's Press, 1996.
5. Stephen M. Silverman, *David Lean*, New York: Harry N. Abrams, Publishers, 1989, 1992. Boulle won the Oscar for adapted screenplay even though he did no work on it and spoke little English. Foreman's and Wilson's credits were restored in 1984.
6. Columbia Pictures synopsis, November 1, 1957 (AMPAS).
7. It surely worked. The film's worldwide gross was $27.2 million. The budget estimate is from Norman Spencer on the *Bridge on the River Kwai* DVD special features.
8. John Milius interviewed on special features, *The Bridge on the River Kwai* DVD.
9. Norman Spencer interview, *Bridge on the River Kwai* DVD special features.

Bringing Up Baby

RKO Radio Pictures, 1938
Written by Dudley Nichols & Hagar Wilde, from a story by Hagar Wilde
Produced by Howard Hawks (uncredited) and Cliff Reid
Directed by Howard Hawks
Code seal #3752

Synopsis
Susan (Katharine Hepburn), a madcap heiress, distracts a befuddled paleontologist, David (Cary Grant), who is trying to raise money to reconstruct a brontosaurus skeleton when Susan's dog George (Asta) steals the final bone and is stalked by an escaped leopard, Baby (Nissa), who has been sent to Susan as a gift. Eventually, after all their adventures, David reciprocates Susan's love.

Background
If you made it through that synopsis, you're more than game for the obstacles that the Breen Office put in place of a Code seal. It's hard to believe, now that it has become a bona fide classic, but *Bringing Up Baby* was a commercial flop, seriously damaging Katharine Hepburn's career. As with *His Girl Friday* (q.v.), one can never be sure what Cary Grant is mumbling at certain times, adding to the subversive nature of Howard Hawks' filmmaking. While it is tempting to "cancel" the film for exploiting scatterbrains, it must be noted that Susan wins in the end, and on her own terms.

Breen happily okayed the script but cautioned the studio about using the word "tramp" applied to a woman, and not to allow Susan's "person" be seen when her dress is torn in the supper club (no view of lace panties, either) when David covers her exposed posterior with his top hat. The Canadian censor, however, insisted on deleting Susan telling David, as he does so, "Will you please stop doing that with your hat."[1]

The censors completely missed a moment early in the film when David, searching where to place a particular bone on his brontosaurus skeleton, suggests to his assistant/fiancée Alice:

David
Alice, I think this one must belong in the tail.

Alice
Nonsense. You tried it in the tail yesterday and it didn't fit.

This is clearly a reference to anal intercourse. There is also the moment when David, wearing Susan's feathery nightgown after a shower, explains his clothing to a baffled Aunt Elizabeth (May Robson):

> *Elizabeth*
> Well why are you wearing these clothes?
>
> *David*
> Because I just went gay all of a sudden!

While *gay* was not in widespread use at the time to mean homosexual, anyone who was aware of the slang would have marked it as running afoul of the Code's prohibition of "sex perversion" (which is what they called homosexuality).

As is well known, *Bringing Up Baby* was not a box office success, and its failure, along with other Katharine Hepburn pictures at the time, caused exhibitors to brand her "box office poison." It's difficult to understand with nearly a century of perspective how anybody could have missed its excellence on every level: writing, performance and direction. Then again, that may be Howard Hawks' great strength: keep it moving, keep talking, and carry the viewers along so fast that they never stop to think about what they're hearing.

Certainly it worked with the censors.

---

1. Breen to Sam Briskin, September 20, 1937.

Casablanca

Warner Bros., 1942
Written by Julius J. Epstein, Philip G. Epstein, Howard Koch, Casey Robinson (uncredited), from the play by Murray Burnett and Joan Alison
Produced by Hal B. Wallis
Directed by Michael Curtiz
Code seal #8457

Synopsis
American ex-patriot Richard Blaine (Humphrey Bogart) goes from isolationist to involvement when a former sweetheart (Ingrid Bergman) shows up in his Moroccan saloon with her resistance hero husband (Paul Henreid). *Or...* A woman who left her lover in wartime Germany when she discovered that her imprisoned husband was alive meets her former lover in a Moroccan bar when she is desperate for his help. *Or...* A corrupt Moroccan police chief (Claude Rains) comes to his senses about national loyalty when he sees his friend fall off the political fence. *Or...* A resistance fighter on the run must put aside questions of his wife's devotion when he meets her former lover who holds the key to his escaping Nazi persecution. *Or...* An American nightclub operator in French Morocco helps an anti-Nazi couple escape to America via Lisbon.

Background
Casablanca stands as one of the finest examples of the old studio system. It was an amalgam of work by at least four writers, a director and cast who didn't know how the film was going to end, a producer who was fighting with his boss over credit, and a real-life war that America was losing when the movie went into production. *Casablanca* succeeds in the way that they say a bumblebee is aerodynamically unsound and shouldn't be able to fly, but nobody ever told it that, so it does.

The strength of *Casablanca* can be seen in the multiple synopses that can be distilled from its rich fabric of character, plot, dialogue, acting and direction that balances everything with the precision of an atomic clock. In fact, the colorless fifth logline (above) is the one used by the Production Code Administration as they tracked the film through its production stages.

It's impossible to write anything new about *Casablanca*, but it is possible to see how the Production Code – just like the people who worked on the picture – had no idea that they were dealing with what would become one of the most popular motion pictures of all time.

As befits a production that came together in pieces, as each successive writer took a whack at the script while facing a shooting deadline, the evaluative letters from Joseph Breen to Jack Warner read like someone taking snapshots of a river. Breen flooded Warner with comments and prohibitions on May 19, 21, 22 and 27, and June 5 and 18. Considering that shooting had begun on May 15 and wrapped on August 3,[1] the Breen office was playing a constant game of catch-up and the filmmakers were on alert in case they needed to revise something they had just shot.

The list of objectionable material is interesting in that not all of it was obeyed, as anyone knows who has seen the film:

> May 19, 1942: The following lines seem unacceptably sex-suggestive and should be changed: "Of course, a beautiful young girl for M'sieur Renault, the Prefect of Police" and "The girl will be released in the morning."
>
> Please submit all lyrics [to "As Time Goes By"] to be used throughout the production.
>
> Also the following lines seem unacceptably sex-suggestive: "I used to take a villa at Cannes, or the very least, a string of pearls – now all I ask is an exit visa" and "How extravagant you are, throwing away women like that. Some day they may be rationed." (See June 5, 1942)

Breen also wanted the Code's Latin-American advisor, Addison Durland, to vet the film's portrayal of a South American singer (Madeline Lebeau).[2]

> May 21, 1942: We cannot approve the present suggestion that Capt. Renault makes a practice of seducing the women to whom he grants visas; the following dialogue is unacceptable [for sex suggestiveness]: "By the way, another visa problem has come up," "show her in," "You'll find it worth your while."[3]
>
> The suggestion that Ilsa was married all the time she was having her love affair with Rick in Paris seems unacceptable, and could not be approved in the finished picture. Hence we request the deletion of Ilsa's line, "Even when I knew you in Paris."[4]

On May 22, Breen wrote Warner that the May 19 changes met the requirements of the Code. On June 5, however (eleven days after the start of principal photography), Breen responded to Warner, saying that Breen and producer Hal Wallis had an understanding that, in the characterization of Renault's seduction-for-visa trade, "the several references to this phase of the gentleman's character will be materially toned down, to wit: the line 'the girl will be released in the morning' will be changed to the expression, 'will be released later'; the line in scene 16, 'Now all I ask is an exit visa' will be deleted; and the line 'someday they may be rationed' will be changed to 'some day they may be scarce.'"⁵ Breen also said that he and Wallis had agreed to delete the dialogue, "they went along with the sound of a tinny piano in the parlor downstairs" because it sounded like a reference to a "bawdy house" (brothel).

> The line "you enjoy war, I enjoy women" would be changed to "you like war, I like women" and Rick's line "Captain Renault is branching out" will be changed to "Captain Renault seems to be getting broad-minded."

These changes, specified in writing, are atypical for Breen. It is almost as though he doesn't trust either Wallis or Warner or both to keep a promise. As anyone who has seen the film will observe, Humphrey Bogart (Rick) and Claude Rains (Renault) managed to convey with a glance much of the dialogue that was ordered cut. Additionally, the line "Captain Renault seems to be getting broad-minded" is more salacious than "branching out" in that the word *broad* is cited on the list of "Don'ts and Be Carefuls" (q.v.) as a pejorative for women.

Casablanca opened in America on January 23, 1943 after its November 26, 1942 New York premiere. Its box office was helped immeasurably by President Franklin Roosevelt's return from meeting British Prime Minister Winston Churchill in the actual Moroccan Casablanca two days before the film opened, and the papers were full of the name. The film went on, of course, to be chosen best picture of the year, among other honors, by the motion picture Academy and to be accepted worldwide as a classic.

Except for Sweden. A confidential report in the Code files dated November 16, 1943 shows two pages of dialogue deletions by Swedish censors, almost all of them having to do with wisecracks about Germany.⁶ Perhaps this sensitivity is because Sweden had surrendered to Hitler on May 12, 1941.

---

1. Charles Francisco, *You Must Remember This: The Filming of Casablanca*. Englewood Cliffs, New Jersey: Prentice Hall, 1980.
2. Lebeau played Rick's spurned mistress who memorably calls out "Vive la France, vive la démocratie!" after the band plays "La Marseillaise."
3. It is also, by today's more enlightened standards, rape. It is therefore noteworthy that the Code furthered the misconception that unwanted or coerced sex was somehow a joking matter.
4. Breen to Warner May 21, 1942.
5. Breen to Warner, June 5, 1942, et seq (AMPAS).
6. Unsigned memo to file October 16, 1943 (AMPAS).

Convention City

Warner Bros., 1933
Written by Robert Lord and Edward Chodorov (uncredited), from a story by Peter Milne.
Produced by Henry Blanke
Directed by Archie Mayo
Code seal: Pre-Code

Synopsis
The convention of the Honeywell Rubber Company in Atlantic City, New Jersey is the setting – make that the opportunity – for countless episodes of drunkenness and romantic dalliances as the head of the company, J.B. Honeywell (Grant Mitchell), has to decide who will be his new sales manager: T.R. Kent (Adolphe Menjou) or George Ellerbe (Guy Kibbee).

Background
Film scholar William K. Everson has said that *Convention City* is the film that almost single-handedly brought on enforcement of the Production Code starting in 1934.[1] While it might be argued that the trigger was *The Story of Temple Drake* (q.v.), why split hairs? Both films made the newly reorganized Code office clutch its pearls and have conniptions. *Convention City* practically uses the "Don'ts and Be Carefuls" list as its screenplay. Or so it is rumored, for no prints of this scurrilous film are known to exist and nobody has seen it in over eighty years. Reportedly, it was confiscated by specific order of studio head Jack L. Warner and wiped off the face of the earth.

This is the most famous film that nobody you know has ever seen. The synopsis itself reads like the plot of a porno movie, and that's practically what the Code thought of it when their James Wingate wrote Jack L. Warner on September 14, 1933 with three single-spaced typed pages of "suggested" deletions topped by a first paragraph that called it "a pretty rowdy picture, dealing very largely with drunkenness, blackmail and lechery, and without any particularly sympathetic characters or elements."[2] Wingate was reassured, he wrote, by producer Hal Wallis's assurance that it would all be played for laughs. In that spirit, he offered a number of items "to which we believe further attention should be given in order to avoid Code and censorship difficulties."[3]

    It would take a flow chart to track all the cuts and changes wrought to *Convention City* along its peripatetic odyssey, but here are the highlights – or lowlights, depending on one's point of view, forming an adventure in understatement.

> Page 20: In line with Mr. Wallis' statement, we recommend much toning down of the indications of drunkenness throughout the

picture. We would call particular attention on this page to the scene of the porter dead drunk on the floor, as well as to other indications of drunkenness in this sequence.

Page 21: This broken "traveling salesman" story may be censorable, and we suggest you protect yourself on it.

Page 27: We suggest modifying the line "stage our honeymoon in Macy's window" under the Code, perhaps replacing it with "our wedding."

Page 49: We believe it will be necessary under the Code to delete the final part of this scene, including the dialogue "Madam, I want my trousers" and the girl's answer, "you can have 'em if you come into the other room and take 'em off me."

Page 58: We recommend deleting under the Code the lines, "You know where you can stick it" and "That's twice the union rate."

Page 70: Care will be needed of this action of George stroking the coat under Nancy's bosom.

Page 96: The word "slut" will probably be censorable.

Page 123: We believe this scene between Bill and Orchard should be modified under the Code, by deleting the lines "I'm taking him out to show him the facts of life. Like to come along"; "No thanks, my mother already told me." Also, the line, "There ain't no ten commandments and a man can raise – a thirst," if used, should be delivered straight.

Delete the lines "Ted, she's only a child" and "She's old enough."

Page 128: Delete the underlined word in the line "Do you think he'd ever let you marry her after–"[4]

Unbelievably, Warner Bros. was somehow given the go-ahead to shoot the picture, although there is no correspondence specifically signaling the all-clear. The closest one gets in the Code files is a letter from Wingate to Warner dated November 17 saying that there are still a few things to be addressed, the implication being that all the others had been handled.[5] When *Convention City* was released on December 14, 1933, however, there was a second wave when a number of city censorship boards sharpened their scissors.[6]

Kansas, which Paramount Pictures Distribution Company's A.H. Cole wrote "is considered extremely dry," objected to the portrayal of drinking, not only in *Convention City* but also in RKO's *Flying Down to Rio* (the first

Astaire-Rogers film).[7] Nevertheless, Kansas cleared the film on December 15, 1933.[8] A month later, Breen wrote Cole a congratulatory letter, toasting, "Long life to you!"[9]

New York's censors would only be placated by removing "indecent action of Joan Blondell's lips as man boards train and snatches letter from her."[10]

> Virginia: "Eliminate suggestive remark made by Negro maid to group of chorus girls who have been discussing fatigue incident to the conventions of various industries held in Atlantic City: 'You'd better leave town before the Hercules Tool Company gets here.' Eliminate ribald laugh which follows remark.[11]
>
> Chicago: The Windy City's watchdogs required two-and-a-half pages of dialogue deletions, the most salacious (especially when taken out of context) are:
>
> "Do I look like a man who would break up a home?"
> "Yes."
> "Huh?"
>
> "I'll lose my job – I'll be disgraced – ruined – if this thing gets out."
> "You should have thought of that before you wrecked my home."
> "Now wait a minute."
> "How much is it worth for you to forget all about this?"
> "Five thousand bucks?"
> "I haven't got that much."
> "Er, how much have you got?"
> "A thousand."
> "I'll take it."
> "Oh!"
> "And your check for the rest."
> "Oh."
> "Hello – what's going on here?"
> "Who are you?"
> "Who are you?"
> "Her husband."
>
> "It's the badger game, Frank."
>
> Eliminate the dialogue: "All I got was this coat and about two hundred and fifty dollars."[12]

Pennsylvania, the brotherly love state, rejected two pages of dialogue having to do with love, or at least sex, among the selections:

Kent: "How did you get away?"
George: "She fell asleep, the old Frigidaire!"

Nancy: "Maybe I would. I could take mother south for her kidneys. I could get out of town before she'd tell father, about us."

Kent: "Twenty! Twenty, darling. That's generous, even for conventions. Are you listening?"

Ontario, Canada: Anyone who might have thought that Canadians were more broad-minded should have visited the provinces. The page of dialogue eliminations includes:

"You haven't seen anything yet, baby."
"Neither have you."
"What are you afraid of? Winchell's out of town."
"With your – uh – these and thosies down."[13]

British Columbia, Canada stated the bleeding obvious on February 28, 1934: "Depiction of a convention of lecherous salesmen as described by one of the actresses in dialogue seems fitting and would make this orgy of drunkenness and sensuality unsuitable for family theatres. Sufficient eliminations would make picture useless from entertainment angle. REJECTED."[14] On June 13, 1934, however, the British Columbia Censor Board informed Breen that they did not reject the film, they rated it "P."[15]

Alberta, Canada: Their sole concerns were two scenes of drunkenness in the picture itself. In the trailer, however, they wanted to shorten the scene of Joan Blondell weeping in Dick Powell's room with the dialogue, "Did you stay here all night?"[16]

Quebec was more tolerant except for: "Eliminate scene of Kent kissing Miss Honeywell (Patricia Ellis) after door is opened."[17]

Quebec, Canada: A page and a half of required dialogue and situation deletions included eliminating this provocative array, here taken well out of context:

"Oh! I can do plenty in a minute."
"She knew the minute she looked into my eyes."
"Father said he'll kill the man who…"
"For her kidneys…"
"Your mother's kidneys?"
"They are awfully big."

"I get the angle."
"That's generous even for convention."
"This house of all."[18]

Australia rejected the film in its entirety,[19] as did Zurich, Switzerland.[20]

What's intriguing about these local board demands is that there is very little consistency. It's as if different people are offended by different things, which of course, they were. No wonder it was impossible to create one set of community standards that fit everyone's community.

On September 3, 1936, Warner Bros., under the rules of the MPPA, applied for Code seals for a number of their pre-Code titles that they wished to reissue. Joe Breen (or one of his assistants) diligently listed, on a film-by-film basis, what would have to be cut in order to qualify for seals under the present Code. *Convention City* was on a list of a dozen films for which the answer was, in effect, "Fat chance":

> With regard to the following, we take the liberty of suggesting that you withdraw your request for a certificate to permit their reissue. The examination of our files would seem to indicate that they contain so much objectionable matter that any attempt to re-edit them so as to bring them within the requirements of the Production Code would be extremely difficult.[21]

On December 27, 1948, Jack L. Warner issued orders to have the negative, all elements, and all prints of *Convention City* destroyed.[22] Despite relentless archive searches by numerous scholars and film restoration experts, no scrap of it has been found. Only the trailer remains, which is readily available online. *Convention City*, the 40-reel uncut version of Erich von Stroheim's *Greed*, the missing scenes from Billy Wilder's *The Private Life of Sherlock Holmes*, and Orson Welles' full *Magnificent Ambersons* head the list of most-wanted lost films among cinephiles. If *Convention City* seems out of place in this heady company, keep in mind that forbidden fruit is the sweetest of all.

---

1. Conversation with the author.
2. Wingate to Warner, September 14, 1933 (AMPAS).
3. Wingate to Warner, September 14, 1933 (AMPAS).
4. Wingate to Warner, September 14, 1944 (AMPAS).
5. Wingate to Warner, November 17, 1933 (AMPAS).
6. Sometimes characters are named, but usually it's just dialogue that's noted.
7. Cole to Breen, January 12, 1934 (AMPAS).
8. Wingate to file, December 15, 1933 (AMPAS).
9. Breen to Cole, January 15, 1934 (AMPAS).
10. Wingate to file, December 7, 1933 (AMPAS).
11. Wingate to file, December 13, 1933 (AMPAS).
12. Wingate to file, February 5, 1934 (noted January 10, 1934) (AMPAS).
13. Wingate to file, February 8, 1934 (noted January 22, 1934) (AMPAS).

14. Wingate to file, March 8, 1934 (noted February 7, 1934) (AMPAS).
15. Breen to file, June 13, 1934 (noted February 28, 1934). Canada's "P" rating is no longer in use.
16. Wingate to file, March 28, 1934 (noted March 10, 1934) (AMPAS).
17. Wingate to file, May 31, 19334 (ASMAS).
18. Breen to file, June 23, 1934 (noted February 29, 1934).
19. Breen to file April 3, 1934 (AMPAS).
20. Unsigned to file, November 23, 1938 (sic).
21. Breen to Warner, September 3, 1936 (AMPAS). The other "difficult" films included *A Modern Hero, Goodbye Again, Lily Turner, Mary Stevens M.D., Picture Snatcher, Merry Wives of Reno, Easy to Love, Blessed Event, Scarlet Dawn, Central Airport* and *Lady Killer*.
22. Details can be gleaned from Ron Hutchinson's authoritative web page: http://www.classicmoviehub.com/blog/vitaphone-view-where-is-convention-city-hiding/

Crossfire

RKO Radio Pictures, 1947
Written by John Paxton, from Richard Brooks' novel *The Brick Foxhole*
Produced by Adrian Scott
Directed by Edward Dmytryk
Code seal #12325

Synopsis
The murder of a Jew in Washington, DC just after World War II leads investigators to a group of people who knew him and, on closer inspection, reveals the issue of anti-Semitism.

Background
Richard Brooks was stationed stateside in the service during World War II and wrote *The Brick Foxhole* based on character types he knew in the Army, although not upon anyone in particular. When the book was published, he faced Court Martial for failing to have it authorized by the brass, but when it started drawing praise from major authors as well as generating news stories, the threats of discipline went away.[1]

The Brick Foxhole is about the murder of a gay man. *Crossfire*, the motion picture that was made from it, is about the murder of a Jew. The changes made from book to screen say a lot about Hollywood's treatment of both Jews and homosexuals, which was played out before the Production Code.

For starters, a gay victim was out of the question. Homosexuality was called "sex perversion" by the Code, which wouldn't even use the word itself, so not only was homosexuality "the love that dare not speak its name," the Code wouldn't speak it either.[2] In changing the victim from a gay to a Jew, screenwriter John Paxton had to face Hollywood's uneasiness with its own Judaism, a sensitivity raised to new levels following the liberation of the concentration camps after World War II and the recognition of the Holocaust.

Converting homosexuality to Judaism was on the mind of William Gordon of RKO Radio Pictures, the studio that had bought the rights to Brooks' novel, when he wrote Breen on July 10, 1945 that he had discussed the book with Geoffrey Shurlock (Breen's assistant): "While we recognize that as presently constituted this novel will probably not pass muster under the Production Code, we yet would appreciate an opportunity to discuss a certain treatment which one of our producers has in mind."[3] A week later, Breen dug in by writing Gordon that "the story is thoroughly and completely unacceptable" and "any motion picture following, even remotely, along the lines of the novel cannot be approved."[4]

Not until nineteen months later does *The Brick Foxhole* – by then called *Cradle of Fear* – cross Breen's desk again, and he responds a week later to Harold Melniker that "the basic story seems to meet the requirements of the

Code."⁵ There were, however, some "minor items" that Breen felt should be addressed, primarily involving the showing or consumption of liquor, as well as:

> Page 13: We suggest rewriting the line, "some soldiers can get away with that sort of thing" to avoid any suggestion that this refers to adultery.
>
> Page 15: We suggest changing the expression, "nigger."
>
> Page 18A: Please change the expression "lousy" (used twice).
>
> Page 25: Please change the line, "I say nuts," as being on the Association's list of forbidden words.
>
> Page 35: We recommend changing the expression "kikes."
>
> Page 47: We feel it will be essential to make some radical change in this scene, which will remove any flavor of prostitution. Our recommendation is that this man who wanders in should definitely be indicated as Ginny's divorced or separated husband who is trying to win her back.
>
> Page 53: We suggest changing the expression "Yid."
>
> It is understood, of course, that there will be no suggestion of a "pansy" characterization about Samuels or his relationship with the soldiers.
>
> In conclusion, we assume that you will make certain that nothing in the finished picture will cause any complaint from the War Department.⁶

After cautioning yet again about showing liquor and liquor consumption or about dialogue referring to it, Breen later reminded RKO to be careful about keeping the women's costumes modest. Then he threw in a P.S.: "On page 1, we suggest the advisability of omitting the name of Jesus Christ in the opening narration, in view of the fact that in its present context, being mentioned along with Genghis Khan and Atilla the Hun, it might prove highly offensive to religious-minded people."⁷ This foreword was eliminated.

Between March 7 and March 21, 1947 there followed twelve letters indicating ninety pages by number on which changes were made. The procedure was for the film company to send the Code office each rewritten page for inspection. The picture was completed, and on March 10, RKO notified Breen that *Cradle of Fear* was being retitled *Crossfire*. A Code seal was issued April 14, 1947 and the picture opened to acclaim in New York on July 22 and across America on August 15.

The film made a profit of $1,270,000[8] on a somewhat larger-than-usual RKO budget of $678,000.[9] That success, however, didn't mean a thing when the film's director, Edward Dmytryk, and its producer, Adrian Scott, were subpoenaed to testify before the House Un-American Activities Committee on October 20 about their alleged ties to Communism. There's a wretched irony that HUAC, whose shameful history includes an anti-Semitic agenda, would call two non-Jewish members of the Hollywood Ten who had just made a film about anti-Semitism, to accuse them of being un-American.[10] But that's another story.

Note: No doubt because of its sympathetic portrayal of a Jew, *Crossfire* was banned in Egypt.[11] The U.S. military showed it only on its bases in the United States with the exception of the U.S. Navy, which refused to show it at all.[12]

1. Ben Terrall, "Book vs. Film, The Brick Foxhole vs. Crossfire," *Noir City* No. 30, filmnoirfoundation.org.
2. Effeminate characters, of course, were rife, most often played by Edward Everett Horton, Eric Blore, Franklin Pangborn, or Grady Sutton. They were never called gay, only "confirmed bachelors."
3. Gordon to Breen, July 10, 1945 (AMPAS).
4. Breen to Gordon, July 17, 1945 (AMPAS).
5. Breen to Harold Melniker, February 27, 1947 (AMPAS).
6. Harold Melniker to Breen, February 19, 1947 (AMPAS).
7. Breen to Harold Melniker, February 27, 1947.
8. Richard Jewell & Vernon Harbin, *The RKO Story*. New Rochelle, New York: Arlington House, 1982.
9. Scott Eyman, *Lion of Hollywood: The Life and Legend of Louis B. Mayer*, New York: Simon and Schuster, 2005.
10. The other two non-Jewish members of the Hollywood Ten were Ring Lardner, Jr. and Dalton Trumbo.
11. Breen to file, November 10, 1947 (reported November 12, 1947) (AMPAS).
12. Gene Brown, *Movie Time: A Chronology of Hollywood and the Movie Industry from Its Beginnings to the Present*, New York: MacMillan, 1995

Design for Living

Paramount Pictures, 1933
Written by Ben Hecht with Samuel Hoffenstein (uncredited), from the play by Noël Coward
Produced and directed by Ernst Lubitsch
Pre-code

Synopsis of the play
Artists Gilda (Lynn Fontanne) and Otto (Alfred Lunt) live together in Paris, but one night while Otto is away, Gilda takes the opportunity to sleep with another artist, their mutual friend Leo (Noël Coward). When Otto returns and discovers this duplicity between his friends, he is furious and leaves. A year and a half later Gilda and Leo are living together when Otto shows up and has an affair with Gilda. Now it's Leo's turn to be furious. When Gilda leaves them both for Ernest (Campbell Gullan), an art dealer, Otto and Leo bond. Two years later Gilda and Ernest are married. She throws a party when Ernest is away. Leo and Otto crash it, disperse the guests, and both declare their love for Gilda. Gilda leaves her house. The next morning, she returns to find that Otto and Leo have presumably slept together. Ernest returns, is livid at the three-way, and stalks off. Gilda, Leo and Otto have a laugh together.

Synopsis of the film
Set in Paris, two Americans – playwright Tom Chambers (Fredric March) and artist George Curtis (Gary Cooper) – fall in love with the same charming woman, Gilda (Miriam Hopkins). Gilda cannot make up her mind which man she loves, so the three decide to live together in a platonic relationship. Friendship turns into competition when George and Tom vie for Gilda's exclusive affections, and she decides to avoid choosing either one of them by marrying her employer, Max Plunkett (Edward Everett Horton). Compared with the ménage, Gilda finds traditional marriage stultifying, and when an uninvited Tom and George attend a party at the Plunkett mansion, Max agrees to a divorce so Gilda can run off with them.

Background
The comedy premiered on Broadway in 1933 instead of London, as otherwise would have been expected for a Noël Coward play, because the producers feared the Lord Chamberlain would put them all in jail over its censorable subject matter. Starring with the married couple of Alfred Lunt and Lynn Fontanne was author Coward himself. Supposedly he drew on the Lunt-Fontanne marriage, which was discreetly open, to inform the play's ménage-à-trois.[1] The characters' names and most everything else were changed for the film. There were so many cuts that Coward said of the adaptation, "I'm told that there are three of my original lines left in the film – such original ones as 'Pass the mustard.'"[2]

Billy Wilder kept a sign on his office wall, "How would Lubitsch do it?" *Design for Living* is the answer, for only Lubitsch could take the panky out of hanky-panky and still retain Coward's intoxicating sexual sophistication. This was astutely recognized by "EEB" of the Code's New York office, who caught the play the night after it opened at the Ethel Barrymore Theatre and reported to Messrs. Wingate (who was pretty much running things) and Shurlock:

> This play is, of course, never really serious for more than a moment, being a vehicle for Coward's sophisticated and witty situations and dialogue. Despite the author's excuse for the unconventionality of the characters' actions on the grounds that they are artists and responsible, accordingly, to their own code of morals, it is somewhat doubtful whether a motion picture audience would take that viewpoint, and a motion picture treatment would be faced with that basic difficulty.

With the gauntlet thus cast, Paramount went to work emasculating the material. On June 14, 1933, Paramount's William H. Wright sent two copies of the script to James Wingate of the Code advising him that the picture was scheduled to start shooting on June 19.[3] On June 19, Wingate sent a three-page letter not to Wright but to Paramount's A.M. Botsford. The first of his numerous notes was an order to make sure that the set is constructed so that even if Gilda, George, and Tom are living together, "there is sufficient accommodation for the three to live separable in the apartment and live up to their bargain of no sex."[4] Among the score-plus "suggestions" for changes are:

> Page A-5: Care will be needed with this scene of the three asleep in the train compartment.
>
> Page A-7: We believe that offense will be taken by the French to the use of Napoleon as the subject of these cartoons.
>
> Page B-1: "It is my unprotected rear that lost me Waterloo" should be deleted under the Code.
>
> Page D-6: Care will be needed in the portrayal of Douglas as an effeminate man.[5]
>
> Pag D-13: We believe this reference to sending orchids should be modified, if it carries a suggestion of sex perversion. This will depend largely on the portrayal of Douglas.
>
> Page E-3: The toilet gag should be eliminated under the Code.

Page G-8: We believe that the dialogue along here indicates a little too specifically that the girl has been having an affair with both men. This will need very careful treatment if the whole sequence is to avoid becoming questionable. It might be possible to cure it by moving up the language on G-9 where Tom says, "You love me" far enough ahead so that the later discussion can be considered as referencing the fact that they have fallen in love, rather than that they have slept together.[6]

Overall, however, Wingate was guarded. "This type of story," he concluded, "will need great care in treatment and direction to avoid making loose and unconventional habits of living appear attractive or condoned. If portrayed in such a manner, it would seem to be a violation of the Code. In a picture of this kind, the finished product must of course be the final criterion. With this in mind, we recommend great care with all details during the course of production."[7]

On Sunday, October 22, Wingate and Shurlock attended a screening of the completed film and, the next day, had a sit-down with Botsford. Three days later they wrote Hays to summarize the meeting: "We attended a preview of this picture last Sunday and noted what we believe to be a major Code violation, as well as a few minor ones. We reviewed it again on Monday, this time in company with Colonel Joy and later had a conference with the studio, at which we went into the matter in some detail. Lubitsch is doing some re-editing and they have promised to let us look at the picture again. We will report on this further."[8]

For another four weeks the matter seemed to be up in the air until, on November 13, the Code's James Wingate rendered the verdict that *Design for Living* "can now be considered as meeting the technical requirements of the Code. We trust it will prove to be a very satisfactory release for your company."[9]

Then the fun started. A new organization called the Legion of Decency, formed by the Catholic Church, released, on May 14, 1934, a list of sixty-three films that they considered "banned." Keeping company on the list with *Design for Living* were such titles as *Convention City* (q.v.), *Easy to Love, George White's Scandals, Jimmy the Gent, Power and Glory* (*The Power and the Glory*), *The Story of Temple Drake* (q.v.), and *Wonderbar*.[10] Confined at this point to Detroit and promoted by Bishop Michael J. Gallagher, the Legion involved having lay Catholics sign a pledge promising to avoid certain films.[11]

Despite this, *Design for Living* was cleared in most of the states where earlier films had found resistance, although some territories demanded additional cuts: Chicago (okay as is), Kansas (two minor dialogue deletions), New York (okay as is), Ohio (minor dialogue deletions and cutting a glance at a store window), British Columbia (extensive dialogue edits), Pennsylvania (moderate dialogue deletions), Quebec (minor dialogue deletions), Australia (cutting whole sequences), Japan (scenes of kissing), Singapore (okay as is),

Britain (numerous cuts), Norway (adults only), Denmark (adults only), and banned entirely in Java, Guatemala, Latvia, Dutch West Indies and Czecho-Slovakia (known as Bohemia-Moravia).

Design for Living was released before films required a Code seal, so when Paramount decided to re-release it in 1935, it was incumbent upon them to apply for a seal. Unfortunately for *Design for Living*, on August 30, 1945, Joseph Breen informed John Hamill of Paramount Productions that the film is "not acceptable under the provisions of the Production Code and the regulations appertaining thereto as now interpreted, and an application for their approval by the Production Code Administration is withheld."[12]

Paramount didn't want to give up. They floated the idea of remaking the film in a manner that could satisfy the Code, only to be flatly informed by Breen, "there are numberless details and lines of dialogue which are completely unacceptable and which could not be approved." Moreover, he recommended that the studio withdraw their application for a seal.[13]

Note: It's interesting to see Gary Cooper playing a sophisticate after seeing him practically trademark the screen image of the strong, silent type (*High Noon, Mr. Deeds, John Doe*, etc.). But he carries off the artist George Curtis so well that Billy Wilder cast him in the equally sophisticated *Love in the Afternoon* (1957), Wilder's charming attempt at making a Lubitsch picture.

And that is how Lubitsch would do it.

---

1. John Simon, "When Icons were Icons," *The New York Times*, December 14, 2003.
2. Dick Richards, *The Wit of Noël Coward*, New York: Sphere Books, 1970.
3. Wright to Wingate, June 14, 1933 (AMPAS).
4. Wingate to Botsford, January 19, 1933 (AMPAS).
5. Good luck with that; Douglas was played by Franklin Pangborn.
6. This is a rare instance in which a Code staffer suggests a substantive change rather than simply a word here or there.
7. Wingate to Botsford, January 19, 1933 (AMPAS).
8. No specifics of the preview were offered in a sweeping report of some two dozen films currently being tracked by the Code office. Wingate to Hays, October 25, 1933 (AMPAS).
9. Wingate to Botsford, November 13, 1933 (AMPAS).
10. EEB to Breen, May 16, 1934 (AMPAS).
11. The Legion of Decency or Catholic Legion of Decency was formed in 1934 by Cincinnati Archbishop John T. McNicholas. In 1965 it was reorganized into the National Catholic Office for Motion Pictures. They shuttered in 1980.
12. Breen to Hammell, August 30, 1935 (AMPAS).
13. Breen to Luigi Luraschi, August 2, 1944 (AMPAS).

East of Eden

Warner Bros., 1955
Screenplay by Paul Osborn, from John Steinbeck's novel
Produced and directed by Elia Kazan
Code seal #17086

Synopsis
In a parable of the Cain and Abel fable set in 1917 in the Salinas Valley in Northern California, brothers Cal (James Dean) and Aron (Richard Davalos) Trask vie for the affection of their Fundamentalist father, Adam (Raymond Massey), who has raised them alone after their mother, Kate (Jo Van Fleet) abandoned the family. Tensions rise when Cal and Abra (Julie Harris) fall in love despite her betrothal to Aron. When Adam loses everything in an agricultural failure, Cal bails him out. Aron joins the wartime Army when Cal reveals to him that their mother is still alive and is a fallen woman. In reaction, Adam has a stroke and Cal takes care of him, choosing to believe that his father forgives him.

Background
East of Eden, the first feature film to be released starring James Dean, instantly established his stardom. Dean, who was reportedly so emotional during the shoot that he frequently broke down in tears, didn't get along with Raymond Massey, who couldn't keep up with his young co-star's changing of lines and physicality, which director Elia Kazan encouraged on the belief that tension between Dean and Massey as actors echoed the estrangement of Cal and Adam.

The film that became a bonanza for Warner Bros., which made three James Dean pictures (*East of Eden, Rebel Without a Cause* and *Giant*), started off at 20th Century Fox. When John Steinbeck's massive novel was scheduled for publication by Viking in 1952, the publisher, as was the tradition, circulated galleys to the studios in search of a film sale. Peter Reid wrote an exquisitely detailed synopsis on April 3, 1952[1] that immediately attracted 20th Century Fox. Jason Joy, director of public relations for the studio, asked Breen what he thought of the property.[2] Breen wrote him back on April 22 that "the novel evidently contains a number of items which could not be approved under the provisions of the Production Code," noting that the most serious offence is that Kate, the boys' mother, is a practising prostitute who escapes punishment for murder by committing suicide."[3] Needless to say, Fox lost interest.

Shortly thereafter, Finlay McDermid of Warner Bros. queried Breen about filming *East of Eden*. Breen responded on September 30 with an exact copy of the cautionary letter he had sent to Joy, including a final paragraph, which included "should you wish to discuss this matter any further, we would be happy to place ourselves at your convenience."⁴ Unlike Fox, Warner took Breen up on his offer. After all, they had on board Elia Kazan, the Broadway sensation who had won an Oscar in 1947 for his direction of *Gentleman's Agreement* (at Fox). On December 1, 1953, Breen, Warner, McDermid, studio operations chief Steve Trilling and distribution head Walter MacEwen sat down with a draft of the screenplay. The next day, Breen confirmed to everyone what they had gone over in the meeting and added that he would be available "to discuss this matter further."⁵

The Code found two objectionable areas in the script, both of them focusing on the brothel where Cal discovers that his mother is a prostitute (he has heard rumors; he is not a customer). The first was the existence and implications of the brothel itself, and the second, to a somewhat lesser degree, is that the sheriff and others in the story do not condemn the brothel because it is so well organized and trouble-free.

The greatest obstacle to filming *East of Eden* was something barely mentioned in the original novel, namely Kate Trask, the mother of Cal and Aron, who left Adam because she didn't want to be a farmer. In Steinbeck's book she sets herself up operating a brothel. As the movie begins, Cal has located her and wants to meet her for any number of reasons, but is rebuffed. Breen asserted the Code's power to deny anything relating to prostitution and cited its recent banning of the Italian film *Bicycle Thieves* because it had a scene in a brothel and so was not suitable for general audiences.

The problem, as anyone knows who has read *East of Eden*, was that the brothel was a central motivation and is the only way to connect the second half of the epic story with the first. "When we discussed this story previously with Mr. Trilling and Mr. McDermid and Mr. Kazan about a year ago," Breen wrote, "we agreed that it would be acceptable to establish the fact that Adam's wife has become a prostitute. But we endeavored to make it clear at the time that we did not feel that we could go any further than merely establishing the fact, which is necessary to bring about the climactic tragedy of the story."⁶

Kazan wrote two letters to Steve Trilling on January 3 and 4, 1954, both of which were passed to Jack Vizzard of the Code office by Finlay McDermid, to whom Trilling had given them. In the first, written from scriptwriter Paul Osborn's house, Kazan says that he and Osborn have made the brothel look as dingy and unwelcoming as possible so as to cast aspersions on prostitution. He also said that they are working on ways to handle the sheriff's apparent tolerance of the brothel, and shared Trilling's concern that too much sympathy was being accorded to Kate.⁷ In his longer, more elaborate follow-up letter, Kazan reiterates that he wants to make the brothel ugly and that he wouldn't show any towels or props that suggest prostitution. He said he faced similar issues on *A Streetcar Named Desire* and managed to overcome them.⁸ Kazan then added an unusual comment saying, in essence, that he always got the feeling from Jeff (Geoffrey Shurlock) and Jack (Jack Vizzard) that if a filmmaker's intent was "honest," he should be accorded more freedom under the Code than if he was simply making entertainment. Kazan, who could manipulate anybody, quickly discovered that the Code was not malleable. In a series of notes "to the file" from Jack Vizzard in which he summarized meetings and phone calls he'd had with Kazan and others at the studio, it was clear that little progress was being made on the matter of the brothel.[9]

Somewhere between May 17 and May 21, Kazan, Osborn and unnamed others devised a solution that now exists in the finished film. Rather than having made her fortune in prostitution, Kate owns a gambling and dancing emporium in Monterey, California. In this way she is able to lend Cal the $5,000 he needs to redeem his father's business loss, but the money still carries a taint. When Cal tells Aron that their mother runs a saloon, it is still a powerful enough revelation to drive Aron to despair.[10] There is a very narrow line, however, between a gambling joint and a full-tilt whorehouse, and from its seedy design viewers can predictably mistake one for the other in the existing film – so Kazan won after all.

Kazan and Osborn solved the uninterested sheriff problem by having the lawman lament a lack of support to clean up the saloon, and that any women seen at Kate's place be clearly indicated as having arrived from the outside, and not be residing there.

A flurry of letters followed confirming that various revised pages had been submitted to the Code and accepted but are without elaboration as to their content. On August 10, 1954, the final cut was sent to the Code for screening, and on October 18, 1954 it was assigned Code seal 17086. *East of Eden* was held back until March 1955. James Dean died in a car crash on September 30, 1955. *East of Eden* was the only one of his films that he ever saw.

---

1. Peter Reid, *East of Eden* synopsis (AMPAS).
2. Joy to Breen, April 17, 1952 (AMPAS).
3. Breen to Joy, April 22, 1952 (AMPAS).
4. Breen to McDermid, April 30, 1953 (AMPAS).
5. Breen to Warner, December 2, 1953 (AMPAS).
6. Breen to Warner, December 2, 1953 (AMPAS). The inference is that her trade is mentioned in passing but not shown.
7. Kazan to Trilling, January 3, 1954 (AMPAS).
8. Nevertheless, *Streetcar* was heavily censored by the Breen Office (q.v.).
9. Vizzard to file, February 16, 1954; April 27, 1954; May 10, 1954; and May 17, 1954 (AMPAS).
10. Breen to Warner, May 21, 1954 (AMPAS).

Ecstasy

Czechoslovakia, 1933
Written by Frantisek Horky and Gustav Machaty with Jacques Koerpel, from the book by Robert Horky
Produced by Moriz Grunhut, Frantisek Horky and Otto Sonnenfeld
Directed by Gustav Machaty
Code seal #13431 (rescinded)

Synopsis
A nature-loving upper-class girl, Eva (Hedy Kiesler), leaves a loveless marriage to Emile (Zvonimir Rogoz) to take up with a construction engineer, Adam (Aribert Mog). The engineer coincidentally brings home the woman's husband, Emile, not knowing who he is, but the husband identifies the engineer and contemplates killing him. Instead, the husband commits suicide. The girl does not tell the engineer about her husband. She and the engineer leave for Paris, but the girl's heart is broken and she abandons the engineer on the train platform.

Background
Stories abound about how this Czech film originated from a five-page script and ran into actor disputes and a shortage of production facilities in addition to having to be filmed in three languages. But the thing that made *Ecstasy* famous is Hedy Kiesler's (later Lamarr) nude frolic in a forest pond, followed by her chasing a horse who has made off with her clothes. Legend has it that in 1933, Lamarr's first husband,[1] arms dealer Friedrich Mandl, supposedly spent $280,000 to buy up all prints of the film, but this has never been confirmed.[2] The film survives because lab technicians made a duplicate negative and hid it.[3]

L'affaire *Ecstasy* is one of the Code's most contentious ongoing cases and, symbolism being what it is, it started off in actual flames. Made in Czechoslovakia in 1933, the film had drawn praise at several European festivals as well as moral opposition (the Vatican's *L'Osservatore Romano* denounced it) when Samuel Cummins and Jacques Koerpel of Eureka Productions secured the American distribution rights. When the print hit U.S. Customs it was seized under tariff decency regulations, put on trial, and banned.[4] But that wasn't enough. As *The New York Times* reported on August 8, 1935, the print of *Ecstasy*, "which a jury of middle-aged businessmen found last June to be 'obscene,'" was burned by agents of the government. In response, Cummins announced, through his attorney, he planned to sue the state for not waiting for him to file an appeal in the obscenity decision. He also said that he would be leaving soon for Europe to buy another copy of the film so it could be shown to the appeals court.[5]

When its distributor sought a wider U.S. release in 1936, it was necessary to submit it to the Breen Office, thus beginning a thirteen-year journey with the censors.

There was a whiff of hypocrisy behind the scenes. Louis B. Mayer, MGM's powerful head, had seen *Ecstasy* on a trip to London and immediately signed Kiesler to a Metro contract, changing her last name to Lamarr. How about: Naturally it behooved MGM to suppress *Ecstasy* while allowing it to be talked about, reaping publicity for their new star without taking responsibility for how she earned it. Her first U.S. film was not for MGM, however; it was *Algiers*[6] (1938), for United Artists, a role for which she is best remembered clothed. Not until 1939 would she appear for Metro in *Lady of the Tropics*. At that time, *Ecstasy* was still entwined in red tape.

The Code's Charles R. Metzger filed a detailed synopsis on July 21, 1936, having caught a showing at the Grand International Theatre, a down-on-its-luck movie house on South Main Street in Los Angeles that showed foreign films. *Ecstasy* had somehow dodged the authorities to play there.[7] Metzger admitted that "the picture is rather delicately done" and that the packed theatre was quiet, but that many viewers emerged saying they had no idea what the movie was about and that they had shown up out of curiosity.[8] Breen reported to Will H. Hays on July 28 that, while they could not determine whether this was the same version that had been screened in New York, "The present one, as can be seen from the attached report, is highly – even outrageously – indecent."[9]

Breen's comment about "the same version" reflects the insertion of a scene, after Eva leaves Emile, in which a lawyer dictates Eva's divorce petition to a secretary. This supposedly sidesteps claims of Eva's adultery with Adam but confuses the motivation for Emile to get her back. The nude scenes were removed for some territories.

Waiting almost a year before alerting the Code, on May 27, 1937 William G. Smith of Jewell Productions Company, which was handling *Ecstasy* in the U.S., wrote Joe Breen informing him that Sidney S. Cummings was going to turn over a print of the film to him for the purpose of securing a Code seal.[10] The very next day Breen wrote Smith that "it is our considered, unanimous judgment that the picture is definitely and specifically in violation of the Production Code." Breen then offered Smith the option of an appeal before the whole board in New York, adding that their decision would be final.[11] Given the close timing of the letter, it might be questioned whether Breen et al. actually screened the film or relied on Metzger's previous appraisal. On December 10, 1937, MPPDA secretary Carl E. Milliken duly notified Breen that Cummins had filed an appeal. Subsequently, Francis S. Harmon in the Code's New York office assembled a file of clippings and correspondence to gird for the December 17, 1937 hearing.[12] On December 12, Samuel Cummins sent a print and a number of documents showing that the film had been cleared in other territories.[13] Breen shot first with a detailed nine-page brief to the MPPDA board stating the case against the film.[14]

The screening and appeal appeared to be more of a formality than a second chance. On December 22, Francis Harmon, who had argued the case on behalf of the Code, wrote Breen a full report and ended with a curiously worded paragraph:

> No vote was taken in the projection room since Cummins was present and since Mr. Kent and one other president who could not attend the projection room showing yesterday are to see the picture today or tomorrow. But there were enough expressions of opinion to indicate that the PCA decision will be sustained.[15]

Breen thanked Harmon for the commentary as well as his report, wished him happy holidays ("you deserve it"), and alerted him that "this same gentleman" (Cummins) would likely be contacting him again about another picture: "We are at loggerheads regarding the picture *Love Life of a Gorilla*[16] and it is more than likely he will take an appeal on this, too."[17]

It would be unfair to ascribe glee to Breen's comments, but surely he and his associates must have felt relief that the *Ecstasy* case was settled. Such a feeling would last less than four years, as in October 1941, Francis Harmon, in the MPPDA's New York Office at 28 West 44th Street, received a story treatment from Martin Licht via his attorney Geza Herczig for a remake of *Ecstasy*. Harmon lost little time sending back a four-page letter elaborating every point on which the remake would be denied a Code seal. The litany included discussion of horse breeding (Eve's father was a breeder), mention of Eve being aroused, her nude swim, drinking, cruelty to animals, and marital infidelity. If all of these issues are addressed, he suggested, then the remake would seem to be permitted under the Code.

One thing that would not be permitted, however, Harmon stressed, was the title. "The question of the suitability of the title *Ecstasy* is within the jurisdiction of the Title Registration Bureau of this Association. Frankness compels us to add that this title has been recently associated in the public mind with a motion picture which this Association could not approve."[18]

There can be no question, given the details of Harmon's response, that Licht wanted to remake the very *Ecstasy* that the Code had already refused to consider. Indeed, Harmon then went on to tell Licht, "This picture in its original form was also the subject matter for a suit in the Federal Court for the Southern District of New York upon the question of obscenity." He then recommended (in uncharacteristically threatening terms) that, given what happened to the first *Ecstasy*, he ought to stop wasting time and money on this one.[19]

Licht wasn't alone. The film's original director-producer, Gustav Machaty, spoke to Geoffrey Shurlock on July 2, 1945 asking about a toned-down remake. Shurlock responded that it would have to omit adultery, Emile's impotence, and the likening of the breeding of horses to human procreation. Machaty proceeded with his project, leaking to Jimmie Fiddler on the gossipmonger's July 8 broadcast that the Hays Office had okayed a remake of *Ecstasy* as long as its leading lady didn't undress.[20]

With the remake wheels turning, Machaty notified the Code office that *Ecstasy* was henceforth to be called *Rhapsody of Love*, to which Breen issued orders to his staff that Machaty was to be told that nothing in his production should mention any connection with *Ecstasy*.[21] Machaty then submitted a twelve-page synopsis titled – guess what – *Ecstasy*.[22] Breen's letter to the filmmaker on August 2 gave wary approval, with the usual caveat that everything would depend on the script.

Here's where it gets confusing. In 1948, *Rhapsody of Love* was released by Pix Distributing Corporation based on a tight cutting continuity in the Code's *Ecstasy* files. *Rhapsody of Love* starred Hedy Lamarr, Aribert Mog, Z. Rogoz and Leopold Kramer with a narration by Joy Williams. Gustav Machaty produced and directed it. Eva is still Eva, but Emile has become Frederick, and Adam has become David. Of course, it was the same film, reedited and retitled. The Code was not fooled and a number of communiques among all the parties addressed the use of the original title (there were somewhat hypocritical threats of getting the Federal Trade Commission involved over the producer trying to fool the public with the title change), and concerns that the Code would be damaged if one was issued. Machaty even swore to Breen that, if he discovered an exhibitor calling *Rhapsody of Love* by the name *Ecstasy*, the engagement would be terminated.[23]

At long last, on February 15, 1949, *Rhapsody of Love*, née *Ecstasy* – or what was left of it – was awarded Code seal #13431.

But wait, there's more. In a frantic memo dated January 31, 1950 from the Motion Picture Association's Gordon S. White and Arthur DeBra to Sidney Schreiber of the Code, a picture called *My Ecstasy* starring Hedy Lamarr was playing at the Rialto Theater. It is a retitling of *My Life* (which was a subsequent retitling of *Rhapsody of Love*). This version carried a Production Code seal but was "not a shortened version of the picture shown to us by Mr. Machaty as having been approved by the P.C.A. It is a completely different version."[24]

Breen was perplexed, although a subsequent visit to the Rialto by White revealed that the same print was being shown, except that the credit footage containing the MPAA seal had been removed.[25] On February 3, Francis Harmon sent a broadside to Pix Distribution threatening withdrawal of the Code seal.[26] The next day, Rose Chatkin of Pix apologized for the confusion and confirmed that they had removed the Code seal from the print shown at the Rialto, sidestepping the *raison d'etre* of the seal, which was to permit public exhibition of motion pictures.[27]

Containing *Ecstasy* by its numerous alternate names – *My Life*, *My Ecstasy*, *Hedy Lamarr in My Ecstasy*, *Rhapsody of Love*, etc. – would prove as useless as trying to put toothpaste back into the tube. By 1953 the Code office was still getting notices of local censorship boards doing their duty, but by then other films had come along that dominated the Code's attention and *Ecstasy* faded away into archives and film societies.

Its Code seal was never restored.[28]

---

1. Mandl and Kiesler were married August 10, 1933. *Ecstasy* was released in Czechoslovakia January 20, 1933 (IMDb).
2. Felicia Feaster, *Ecstasy*. Turner Classic Movies. Posted July 22, 2016.
3. Gerald Gardner, *The Censorship Papers: Movie Censorship Letters from the Hays Office 1934-1968*, New York: Dodd-Mead and Company, 1987.
4. Fred Stein, "New York Spectator," *Hollywood Spectator*, May 23, 1936 (AMPAS).
5. Ecstasy Burned Despite Appeal, *The New York Times*, August 8, 1935.
6. This is the film in which Charles Boyer almost says, but does not, "Come viss me to zee Casbah," although everybody thinks he does.
7. As noted with *The Birth of a Nation*, independent distributors were not monitored by the Code.
8. Metzger report, July 21, 1936 (AMPAS).
9. Breen to Hays, July 28, 1936 (AMPAS).
10. Smith to Breen, May 27, 1937 (AMPAS).
11. Breen to Smith, May 28, 1937 (AMPAS).
12. Harmon to Breen, December 10, 1937 (AMPAS).
13. Cummins to Breen, December 12, 1837 (AMPAS).
14. Breen to Board, December 21, 1937 (AMPAS).
15. Harmon to Breen, December 22, 1937 (AMPAS).
16. A big game hunting film made by Major Frank Brown released by Jewel Productions in 1937.
17. Breen to Harmon, December 27, 1937 (AMPAS).
18. Harmon to Licht, October 29, 1941 (AMPAS). Titles cannot be copyrighted so the Association established a Title Registration Bureau where producers could register a title to prevent another producer from using it. The Bureau still exists, and only regulates producers who are members.
19. Harmon to Licht, October 29, 1941 (AMPAS).
20. Arch Reeve to Breen, July 11, 1947 (AMPAS).
21. Breen memo July 29, 1948 (AMPAS).
22. Undated in file, most likely late July 1948 (AMPAS).
23. Machaty to Breen, February 15, 1949 (AMPAS).
24. White and DeBra to Schreiber, January 31, 1950 (AMPAS).
25. White to DeBra, February 2, 1950 (AMPAS).
26. Harmon to Pix, February 3, 1950 (AMPAS).
27. Chatkin to Harman, February 6, 1950 (AMPAS).
28. Anybody of any age who wants to see it can now find it on YouTube: https://www.youtube.com/watch?v=FTvFeuUjZ44&list=WL&index=14.

The Gay Divorcee

RKO Radio Pictures, 1934
Written by George Marion, Jr. & Dorothy Yost and Edward Kaufman from the book by Dwight Taylor. Musical adaptation by Kenneth S. Webb and Samuel Hoffenstein. Contributors to dialogue: Robert Benchley, H.W. Hanemann, J. Hartley Manners (unproduced play *An Adorable Adventure*), Stanley Rauh and Dwight Taylor (play *Gay Divorce*)
Produced by Pandro S. Berman
Directed by Mark Sandrich
Code seal #282

Synopsis
Mimi Glossop (Ginger Rogers) wants to divorce her husband Cyril (William Austin) so her Aunt Hortense's (Alice Brady) bumbling lawyer, Egbert Fitzgerald (Edward Everett Horton), arranges for Rodolfo Tonetti (Erik Rhodes) to be the co-respondent. Fitzgerald forgets to coordinate the mock scandal with Tonetti, and Mimi mistakenly thinks that Guy Holden (Fred Astaire) is her fake lover. By the time Tonetti finally arrives, Guy and Mimi have fallen in love for real and Cyril is exposed as an adulterer.

Background
Written by Dwight Taylor as *Gay Divorce*, the show opened on Broadway at the Ethel Barrymore Theatre on November 29, 1932 and moved to the Shubert Theatre on January 16, 1933, where it ran until July 1. Never a hit, and receiving criticism because Astaire's light voice couldn't be heard over the orchestra, it had eleven songs by Cole Porter, only one of which, "Night and Day," made it into the movie. But mostly it had Fred Astaire, although he didn't gain recognition until he went to Hollywood.[1] When the rights were bought by RKO, who, in 1933, had signed Astaire to a contract, they submitted the material pro-forma to the Production Code Administration, little suspecting that the whole premise of the story was unacceptable.

What could possibly be censorable about a Fred and Ginger picture? Okay, there's the title.[2] But even then, in 1934, only the closeted gay community used "gay" to mean homosexual, and that would include Cole Porter, who wrote the songs. When H.N. Swanson ("Swanie") of RKO asked Dr. James Wingate of the Producers' Association (sic) on November 14, 1933 if the play was censorable,[3] he was probably surprised to learn, during a meeting he held with the Code's Wingate and Shurlock, that, whereas the element of divorce by collusion admittedly had been a plot point in other pictures, "it was generally used only as an incident and seldom constituted the entire picture."[4] Clearly, in *The Gay Divorce*, Mimi's agreement to an assignation with Tonetti would meet that standard.

Joseph Breen was remarkably accommodating with Swanson in a December 30, 1933 communique explaining that, were a film to be made of the material, it "would be largely mutilated by censors in important areas," and offering, "if you should decide to attempt an emasculated version of the story, we will be glad to discuss it with you further."[5]

In his RKO offices, producer Pandro S. Berman stewed for a month. Then he wrote Colonel Jason Joy, with palpable impatience: "I would appreciate it if you would allow me to tell somebody in your organization exactly why I think we should be allowed to make this. I consider it perfectly beyond reproach from both our angle and your's (sic), and I am sure you would feel likewise had you seen the Play and lightness of handling the theme."[6]

It worked. Joy arranged a meeting among himself, Berman and Breen on the morning of February 1 in which Berman assured Breen that the material would be treated as "a broad farce comedy" and that "the attempts at collusion will not be successful." He concluded, "In the face of all these facts, we think you would be safe in going ahead with this particular play." That said, he still wanted the opportunity to "check with you as you go along in the writing of the screen play."[7]

With this breakthrough, the *Gay Divorce* conversion therapy began with a four-page letter from Breen listing the changes to the script he otherwise found "highly amusing." It was a happy divorce, and that was the problem. His over-arching rule was to remove any reference that collusion was an organized practice but that it was just for this marital situation. Beyond that:

> Scenes 5 and 6: The word "nudist" is objected to by censors
>
> Scene 33: remove dialogue "arouses the beast in me"
>
> Drop the lines "assumed name," "professional co-respondent," "he has several children of his own," "what name shall they register under?" "watch the men at work," "when I think of being in a strange room with a strange man," "that would make us guilty of collusion or something," "undressed in the car? But he was busy driving," and an offensive line, "No, Mimi says she can take dictation."

There were other nibbles that Breen included that, despite their use in a highly amusing broad farce comedy, were likely to run into censorship problems from local boards.[8]

The Gay Divorcee being a musical, the songs also came under Code scrutiny. There was a bit of a go-round in mid-June when nobody at RKO could learn anything about a song called "Pet's Knock Knees" that was in their own picture, and to which Breen raised a written eyebrow.[9] This was resolved on June 11 when Carl Milliken, Will Hays' secretary, reported that the title was a typo and that the song was actually called "*Let's* Knock

Knees."¹⁰ The song (by Mack Gordon and Harry Revel and sung by Betty Grable and Edward Everett Horton) eventually passed, but not before phrases such as "so if we can't be good, let's be careless" and "is this love or is it wrestling," among others, were changed.¹¹

With the picture set to roll on June 26, 1934 Breen was still ordering changes including use of the words "brassieres" and "co-respondent."¹² That same day, Berman received a letter from James Wingate informing the producer that, based on the third script and the existing problems with Code content, RKO should not make the film. Berman and his production team immediately conferred with Geoffrey Shurlock and Iselin Auster (Breen's assistant) who reported that Berman said it would cost them as much to shut down the picture as if it was made and then banned. A fourth "final" script was sent on June 27, and the next day, June 28 – two days late – production began. Oddly, official notice from the Breen Office that production could commence was sent to RKO on July 13.¹³

Adjustments that could only be called niggling were made and implemented to script and song lyrics throughout production, and guidance ordered as to how much skin was shown (or not) by the women's costumes. Several screenings of the completed (workprint) film for Code staff on September 17-20 resulted in demand for deletion of the phrases, "a co-respondent, could anything be more degrading?," "you ought to be at work," and "all the shots of the girls dancing with the men where their hips move back and forth" in the picture's big production number, "The Continental."¹⁴

There was one wisecrack Breen missed. When Mimi's husband shows up at the end, he disparages Tonetti ("Your wife is safe with Tonetti, he prefers spaghetti"), charging that he couldn't be anybody's professional co-respondent and then calls him a hairdresser.

Finally, on October 18, 1934, Carl Milliken, secretary to Hays, wrote Breen to confirm that the film's title had been changed from *Gay Divorce* to *The Gay Divorcee*.¹⁵ As would be said in another picture at another time, so let it be written, so let it be done.¹⁶

Breen was not a man to look back, but he did like to look ahead. In a letter to Hays on February 12, 1937, he expressed concern over offending people of other nationalities by several actors' broad characterizations in comedy films such as with Erik Rhodes's Tonetti.¹⁷ "This is all very much to be regretted," he wrote. "It suggests enormous difficulty for our producers, because, once we establish this kind of rule for Italians, it is only a mere matter of a few months before we shall have to do the same thing for the Chinese, Japs, Spaniards, Russians, Germans, French, Czechs, and Poles."¹⁸

---

1. Fred was always in his sister Adele's shadow on stage and did not blossom until he left her for Hollywood.
2. Not until 1951 did the word *gay* cross over from the homosexual sub-culture into mainstream use, before which it meant happy or carefree. This rather specific date is offered by Jordan Redman citing the *Oxford English Dictionary* in *The Gayly*, June 17, 2018.

3. Swanson to Wingate, November 14, 1933 (AMPAS).
4. Unsigned (likely Wingate) memo to file, November 17, 1933 (AMPAS). Divorce by collusion occurs when parties seeking a divorce arrange for acts to be committed that would constitute grounds for divorce, i.e. appearance of, or actual occurrence of, adultery.
5. Breen to Swanson, December 30, 1933 (AMPAS).
6. Berman to Joy, January 29, 1934 (AMPAS).
7. Breen to Merian C. Cooper (head of RKO), February 1, 1934 (AMPAS). Apparently Breen didn't deal with underlings, only studio brass.
8. Breen to Cooper, April 26, 1934 (AMPAS).
9. Breen to Paula Kelly (MPPDA), June 5, 1934 (AMPAS).
10. Milliken to Hays, June 11, 1934 (AMPAS).
11. Wingate to Berman, June 17, 1934 (AMPAS).
12. Breen to Berman, June 14, 1934 (AMPAS).
13. Breen to B. B. (Ben) Kahane, July 13, 1934 (AMPAS).
14. Doug Mackinnon memo to the Code files, September 20, 1934 (AMPAS).
15. Milliken to Breen, October 18, 1934 (AMPAS). The stage title meant a happy divorce, not a homosexual one.
16. Pharaoh Yul Brynner in *The Ten Commandments* (1956) (q.v.).
17. An aspect of the Code was to avoid offending persons of various ethnic nationalities. Although this was enforced in dramas, comedies enjoyed some elasticity.
18. Breen to Hays, February 12, 1937 (AMPAS).

Gentleman's Agreement

20th Century Fox, 1947
Written by Moss Hart (uncredited revisions by Elia Kazan), from the book by Laura Z. Hobson
Produced by Darryl F. Zanuck
Directed by Elia Kazan
Code seal #12488

Synopsis
A gentile journalist, Philip Schuyler Green (Gregory Peck), poses as a Jew in order to sample the depth of American anti-Semitism. His masquerade upsets a woman he has met, Kathy Lacey (Dorothy Maguire), because she is uncomfortable not only with the ruse but also, it turns out, with Jews.

Background
Hollywood has always had a Jewish problem. Although the industry as it came to be known was founded by Jews, all of whom came from roughly the same area in Eastern Europe, the town in which they chose to set up shop was staunchly Christian. When the founding moguls, seeking legitimacy, were denied membership in L.A.'s country clubs, schools and business organizations, they formed their own society. Loving their new country despite being rejected, they created, on screen, an idealized version of their new land which the rest of the world came to believe was the real America.[1] At the same time, they clouded their Jewish roots. They had actors "Americanize" their names. They minimized the presence of Jewish characters in their films. They divorced their Jewish first wives and married gentile woman. And they ignored the rise of Hitler and held off making anti-Nazi pictures prior to World War II so as not to lose the market in what was becoming occupied Europe.[2] Only one mogul dared make this picture.

In the 1940s there were two major studios that weren't run by Jews: RKO and 20th Century Fox.[3] Of Fox's three co-founders – Joseph Schenck, William Goetz and Darryl F. Zanuck – Zanuck was Protestant. Born in Wahoo, Nebraska, he tasted anti-Semitism when he arrived in Hollywood as a young man and was refused a room at the Los Angeles Athletic Club because they thought Zanuck was a Jewish name.[4] He never forgot the sting and, first at Warner Bros., and then at Fox, he had the courage to greenlight films about social issues including racism (*Pinky*, 1949), mental illness (*The Snake Pit*, 1948) and anti-Semitism (*Gentleman's Agreement*, 1947). Interestingly, RKO, the only other major film company to produce a film about anti-Semitism (*Crossfire*, 1947), was also run by gentiles.

The Breen Office was in a tight spot when it came to vetting these films. They were run by Christians. This was no accident. Made paranoid by the scandals of the 1920s, the heads of the studios sought a Christian figurehead to appease the anti-Semites across America. They found him in Will H. Hays who was, in addition to being a former Postmaster General, a deacon in the Presbyterian church. When Hays retired in 1945, the MPAA Board hired Eric Johnston, former head of the U.S. Chamber of Commerce, a native of Seattle, Washington, and as non-Jewish as a jar of mayonnaise. Under them were Joseph Breen, Geoffrey Shurlock and their staffs, no more than three or four (if names are any indication) could have been expected to go to a synagogue except to attend a friend's son's bar mitzvah.

With the stage set, *Gentleman's Agreement* enters the picture.

By this time. Colonel Jason S. Joy was at 20th Century Fox. In early March 1947, he sent Laura Z. Hobson's bestselling novel and a synopsis to the Breen Office for their consideration. On 21 March, Breen wrote Joy expressing confidence, couched in his customary "if/then"s, that "the basic story seems to meet the requirements of the Code." Otherwise, Breen urged that the lead characters of Phil and Kathy not have an affair, and that Kathy not be a divorced woman.[5]

Zanuck, who was personally producing the picture, was having none of it. "Phil and Kathy are in love," he wrote. "They will behave on the screen as well-bred adults behave when they are in love. Kathy is a divorcee. Anyone who has read the book knows it is impossible to tell the story unless she is a divorcee. Your suggestion in this regard cannot be complied with."[6] On April 2, Breen, knowing he had poked the bear, ventured a cautious reply: "I suggest we defer any further discussion about this story until we have had an opportunity to read the first draft script."[7] On May 16, two copies of the script were delivered to Breen. Over the next few weeks, Joy also sent wardrobe test photographs of Dorothy Maguire, Anne Revere, Celeste Holm, Marion Marshall, Kathleen Lookhart, June Havoc and Jane Wyatt, all of which were provisionally accepted.

Still in contention as of May 23, 1947 was Kathy's marital status. Breen insisted that divorce not be a story point, saying that its use in what was going to be a prestigious film would legitimize the practice in the minds of audiences. He also requested minimizing instances of liquor consumption and wanted the removal of a bar from one of the living room sets.[8] These were obeyed – with the exception of eliminating Kathy's divorce.[9]

On November 19, 1947 *Gentleman's Agreement* was given a Code seal without changes.[10] It went on to win Oscars at the 1948 Academy Awards for best picture, best director (Kazan), supporting actress (Celeste Holm) and nominations in six other categories.

Note: The adapted screenplay was written by Moss Hart, a Pulitzer prize co-winner in 1936 for the play *You Can't Take It with You*. In one oft-cited story about the production, Hart visits the set of *Gentleman's Agreement* and is stopped by one of the crew members. "I want to thank you for this script," the man tells Hart. "I learned something important from it." Beaming with pride, Hart asks the man, "What did you learn?" The man tells him, "I learned to always be nice to a Jew because he might be a gentile in disguise."

1. Neal Gabler, *An Empire of Their Own: How the Jews Invented Hollywood*, New York: Crown Publishes, 1988.
2. Many Hollywood Jews, and not just the moguls, quietly arranged and financed the emigration of European Jews as Hitler rose to power and supported them once they arrived in America.
3. Disney, Hal Roach, and a few others were considered "minors" who did not distribute their own films.
4. Stephen M. Silverman, *The Fox That Got Away*, Secaucus, New Jersey: Lyle Stuart, Inc., 1988.
5. Breen to Joy, March 21, 1947 (AMPAS).
6. Zanuck to Breen, March 27, 1947 (AMPAS).
7. Breen to Zanuck, April 2, 1947 (AMPAS).
8. Breen to Joy, May 23, 1947 (AMPAS).
9. Breen to Joy, June 18, 1947 (AMPAS).
10. MPPDA Certificate (AMPAS).

Gone with the Wind

Metro-Goldwyn-Mayer, 1939
Written by Sidney Franklin (and Ben Hecht, David O. Selznick, Oliver H. P. Garrett, Jo Swerling and John Van Druten, all uncredited), from Margaret Mitchell's novel
Produced by David O. Selznick
Directed by Victor Fleming, George Cukor (uncredited), Sam Wood (uncredited)
Code seal #5729

Synopsis
The sweeping story of Southern belle Scarlett O'Hara, her tempestuous romance with blockade runner Rhett Butler, her serial marriages, the rebirth of her family estate Tara, and the passing of a way of life before, during and after the American Civil War 1861-65.[1]

Background
David O. Selznick's 1939 film of Margaret Mitchell's bestselling 1936 novel of the Old South has gone from headlines to screen to classic to anthem and back to headlines as each generation celebrates different things in its complex soap opera plot. It is at once a story about a culture's defeat, a strong woman's business and romantic travails, a scoundrel's impatience, and Hollywood at its zenith. It is also a magnet for unquestioned revisionism and racism.

If there is one thing everybody seems to know about *Gone with the Wind* it's producer O. Selznick's snit with the Production Code over Rhett Butler's use of the word *damn* as he leaves Scarlett O'Hara in the film's final scene. What the film has become increasingly known for, however, is it racially insensitive portrayal of Black people, its romanticizing of the evils of slavery, and its disguising the Ku Klux Klan as mere vigilantes – literally making the "invisible empire" invisible. Many social critics today rank *GWTW* second only to *The Birth of a Nation* (q.v.) as a dangerous misrepresentation of history.

What role did the Production Code play in what *GWTW* was, is, and isn't? A massive 172-page file in the PCA archives speaks to that.

The cuts, compromises and allowances rendered unto *Gone with the Wind* serve primarily to tone down the novel's sexual content which is, after all, one of the reasons for its popularity. When independent producer David O. Selznick bought Margaret Mitchell's 1,037-page novel in July 1936, a month after it was published, for $50,000, he lit a fuse that could have – and, as a matter of fact, did – ignite the burning of Atlanta. Not only did everybody seem to want the movies' king, Clark Gable, to play Mitchell's hero Rhett Butler, every actress in Hollywood wanted to play his consort, Scarlett O'Hara.

But while the gossips were measuring the casting couch for slipcovers, the Breen Office – in particular, Iselin Auster, Breen's assistant, who was handed the book to vet – was girding for battle. It had taken Selznick and a succession of screenwriters a year to tame the novel and get a screenplay to the Production Code office knowing full well what lay ahead. Auster's three-page letter to his boss on September 29, 1937[2] primed Breen's pump. On October 11, 1937, Breen met with Selznick, screenwriter Sidney Howard and director George Cukor. He summarized their meeting in a remarkable seven-page letter to Selznick three days later.[3] It laid the groundwork for a negotiation that would continue throughout the film's principal production from January 26 to July 1, 1939 and practically until its December 15, 1939 world premiere in Atlanta.

Fans of the resulting motion picture will recognize each of these scenes and know what's missing. They should also marvel at the contrivances that were used to accommodate the prohibitions. The Breen encyclical began by requiring the toning down of anything involving Rhett's obvious marital rape of Scarlett; the removal of any indication that Rhett has had affairs; minimizing the childbirth scene; Scarlett should not offer her body to Rhett in jail for money to pay the taxes on Tara; and Belle Wattling must not be a prostitute. A summary of other details – some that would be followed and some that would thankfully be ignored – includes:

> Remove Gerald O'Hara's line suggesting that the overseer Wilkerson is the father of the white trash Slattery woman's child.
>
> Showing religious ceremonies will be prohibited in England. No sign of the cross.
>
> Referring to a woman who had an affair with Rhett, cut Cathleen's line, "She was ruined, though."
>
> Cut Scarlett's expression, "damned to you."
>
> Belle Wattling's place of business should not be a bawdy house or a house of assignation. Could it not be a drinking or, possibly, gambling establishment?
>
> We urge and recommend that you change the expression "Fo de Lawd" to possibly the expression "Lawsy" or "Law-see."
>
> Don't show the dead as being too gruesome. These scenes might be removed in toto by political censor boards.
>
> With the birth of Melanie's child, delete such action and dialogue which *throws emphasis upon the pain and suffering of childbirth.*

This, likewise, is of *very great importance*. Eliminate Scarlett's speech, "Miss Melly's baby is coming" and Prissy's reply, "Oh, Lawd!" Please do not over-emphasize the anguish in Melanie's voice. There should be no *moaning* or *loud crying* and you will, of course, eliminate the line of Scarlett, "And a ball of twine and a scissors." [emphasis Breen's]

Eliminate Melanie's line, "I hope I'll be like one of the darkies."

Prissy's line, in scene 219, "Miss Meade's Cookie say effen de pain git too bad, jes' you put a knife unner Miss Mally's bed an' it cut de pain in two," and Scarlett's line at the bottom of the page, "I think it's coming now," – these scenes, together with all the business set forth on page 107, are enormously dangerous from the standpoints of both the Production Code and of political censorship.

We recommend that you merely suggest the body of the dead Confederate soldier and not actually photograph it.

Scenes 277 et seq[4]: Here, and elsewhere throughout your script, we urge and recommend that you have none of the white characters refer to the darkies as "niggers." It seems to us acceptable if the negro characters use the expression; the word should not be put in the mouth of white people. In this connection you might want to give consideration to the use of the word "darkies."

Scene 320: Please delete Scarlett's expression, "As God is my witness."

Scene 353: We suggest that you substitute the word "Freedman" for the expression "Free niggers" in Scarlett's speech.

When Scarlett visits Rhett in jail she should not offer him her body, she should want him to marry her.

Scene 409: We suggest the elimination of Scarlett's line at the bottom of the page, "I've decided I'm not going to have any more children" as well as Rhett's reply; Scarlett's line at the top of page 214, "You know what I mean, I think," and Rhett's reply, "Lock your door, by all means. I shan't break it down." Also his line, "I've never held fidelity to be a virtue" Scarlett's line, "I shall lock my door every night," and Rhett's line, "Why trouble? If I wanted to come in, no lock would keep me out."

> All this dialogue is questionable from the standpoint of audience reaction.
>
> Please eliminate Rhett's line (about Ashley), "he can't be faithful to his wife with his mind, or unfaithful with his body."
>
> Scene 423: There should be no suggestion here that Rhett is about to rape Scarlett. It is our thought, in line with the suggestion made on Monday by Mr. Cukor, that you merely have him take her in his arms, kiss her, and then gently start with her toward the bedroom. It is our thought that you should not go so far as to throw her on the bed.[5]

Breen then concluded with uncharacteristic magnanimity: "you have done a magnificent job with this first draft script… even the present draft suggests great possibilities for a superb picture which will add much to the prestige, the dignity, and the artistry of the screen."[6]

With the ground rules set, the haggling began. Letters and new script pages flowed between the Breen Office and Selznick's production executive, Val Lewton (later to become a legendary, stylish filmmaker at RKO), over words, lines and sometimes even the inflection of their delivery. With the final shooting script submitted by Lewton on January 17, 1939,[7] nine days before principal photography was scheduled to begin, Lewton may have been shocked when, on January 24, Breen wrote him, "I regret to be compelled to advise you that this material, in our judgment, is unacceptable under the provisions of the Production Code and cannot be approved. A motion picture, based upon the material, as set forth in the script before us would have to be rejected."[8] The objections – and there were eight pages of them this time – centered almost entirely around the intimacy of marriage and of Belle's establishment, reiterating the complaints that were in place from the start. Almost swamped in the deluge is a note on page eight of the missive:

> Scene 690: Please eliminate Scarlett's line, "for God's sake" and Rhett's reply, "I don't give a damn."

Typed below it, however, is a more significant one:

> We note, in several speeches throughout the script, the use of the word, "nigger." As we told you before, this word is highly offensive to negroes throughout the United States and will be quite forcefully resented by them. We suggest that you find some other word – possibly the word "darkie" in its stead.[9]

While Breen and Selznick were re-fighting the battle of Atlanta with dozens of nearly daily rewritten script pages and their responses while shooting was going on, members of the public were spontaneously writing Will Hays about ethnic slurs that they feared might appear in *GWTW*. Hays' executive assistant Francis Harmon responded to these people, "It has been the established practice of our Production Code Administration to request the deletion of such expressions as 'nigger,' 'wop,' 'chink,' 'dago,' etc. derogatory to any racial or national group. I do not believe you have any occasion to worry in connection with their insertion in the dialogue for the forthcoming picture which you mention."[10]

There were occasional victories for the filmmakers thanks to the direction and performance setting the writing in acceptable context. After Scarlett kills the renegade soldier (Yakima Canutt), she tells Melanie, "Well, I guess I've done murder." Breen wanted the line excised, "as it is important from the standpoint of the Code that this killing definitely be in self-defense, and not cold-blooded murder." As staged by director Victor Fleming (Cukor having by then been replaced), it is indeed self-defense, although the distinction between killing and murder is a Talmudic one.[11] The scene was criticized by the Department of Ohio, Sons of Veterans of the Civil War as "the soldier in the uniform of his country is shown as a person of ill repute."[12] Francis Harmon's response to Ryan of July 25 is a model of diplomacy, both assuring the man that the film will adhere to the Code and explaining that, were the producer to depart from the novel, it would engender negative public reaction.[13]

While the thrust of the Code's relentless supervision involved neutering sex and downplaying the toll of war,[14] there were occasions when the public had a say. Apparently citing the book, but possibly having seen the ever-changing script, Minnie L. Johnson and Arthur O. Waller of Neighborhood Councils of Washington, D.C. wrote Hays on May 12, 1939, astutely noting "the story fails to show repentance for selling human beings as cattle, nor for poor food, clothing, and shelter given them during their many years of slavery."[15] No response from Hays is noted. Mrs. Johnson wrote to both Hays and Selznick on June 10 asking that the man who attacks Scarlett on the bridge not be a negro "as it might engender race hatred and prejudice in many people," as well as not to portray the negroes at the mill as being lazy. She was joined by three others of the YWCA. There is no response in the files from either man.[16]

By June 6, Breen was back on "my dear, I don't give a damn," insisting that it be removed. On June 8, in response to new pages, he repeated his order, expanding the line to "Frankly, my dear, I don't give a damn."[17]

A successful sneak preview[18] of the mammoth production led to a Code review on September 15, 1939 by Breen, Shurlock, and others. In their report, they noted that the film was significant because it showed that "tragedy will pursue a willful woman" and remarked, "the whole negro element is predominantly sympathetic." What has been lost over the years is that this preview ended with Rhett telling Scarlett, "Frankly, my dear, I don't care." With the December 14 premiere staring Selznick in the face, the producer again petitioned Breen to allow him to change it to the way it is in the book, using "damn." Breen opposed it, citing the Code, but advised Selznick that he could appeal to Hays and the Code Board.[19] This was in fact done on October 25, 1939. The decision smacked of contrivance – it was decided that "damn" was spoken within historical context and was therefore permissible under the Code – but Selznick paid a token $5,000 fine for using it. For nearly a century, audiences, of course, have been giving one hell of a damn about *Gone with the Wind,* sometimes for it but increasingly against it. They have remarked about the film's continuation of the "happy, smiling slaves" stereotype used by those who romance the Old South or downplay the evil of the "peculiar institution" that has never been washed from America's soul.

Despite what they believed to be sensitivity, the mission of the Production Code Administration was, after all, to maintain the standards of its time, not to advance them. This was what eventually drove the necessity for its overhaul.

---

1. Or as *Mad* magazine once memorably summarized the sprawling plot, "Fiddle-dee-dee" "Boom!"
2. Auster to Breen, September 29, 1937 (AMPAS).
3. Breen to Selznick, October 14, 1937 (AMPAS).
4. "and the following sequence" (abr).
5. This was still on Breen's mind on May 29, 1939 when he wrote Selznick during the film's production, "All the business of Scarlett stretching luxuriously, the patting of her hair, her gay mood, etc., all emphasize this marital experience and should, we think, be toned down to the absolute minimum." Viewers of the film will note that this note was largely ignored, but also that it appears to justify marital rape (AMPAS).
6. This is pure speculation, but here and elsewhere it appears that "political censorship" refers to decisions based on race or religion, not sexuality.
7. Lewton to Breen, January 17, 1939 (AMPAS).
8. Breen to Lewton, January 24, 1939 (AMPAS).
9. Breen to Lewton, January 24, 1939. At one point in finished film Rhett refers to Prissy as a "simple-minded darkie."
10. Letters to Harriet F. Davis and Evelyn Hickens, February 16, 1939 (AMPAS).
11. Breen to Selznick, May 12, 1939 (AMPAS).
12. W. Gordon Ryan to Hays, July 20, 1939. The scene had been reported in the *Cincinnati Times-Star,* July 3, 1939 (AMPAS).
13. Harmon to Ryan, July 25, 1939.
14. A side note: *Gone with the Wind* is technically a war picture yet contains not one battle scene.
15. Johnston and Waller to Hays, May 12, 1939 (AMPAS).
16. Johnston to Selznick, June 10, 1939 (AMPAS).
17. Breen to Selznick (AMPAS), June 8, 1939.
18. For the record: Saturday, September 9, 1939 at the Riverside Theater in Riverside, California.
19. Breen to Hays, October 21, 1939 (AMPAS).

The Grapes of Wrath

20th Century Fox, 1940
Written by Nunnally Johnson, from the novel by John Steinbeck
Produced by Darryl F. Zanuck and Nunnally Johnson
Directed by John Ford
Code seal #5789

Synopsis
The travails of the Joad family as they migrate from parched, bankrupt Oklahoma to the promised land of California, only to find further distress and hardships there.

Background
Inasmuch as John Steinbeck's novel of the dust bowl has faced continual repression and banning by right-wing ideologues since its April 1939 publication, it's noteworthy that it practically sailed through the Production Code gauntlet. Nevertheless, the honors that the film has received, contrasted with the criticism that the book has drawn, compel a look at a schism between moral and political Hollywood.

Darryl F. Zanuck's decision to film *The Grapes of Wrath* was a continuation, if you will, of his taste for the socially relevant stories that he had favored when he was production head of Warner Bros. in the 1930s before co-founding 20th Century Fox. His brilliance as a producer consisted of hiring Nunnally Johnson to write the script, Gregg Toland to photograph it, and John Ford to direct. This is one of those films where everything came together: American everyman Henry Fonda as the American everyman Tom Joad, Jane Darwell as everyone's beloved mother, John Carradine as Muley, the awakening conscience of a country, Alfred Newman's rich musical score that captured American traditional folk themes, and, of course, the team of director Ford and cinematographer Toland, whose images look like Dorothea Lange photographs brought to life.

Steinbeck, himself a former journalist, brought objectivity and compassion to his novel, which he had written after spending time with displaced persons in the 1930s when nature did to middle America what the banks had also done. In the wake of the Depression, banks had loaned farmers money to grow crops, but when the dust storms came and destroyed the topsoil, they foreclosed and made thousands of people homeless. Businesses, of course, hated Steinbeck for exposing the facts. In California, particularly, efforts to ban the book came from the Associated Farmers of the California Farm Bureau Federation and the state Chamber of Commerce to fight organized labor. Areas such as Kern County passed resolutions against the book.[1] More broadly, there was reaction against the novel's use of profanity, sexuality (the book's final image is a woman who has just lost her newborn child breastfeeding a starving man) and a tinge of Communism drawn from Steinbeck's New Deal liberalism. John Ford's politics have been even harder to describe; he opposed the Blacklist while joining a Hollywood group that helped implement it; supported unions yet voted Republican in his later life.[2] He said he took the film because it was about simple people and reminded him of the famine in Ireland.[3] Zanuck's politics are downright impenetrable. If anything, he was an internationalist, given his single-minded love of Woodrow Wilson and of Wilson's doomed League of Nations.

Breen instantly recognized the political nature of the property when Jason Joy of Fox submitted a report that Breen forwarded immediately to Will Hays in New York. "There is little to worry about from the standpoint of general policy," his letter of September 29 began. "The 'heavy' in the story is really a two-headed monster: The one, certain employers, who take advantage of the tragic plight of a number of people and get them to work for starvation wages; the second, the elements of nature." Of importance, he noted, was that not every employer in the picture was unsympathetic, nor are some policemen, but that there are positive characters in these roles too. "We get out of the whole story the suggestion that we are dealing with a great epic in the history of the development of the west. Frankly, we here do not worry very much about the question of policy, which may have been suggested by the original novel. We feel, of course, that there will be some who object to any picture on the screen made from the Steinbeck book, but any serious objection on this point may not be quite fair, we think, in the face of the first draft script, which we have just finished reading."[4]

That said, Breen still had three pages of very specific notes for Joy: don't portray the radical character Muley as insane or the British will cut it; be careful what words you use to described Rosasharn's pregnancy ("goin' to have a baby" for the word "due"), and not to mention Tulare County or the town of Pixley by name[5] (this was ignored), delete the toilet gags, and don't be excessively brutal in showing beatings.[6]

Unusual for Hays, he wrote Breen on October 2 saying that he was taking a personal interest in *The Grapes of Wrath*, but didn't say why.[7] On December 7, after viewing the film, Breen wrote Hays a remarkable letter offering his personal reaction and offering phrases and ideas for a press response should Hays be asked about it.

> The story is really of mother love, of the efforts on the part of the mother to keep her family together against odds which at times are insurmountable. True, the entire story is a shocking indictment of present-day conditions among agricultural workers in California and, as such, is likely to be seriously resented by those who seem to feel that any effort to expose to public view these unjust conditions is, in a way, a part of the alleged communistic enterprise, which is said to be active hereabouts. There are in the picture some potent lines, with reference to the practice some people have of calling a man "red"

because he refuses to work for starvation wages, but this, we feel, is counter-balanced in some measure by the presence, in these parts, of the camps, set up by the Department of Agriculture of the national government, to provide living quarters for the migrant workers, who either cannot secure employment and thus earn enough to make a living, or whose wages are so low as to not permit them to live in decent frugal comfort.

The Grapes of Wrath went into general release on March 15, 1940 after premieres in New York and Los Angeles. The Breen Office received notices of several censors' cuts from international territories involving perceived violence and anything related to pregnancy. When shown in England, a pre-title crawl was added explaining the American dust bowl to unfamiliar audiences. It won Oscars for best director and best actress in a supporting role (Jane Darwell), with nominations for best picture, best actor (Henry Fonda), screenplay (Nunnally Johnson), sound recording (Edmund H. Hansen) and editing (Robert L. Simpson).

Of note is that the film, unlike the book, does not end with the stillbirth of Rosasharn's child and her breastfeeding a man. It was, in fact, supposed to end with a now-radicalized Tom Joad walking up a hill intent on fomenting dissent after what his family had been through. Instead, Zanuck tacked on a scene in which the Joads hit the road again for who-knows-where with Ma Joad saying that nothing can keep them down because "we are the people."

---

1. Linda Gershon, *JStor Daily*, March 27, 2022.
2. Kyle Smith, "The Politics of John Ford's Cinema," *National Review*, January 31, 2018. He was also a member of the reactionary Motion Picture Alliance for the Preservation of American Ideals.
3. Peter Bogdanovich, *John Ford*, Los Angeles, California: University of California Press, 1968, reprinted 1970.
4. Breen to Hays, September 29, 1939 (AMPAS).
5. On December 13, Francis Harmon notified Hays that it would be a good idea for Fox to allow exhibitors in Tulare County to cancel bookings of any film they feel is "obnoxious" (without mentioning *The Grapes of Wrath*). This exemption was necessary in light of Fox's block booking policy that compelled a theater to play all of the studio's films without exception. (Harmon to Hays, December 13, 1939; AMPAS). Thirteen days later Zanuck capitulated and had the offensive lines redubbed. (Harmon to Breen, December 6, 1939) (AMPAS).
6. Breen to Joy, September 29, 1939 (AMPAS).
7. Hays to Breen, October 2, 1939 (AMPAS).

His Girl Friday

Columbia Pictures, 1940
Screenplay by Charles Lederer from the play *The Front Page* by Ben Hecht and Charles MacArthur (uncredited additional writing by Ben Hecht and Morrie Ryskind)
Produced and directed by Howard Hawks
Code seal #5823

Synopsis
Morning Post editor Walter Burns (Cary Grant) will do anything to keep his ex-wife/star reporter, Hildy Johnson (Rosalind Russell), from marrying boring insurance salesman Bruce Baldwin (Ralph Bellamy). He contrives for her to cover the hanging of anarchist Earl Williams (John Qualen), but when Williams escapes and Hildy hides him, her reporter's instincts kick in. She and Walter find themselves in the thick of a manhunt, a municipal corruption story, and their rekindled love.

Background
The 1929 stage hit *The Front Page* by former newspapermen Ben Hecht and Charles MacArthur had been filmed once, in 1931, but Howard Hawks thought it would work again if its two male characters were changed to male-female characters, adding the element of romance.

When Howard Hughes produced and Lewis Milestone directed *The Front Page*, they gave the then-new Production Code plenty of reasons to have seizures. In violation of a litany of Don'ts and Be Carefuls, the film had a character casually flipping the bird, toilet gags, a reporter asking Mollie, who was obviously a prostitute, "How's tricks?," blatant disrespect for a policeman they called Woodenshoes, portrayed editor Walter Burns as having been divorced ("I was in love once – with my third wife"), and used various ethnic nicknames in questionable context. By the time Howard Hawks got the idea to remake it with a sex change, Code seals were in force. The happy result, *His Girl Friday*, has withstood the test of time thanks to Hawks's straightforward eye-level style as opposed to Milestone's camera acrobatics that drew praise at the time but today seem distracting and indulgent.

Hawks also had his actors overlap their dialogue, just as people talk in real life, giving the newspaper picture a sense of urgency as well as making audiences ask themselves, "did I just hear that?" A case in point occurs in the last act in which Hildy Johnson is madly typing her story as Walter Burns calls the City Desk to prepare them for an extra edition:

>Hildy: The mayor's first wife. What was her name?
>Walter: You mean the one with the wart on her?

> Hildy: Right.
> Walter: Fanny.[1]

If you say it quickly, you get the playful joke. (It would also have to be bleeped in England where "fanny" has a distinctly different meaning.)

Given the pre-production title *The Bigger They Are*, an allusion to the degree of political corruption in the film's unnamed city (but clearly Chicago), the screenplay was duly submitted as a work-in-progress to the Breen Office. Breen responded to Columbia Pictures head Harry Cohn on August 24, 1939 with three pages, most of which were his concern that the escaped murderer, Earl Williams, was written as an insane man, a diagnosis that would result in heavy censorship in England and other foreign countries. Breen's other comments were the essence of tact:

> Scenes 25, et seq.: Here, and elsewhere, we suggest that you do not emphasize, even by suggestion, the thought that newspaper men are "drunks." (He also ordered deleted a character calling newspapers "the scum of modern civilization" for "obvious reasons.")

> Scenes 81, et seq.: We suggest that your several references to "Moscow" and to the alleged "Red Menace" be not made to appear as a dishonest or "trumped up" charge against Williams. The point here is to get away from throwing out the suggestion that the police and other municipal officials are in the habit of shouting about a "Red Menace" when there is no valid reason for so doing.

Less blatant but no less political examples of changes are to avoid making Mollie a prostitute, not to show gallows (which will be censored abroad), make the man whom Hildy bribes for access to Williams not the prison warden but just a guard, and switching the "production for use" philosophy to a version of the golden rule. (This makes no sense, which is why Hawks ignored it. In the film, Hildy puts words in Williams' mouth that a gun is made to shoot, ergo "production for use.[2]")

By September 7, 1939, the picture's title had been changed to *His Girl Friday* and the Code's overriding concern was how poorly the picture treats journalists. There was no specific prohibition in the Code that prevented the vilification of the press, but it didn't take a genius to realize that the industry as a whole, and *His Girl Friday* in particular, would be at the mercy of the Fourth Estate. Rather than call for sweeping changes, Breen notified Hays on September 20 of thirteen offenses that the script commits (and which those familiar with the play and film will immediately see as the reasons for its success). Among them:[3]

The indication that the managing editor employs a criminal for a body guard

The insurance gag [Walter making fun of Bruce's paperwork-filled profession]

Hildy's several belligerent speeches to Burns[4]

Two scenes of a newspaper reporter bribing the jail warden

The gag about the blond (sic) which results again in Bruce's arrest:
Hildy: You and that albino of yours.
Louie: You talkin' about Evangeline?
Hildy: None other.
Louie: She ain't no albino. She was born right here in this country.

The $450 counterfeit money

The scene in which the reporters brow-beat Mollie to the extent that she jumps out of a window

The kidnapping [by] Louie [of] Mrs. Baldwin

The smuggling of the prisoner out of the court building

Burns' thoroughly unethical dealings with Benzinger[5]

To the filmmakers' credit, they ignored every last one of these orders and made up new lines on the spot to replace some of those that were approved. Apparently the Code office was more concerned about a larger matter: how the film treats the press. The film's irreverence for the Fourth Estate caused Breen to notify Hays and Columbia Pictures' Sam Briskin that he wanted to bring the matter before the Standing Committee of the Newspaper Publishers Association. Jack Cohn (Harry's brother and a Columbia Pictures executive) thought that this would call undue attention to the film's treatment of the press.[6] Perhaps this was in response to a December 5 letter from Donald J. Sterling, president of the American Society of Newspaper Editors, who objected to the movie industry's ongoing portrayal of reporters as "amiable drunks."[7]

With everybody having huffed and puffed, *His Girl Friday* went into release on January 18, 1940 and received, as expected, qualified reviews from the critics.

Of note is the famous curtain line of *The Front Page* that Howard Hughes struggled to preserve nine years before *His Girl Friday*. In the play, Walter Burns disingenuously gives his blessing to Hildy's marriage and, lacking a proper wedding gift, presents him with his prized pocket watch "given to me by the chief." Inside is the inscription, "To the best newspaperman I know." It's a gallant gesture, and Burns wishes Hildy and his fiancé well as they leave the City Room. Once they're gone, however, Burns phones his city editor and tells him to call the police to arrest Hildy Johnson because "the son of a bitch stole my watch."

Whatever else Hughes and Milestone put into their version, "son of a bitch" wasn't something they could finagle past the Hays Office. Their solution in 1931 was to have Adolphe Menjou, playing Burns, make the phone call leaning on a typewriter and, when he gets to "son of a bitch," he pushes the noisy carriage to one side, making a scraping sound that obscures the words.

His Girl Friday avoids the moment entirely as Hildy's engagement has gone up in smoke and, no longer needing a wedding gift, Walter proposes to her as they leave town to cover another big story – and get married.

What explains the Code's sensitivity about *His Girl Friday* is not that they so much wanted to protect the public from its ribald content as to protect the motion picture industry from the press. The Motion Picture Association then as now is more than a ratings or self-censoring enterprise. It is the trade group and lobbying organization for the American motion picture industry. They influence legislation in Washington, DC, across the country, and around the world. They need the cooperation of civic groups, politicians and, above all, the press to do their job.

---

1. This dialogue was substituted during filming. The original lines were to be: Hildy: "What was the name of the Mayor's first wife? Walter: You mean the one who drank so much? Tillie!"
2. Breen to Cohn, August 24, 1939 (AMPAS).
3. Breen to Hays, September 20, 1939 (AMPAS).
4. Walter and Hildy had been married but, after their divorce, she is engaged to Bruce.
5. Walter offers Benzinger, a competing reporter, a job to prevent him from looking inside his desk where Williams is hiding, then rescinds the offer after Benzinger has given notice to his own editor.
6. Breen to Hays, December 7, 1939 (AMPAS).
7. Sterling to Hays, December 5, 1939 (AMPAS).

Hud

Paramount Pictures, 1963
Written by Irving Ravetch and Harriet Frank, Jr. from Larry McMurtry's novel *Horseman, Pass By*
Produced by Irving Ravetch and Martin Ritt
Directed by Martin Ritt
Code seal #20308

Synopsis
Hud Bannon (Paul Newman), an attractive but thoroughly unprincipled lothario in Texas ranch country, lives with his father (Melvyn Douglas), nephew Lon (Brandon DeWilde) and their housekeeper Alma (Patricia Neal). When financial tragedy strikes, Hud's amorality threatens the family.

Background
Hud has seldom been accorded the praise it deserves as a milestone in American cinema. It single-handedly codified, if it didn't originate, the concept of the anti-hero. Hud Bannon is a bastard – a selfish libertine, a thoughtless lothario who is the same, or worse, at the end of his story as he was at the beginning. Character arcs be damned. But because he is played by Paul Newman – one of the most charismatic stars and consummate actors in Hollywood history – audiences for over sixty years have been cutting him slack.

The Production Code was not ready for *Hud* when the married writing team of Irving Ravetch and Harriet Frank, Jr. sent their adaptation of Larry McMurtry's short novel to the Shurlock Office in November 1961. Shurlock's stinging report to Edward Schellhorn of Paramount Pictures said, "While a basically acceptable story could be derived from this material, in its present form this script is unacceptable under the Code." His reasons were "vulgar and unacceptable dialogue," Hud's crude and promiscuous character, and the possible murder or suicide of Granddad. Ultimately the changes rendered unto *Hud* were massive, yet the film survives on its power and integrity.[1]

On November 13, Shurlock and Schellhorn met at the home of Paramount production VP Marty Rackin, himself a successful producer, to hammer out a solution to the project, which had already been given the studio's greenlight. The race was on. Shurlock's points were almost entirely profanity-based, chiefly a littering of "hell"s, "damn"s, "bastard"s and an occasional "crap." Interestingly, he left the damn in Granddad's phrase, "You don't give a damn, Hud," while a second "damn" on the same page was verboten. He nixed the line "What're you saving it for?" for exactly the same reasons that a rude guy asks a girl that question, and wanted the line "Fight to keep your pants on" revised.

The major change was in the treatment of the grandfather, Homer Bannon, a grizzled, eighty-year-old westerner on whose cattle ranch in the town of Thalia, Texas, the story is set. Homer's son, Hud, lives there with his teenage nephew, Lon, who is enamored of him. Homer detests Hud for Hud's involvement in the death of Lon's father, Norman (Hud was driving the car when Norman was killed). Also on the ranch is Alma Brown, a world-weary housekeeper, whom Lon treats as a second mother and whom Hud desires carnally. In the course of the story, Homer's herd of cattle develops foot-and-mouth disease and must be slaughtered and buried in a lime pit. Hud suggests quickly selling them to a neighbor, a dastardly scheme that Homer instantly rejects. Once the killing is done, Homer is emotionally destroyed and one night, as Hud and Lon drive home from town, they see grandfather crawling across the road, having been thrown by his horse. He dies. In the original Ravetch/Frank script, Hud hits Homer with his truck and sends Lon to get help. As Lon is leaving, he hears a shot and quickly runs back to find Homer dead and holding a gun in his hand. It is left open whether Hud killed his father a) at all, b) in revenge, or c) as a mercy killing.

"As presently treated," Shurlock began, "the suicide by Granddad is unacceptable under the Code. As discussed at our meeting, dialogue should be given to Lon wherein he both condemns the suicide and charges Hud with responsibility for it. He should make it quite clear that what Hud did was to give a gun to a man who was clearly out of his mind. Most importantly, Lon's viewpoint should be the concluding one of this scene, and effectively top Hud's attitude of condonation and justification regarding Ganddad's death."[2]

By March 15, Shurlock reprimanded the studio for their revised shooting script which "contains almost all of the unacceptable lines of dialogue to which we called your attention in our letter of November 24, 1961." He added objections to Hud departing his mistress's house tucking in his shirt, the expressions "take the cock out of his doodle-do," "charge a stud fee" and a couple of uses of the word "ass."[3] The next week, Shurlock, Rackin and Schellhorn held a horse-trading pow-wow where "stud fee," "below the belt" and "bastard" were deemed acceptable, but that the "hells" and "damns" would be cut.[4] The film was at the time named *Hud Bannon*. The dust finally settled on April 30 and the film was given the go-ahead with the Code's traditional caveat, "You understand, of course, that our final judgment will be based on the finished picture."[5] Sometime after it received its Code seal on September 6, 1962[6] its title was changed to *Hud*.

After the shooting stopped, another kind of shooting started. John Hall of the Royal Society for the Prevention of Cruelty to Animals queried the American Humane Association on July 12, 1963, after *Hud* opened in the UK, about the treatment of animals in the film's "greased pig" rodeo sequence. Hall wanted assurances that the AHA had supervised the scene, whether any pigs were hurt, and if the slaughter of cattle in the story is how such things are handled in the USA. Rutherford T. Phillips, executive director of the AHA, responded to Hall's and other such enquiries by explaining that several shifts of pigs were used, that the men's hands slipped off of them, and that none was injured in the course of being dragged across the ground. Moreover, the slaughter of the cattle was accomplished by simulating foot-

and-mouth disease with a mixture of water, sodium silicate, and mineral oil; the 400 animals were kept in a pasture until needed; the pit was empty when the men appeared to fire rifles into it; and the cattles' remains were fabricated. He added that falling horses in the rodeo were specially trained to do so.[7]

One matter that appears to have been either overlooked or accepted is Hud's attempted rape of Alma, a horrifying sequence in which Lon comes to Alma's aid and is set to kill his beloved uncle in revenge. The attack foments Alma's quitting her job and leaving the ranch, consigning Hud – whom Lon appears to abandon as well – alone and unrepentant. Patricia Neal won an Academy Award for playing Alma, as did Melvyn Douglas as Homer, but the only objection found in the Code file to this assault is from the British Board of Film Censors who wanted it minimized, along with their demand to reduce the cattle slaughter sequence. Perhaps the Code was as seduced by Paul Newman as audiences were. Except Alma.

Note: *Hud* continued a superstition – or perhaps it was merely a coincidence – that when a Paul Newman film had an "H" in the title it did well. *The Hustler, Hud, Harper, Hombre, The Secret War of Harry Frigg, Harry and Son* and, who knows, finally *The Hudsucker Proxy* suggest this. By Hollywood's desperate logic, this makes some kind of sense.

Note: The censors had to approve the lyrics for the film's diegetic music, such as the American folk song "Clementine," which was composed in 1884 by Percy Montross. Other songs such as "Wabash Cannonball," "Bonaparte's Retreat," "Driftwood on the River," "Fraulein," "Honey-Love" and "Why Don't You Haul Off and Love Me" were likewise approved.[8]

---

1. Shurlock to Schellhorn, November 10, 1961 (AMPAS).
2. Shurlock to Schellhorn, November 24, 1961 (AMPAS).
3. Shurlock to Schellhorn, March 15, 1962 (AMPAS).
4. "A.V.S." to file, March 23, 1962 (AMPAS).
5. Shurlock to Schellhorn, April 30, 1962 (AMPAS).
6. AMPAS.
7. Rutherford to John Hall, July 29, 1963 (AMPAS).
8. May-July, 1962 (AMPAS).

In the Heat of the Night

United Artists, 1967
Screenplay by Stirling Silliphant, from the novel by John Ball
Produced by Walter Mirisch
Directed by Norman Jewison
Code seal #21423

Synopsis
A black police detective (Sidney Poitier) from the North is impressed into helping a white Southern sheriff (Rod Steiger) solve a businessman's murder and, in so doing, runs up against prejudice and violence. All eventually ends in cross-racial understanding.

Background
In the Heat of the Night is as important in the development of the Production Code as it is in the civil rights movement and the history of American cinema because of a single moment. It's also a ripping good detective story.

The movies were growing up. This was due, in part, to the fact that audiences were getting younger. The social changes in the 1960s, from sexual liberation to the anti-war movement and the civil rights struggle, were finding a voice among the baby boomers whose media of choice were music and motion pictures. With the FCC still controlling broadcast program decency and cable and streaming many years off, it fell to the movies to open doors and eyes. A growing influx of underground, imported, and independent films thumbed their noses at the Code. Art houses, campus film societies and underground newspapers drew young audiences away from mainstream theaters in major cities and the Code found itself powerless. Hollywood studios began demanding the same freedom as their foreign and independent competitors.

Jack Valenti was hired as President of the Motion Picture Association of America in May 1966, replacing retiring Eric Johnston. Geoffrey Shurlock, who ran the Code under Valenti, would continue to do so until his retirement in 1969.[1] One of Valenti's first moves in a larger effort to revamp and update the Code was instituting the designation Suggested for Mature Audiences (SMA). One of the first films so labeled was *In the Heat of the Night,* which was released August 2, 1967.[2]

SMA was warranted. One of the subplots of the steamy story of murder in the town of Sparta involved the young minx Delores Purdy (Quentin Dean) showing herself off in her bedroom window to officer Sam Wood (Warren Oates), a scripted moment that inspired Shurlock to write producer Walter Mirisch on September 23, 1966, "we will be unable to approve nudity in this scene." There was also objection to the overuse of "damn" and "hell" in dialogue and to a "calendar girl" wall calendar in one scene."[3]

The Code file on *In the Heat of the Night* is remarkably brief, only twenty-seven pages, mostly reviews and perfunctory screening reports. In fact, only the one letter just quoted contains cautions about content. The explosive element came at the bottom:

> Pages 87, 88, 113 & 124: The expression "nigger" as used in this script is quite valid. However, unnecessary repetition could prove objectionable. We urge that you eliminate one or two uses of the word.[4]

The use of the N-word was key, but so was something else that the Code accepted without comment. It was "the slap."

"There was a scene in the [script] in which Rod Steiger and I went to the home of one of the official bigwigs in the town and I asked him a couple of questions and he slaps me," Sidney Poitier said. "And I slapped him back." In agreeing to make the film, Poitier, as a major star and an icon among black Americans, was concerned that the slap would be filmed but then cut, or worse. "I told the people who were making the film that I have no interest in it if that is what I have to endure – that he slaps me and I just take it and walk away. No, I will not take it and walk away so pass me and I hope you find someone. There are many young actors who would like to play it and play it wonderfully well. I said I cannot. And they were very understanding. I worked with a very, very successful filmmaker [Norman Jewison] and said, 'I simply can't play this. There are some things I won't play.' They had their sessions with the United Artists people. They said they would take care of it and I told them that 'taking care of it' means that either I do it that way or I don't do it; I couldn't possibly do it, it's just against my value system. So they said that they would do it, they would shoot it that way. I said, No, you won't only shoot it that way, you will give me the promise that it will be released that way."[5]

It was the first time in a major American film that a black man returned a white man's hostility. As important as it was to the black community while the civil rights struggle was in full gear, it was also an indication that, after thirty-three years, the Code was ready to open its eyes.

The film, actor Rod Steiger, screenwriter Stirling Silliphant, editor Hal Ashby, and the Samuel Goldwyn Studio Sound Department all won Oscars.

---

1. Shurlock died on April 27, 1976 at the Motion Picture Country Home and Hospital in Woodland Hills, California. (*The New York Times*, April 28, 1976).
2. Michael Linden, director of the Code for advertising, to Fred Goldberg, vice president for advertising and publicity, United Artists, May 22, 1967 (AMPAS).
3. Shurlock to Mirisch, September 23, 1966 (AMPAS).
4. In some instances, but not all, the N-word was replaced by "boy."
5. Author interview, November 16, 2012.

Irma La Douce

United Artists, 1963
Written by Billy Wilder & I.A.L. Diamond, from the play by Alexandre Breffort
Produced by Edward L. Alperson, I.A.L. Diamond, Doane Harrison and (uncredited) Alexandre Trauner and Billy Wilder
Directed by Billy Wilder
Code seal #20447

Synopsis
A policeman (Jack Lemmon) in Paris's red light district falls in love with one of its working girls (Shirley MacLaine) and, to keep her off the streets, disguises himself as her only john, effectively cuckolding himself. This works out (except for tiring him) until he decides to "kill" his sugar daddy alter-ego and becomes accused of his own murder.

Background
Years ago nobody could even mention a prostitute in a film, and in 1963 Billy Wilder made a whole movie about one.

Prefaced that the stage musical had enjoyed runs in London and Paris and was slated for a New York opening, Luigi Luraschi of Paramount submitted the playscript for *Irma La Douce* to Geoffrey Shurlock on September 10, 1959, only to hear back five days later with the news that the film was a non-starter.
"It's unacceptability," Shurlock decreed, "stems from the fact that the leading lady is a practicing prostitute who, additionally, falls in love with the leading man, bearing his child out of wedlock. She is also carrying on a second affair with the leading man who has disguised himself as somebody else. This relationship is not treated with any semblance of the compensating moral values and voice for morality required by the Code." Shurlock added that there were other details not worth going into because of the overall nature of the project, for which, he concluded, "we have no alternative." [1]
Dissuaded thus, Paramount dropped the project, which was picked up in January 1961 by producer Joseph Pasternak, best known for his lower-budget MGM musicals during the golden era when Arthur Freed commanded the big budgets and prestige at that studio.[2] Pasternak announced that he was producing *Irma La Douce*, reuniting Billy Wilder with Jack Lemmon and Shirley MacLaine, who had just triumphed with *The Apartment*.[3] By June of 1962 Pasternak was gone and so were all the songs from what had been a musical.[4]
Also abandoned was the Code. In October 1962, Wilder told *Daily Variety* that he was willing to make his picture for United Artists and release it without a Code seal. No doubt he was emboldened by remembering that

his old friend, director-producer Otto Preminger, had released his 1953 film *The Moon is Blue*, also through United Artists, without a Code seal and the world did not end. Nevertheless, he shot two endings for *Irma*: one in which she (MacLaine) gives birth to her baby in a church right after she and Nestor (Lemmon) are wed, and another in which she has her child in the restaurant across the street from the church. The first ending was the one that was used.[1]

On May 23, 1963 *Irma La Douce* was given a Code seal and entered release on June 5 to become one of the most successful films Wilder had ever made.

This doesn't mean that the picture got away without opposition. A confidential report in the Code files says that Germany approved the film for over-18 audiences only and was not to be shown on holy days. The British demanded removal of several suggestive lines of dialogue and trimming the end wedding scene so that it no longer looked as if the priest was hurrying the ceremony so Irma and Nestor could be married before she delivered. (Yes, speeding up a scene to slow it down.) Australia wanted cuts in fights and girls and their johns entering and leaving hotel rooms. The reviews were generally favorable if occasionally condescending. None expressed outrage.

In fact, the only damning review in the files came not from the press but from esteemed producer Hal Wallis who quoted Wilder as saying, in a *Life* magazine article, "We don't make movies under the Code anymore." Wallis then commented in high dunder:

> Watching the workings of whores and their frequent trips into a hotel, glorification of pimps and detailing of their operations, cleavage of the whores, and particularly MacLaine, down to their navels, MacLaine completely nude shown down to her buttocks getting out of bed where she has spent the night with her pimp, the seduction scene in the hotel room which might have been something out of Frank Harris or Henry Miller – these, I suppose, are the elements that mean something to an audience. Possibly they do in the same way that exhibitions in brothels and looking at stag films mean to them.[2]

Shurlock's reply – sent after Christmas and New Year – informed Wallis that he had asked Eric Johnston's people in the MPAA office in the east to screen the film and that they, other than agreeing with Shurlock's people that it should be marked for adults only, had no objection. Even the Catholic church's Legion of Decency rated the film B but did not condemn it. "We were at first somewhat apprehensive," Shurlock said in his defense, adding that it would be one of the year's top grossers, and then added, "from what we can find out it is mostly men who complain about it. Women generally seem to find it hilarious."[3]

1. Luraschi to Shurlock, September 10, 1959 and Shurlock to Luraschi, September 15, 1959 (AMPAS).
2. *Daily Variety*, January 19, 1961.
3. *Los Angeles Times*, February 1, 1961.
4. *Daily Variety*, June 25, 1961.
5. *Daily Varity*, January 23, 1963.
6. Wallis to Shurlock, December 23, 1963 (AMPAS).
7. Shurlock to Wallis, January 6, 1934 (AMPAS).

Jezebel

Warner Bros, 1938
Written by Clements Ripley & Abem Finkel and John Huston, from the play by Owen Davis, with uncredited contributions from Robert Buckner and Louis F. Edelman
Produced by Hal Wallis, Henry Blanke and (uncredited) William Wyler
Directed by William Wyler
Code seal #3915

Synopsis
In 1852, before the Civil War, wilful Juli Kendrick (Bette Davis) outrages her fiancé, Preston "Pres" Dillard (Henry Fonda), by wearing a flame-red dress to a ball, something no decent southern girl would ever do. Pres teaches her a lesson by insisting on dancing with her to shame her. Then he breaks their engagement and marries Amy Bradford (Margaret Lindsay). When a yellow fever epidemic strikes the south and Pres falls ill, Julie accompanies him to quarantine, nobly lying to Amy that it is she whom Pres loves, not her.

Background
When Bette Davis was passed over as Scarlett O'Hara in *Gone with the Wind*, Warner Bros. created a competing story about a headstrong Southern belle especially for her. The result is a film that has likewise withstood the test of time, as has Davis's performance, which won her an Oscar the year before Vivien Leigh won hers for *GWTW*.

While David O. Selznick was sweating the word "damn" in *Gone with the Wind*, Warner Bros. was looking forward to clear sailing with their production of *Jezebel*. As a William Wyler film, it was automatically a class act. On October 15, 1937, Joseph Breen told Jack L. Warner, on reading part I of the final script, "that this material seems to us to be basically satisfactory from the standpoint of the Production Code, and of censorship.[1] (It's perhaps noteworthy that Breen did not view the Production Code as *de facto* censorship; he was referring to local and foreign censors.) Part II got the same response on October 20, and so did revised pages on October 27. Two weeks later, however, he advised that "the scene of the negress crossing herself" and "two uses of the word 'bugs'" would likely be cut by British censors.[2] In subsequent letters he repeated that the action of Julie slapping Pres on the face would be deleted by censors.[3]

The big shock came just before Thanksgiving when Breen had problems with the very title of the film, *Jezebel*, because of its scriptural allusion to "a woman who did evil in the sight of God," again citing the British censors' sensitivity to any screen portrayal of religion.[4] This began a dash to establish, checking Code files on both coasts, whether Will Hays had approved the title in late 1936. Either the Code covered for Hays or they found the authorization (no record of it is in the file), but *Jezebel* got its seal on February 1, 1938, and went into a highly successful release on March 28. Many of the critics then and since have noted that it made no sense for Julie to suddenly become noble at the end of the film, given her selfishness up until that point, but Davis's skill pulled it off.

Contrary to Breen's warnings, no cuts by British censors are noted in the Code files, although the Canadian province of Quebec deleted a shot of a man and woman kissing. The report doesn't specify which man and which woman.

---

1. Breen to Warner, October 15, 1937 (AMPAS).
2. Breen to Warner on October 20, 27, and November 12, 1937, respectively (AMPAS).
3. Breen to Warner, November 17 and 20, 1937 (AMPAS).
4. Breen to Warner, November 26 and 29, 1937 (AMPAS).

Kiss Me, Stupid

Lopert Pictures, 1970
Written by Billy Wilder and I.A.L Diamond, based on the play *L'Ora della Fantasia* by Anna Bonacci
Produced by Billy Wilder, I.A.L. Diamond and Doane Harrison
Directed by Billy Wilder
Code seal #20712

Synopsis
Two amateur songwriters,[1] a musician (Ray Walston) and a garage mechanic (Cliff Osmond) living in Climax, Nevada, conspire to detain singing star Dino (Dean Martin), whose car breaks down en route to Las Vegas, long enough to make him hear their songs. The insanely jealous Walston fears that Dino will become attracted to his wife (Felicia Farr), so he arranges with the town floozie (Kim Novak) to swap places with her. But Dino goes after Farr, whom he believes to be the town floozie.

Background
Although *Kiss Me, Stupid* has its supporters, it may be Billy Wilder's least successful film on nearly every level. The production was beset with problems: costume designer Orry-Kelly died, Kim Novak hurt her back, and Peter Sellers dropped out due to illness, to be replaced by a miscast Walston.

Sex farces run on precocity, not necessarily in the material itself but in the minds of the audience, who are tricked into expecting more than what's delivered. *Kiss Me, Stupid* reverses that equation by asking the audience to see the innocence despite the characters striving for guilt. Wilder and Diamond, known for their deft handling of risqué situations, saddled themselves with an actress who exuded sex and had laudable sweetness but slim comedic chops (Novak), and a replacement performer (Walston) whose frantic over-acting pushed moderately suggestive situations into the realm of vulgarity. Had they managed to hire Danny Kaye or, better, master farceur Tony Randall, to replace Sellers, as was first suggested, they might not have thrown their project off balance. As it is, recasting and re-shooting after Peter Sellers departed took three weeks.[2]

Filmed as *The Dazzling Hour* from March 6 to late July 1964, the film was eventually submitted for a Code seal under the title *Kiss Me, Stupid* (the film's happy ending's last line) and received it on October 13.[3] There are no records in the Production Code file noting any revisions in either the script or the final film. It was as though it sailed through the vetting process unscathed, a tribute to the sophistication of the Shurlock office. Instead, it was the audience that had a thing or two to say. Following a test screening at which some members of the audience were disturbed by coarse language, Wilder and Diamond did re-shoots.[4] Now wary of the wider reaction, United Artists decided to release *Kiss Me, Stupid* under their off-brand subsidiary, Lopert Pictures.[5]

The National Legion of Decency was not fooled, and the maelstrom began when they branded the film "C-Condemned" in early December.[6] "It is difficult to understand," the Legion's notice stated, "how such approval is not the final betrayal of the trust which has been placed by so many in the organized industry's self-regulation." They also criticized the film's release, timed for the Christmas and Chanukkah season.[7]

Their blast was not a knee-jerk reaction. They appreciated Wilder's use of satire in such earlier films as *The Apartment*, but said that "In *Kiss Me, Stupid* not only has Wilder failed to create a genuine satire... but he has regrettably produced a thoroughly sordid piece of realism which is esthetically as well as morally repulsive."[8]

Martin Quigley, Jr., publisher of the Motion Picture Herald, and son of the man who secretly helped to write the original Production Code, chimed in on December 8. Quigley was the son of the paper's founder, Martin Quigley, who had been one of the secret founders of the original Production Code (with Father Daniel A. Lord) and then a force in the creation of the National Legion of Decency with Archbishop John T. McNicholas. "The fact of the matter," Quigley wrote, "is that industry support of the Production Code has been falling away for years. Now the Production Code Administration could be blown away by a gentle zephyr... Let us leave to the historians of the future any apportionment of responsibility – or whether there is personal responsibility – for the current state of affairs. But let those of us who are interested in the welfare and progress of the theatrical motion picture face up to the situation and decide now – before it is too late – what is to replace the Production Code system."[9]

Quigley was prescient. The Code would indeed be replaced in 1968 by Jack Valenti, two years after he became MPAA president. But the fallout from Quigley's influential broadside intensified as the news media, rather than simply dismissing *Kiss Me, Stupid* and moving on, covered the scandal instead of the film. *Variety* disclosed that producer Walter Mirisch had attempted to re-edit the film to please the Legion of Decency, but failed to meet their criteria.[10] Reactionary columnist Paul Harvey echoed the Legion's astonishment that the film had opened in time for the holidays[11]

Writing sympathetically and analytically in *Billy Wilder: Dancing on the Edge*, Joseph McBride quotes I.A.L. Diamond's view that *Kiss Me, Stupid* was a Restoration comedy and nobody noticed. McBride notes that the theme of both the film and the source play[12] is that adultery can solve problems, and that there is a basic kindness to all the characters. What outraged audiences, both McBride and the filmmakers discovered, is that audiences hated to be called out on their foibles.[13] It might be added that, however Lubitschian *Kiss Me, Stupid* may have appeared on the page, that adroitness didn't carry across to the screen.

With the luxury of hindsight, it is easy to see that *Kiss Me, Stupid*, while not the apocalypse, was an opportunity for the Code to cross the line from past to future. The civil rights struggle, the rise of folk and protest music, the maturing of the baby boomers, the American commitment in Southeast Asia, and the intellectual stimulation of the Kennedy years were coming together to forge what became known as the generation gap. The emergence of the youth market – and Hollywood's discomfort in addressing it – made the schism even more profound.

Billy Wilder, who lit the fuse, was out of the country when his picture opened in the States. On January 11, 1965 he wrote a personal letter to Geoffrey Shurlock in which he noted that "the [American] Legionnaires have been lying in the bushes, biding their time until they could waylay a picture-maker of import and use him as a whipping boy for the entire industry." Confessing that it would be useless to defend himself at this point, he apologized for causing Shurlock "considerable trouble, and for this I am genuinely sorry."[14]

Shurlock responded immediately, saying, "That is, among other things, what I get paid for. But in your case, please believe me, I was motivated primarily by my esteem and affection for you, over and above the normal call of duty."[15]

---

1. How amateur could they be? The film used three unpublished George Gershwin songs with new lyrics written by Ira Gershwin.
2. American Film Institute catalogue.
3. AMPAS.
4. *Daily Variety*, October 21, 1964 (AMPAS). This was after the film had been awarded a Code seal.
5. Producer Ilya Lopert (*Summertime*, etc.) handled films that UA was cautious about releasing. When the company was bought by TransAmerica in 1966, the parent company sought to distance themselves from pictures that might attract scandal, such as *Last Tango in Paris*, on which the TA logo did not appear. This was not an uncommon practice (q.v. *Blow-Up*).
6. *Daily Variety*, December 7, 1964 (AMPAS).
7. *Daily Variety*, December 7, 1964 (AMPAS).
8. *Daily Variety*, December 7, 1964 (AMPAS).
9. *Motion Picture Daily*, December 8, 1964 (AMPAS).
10. *Variety*, December 8, 1964 (AMPAS).
11. Paul Harvey, "Sex for Yuletide Sickening Diet," *Citizen-News*, Los Angeles, CA, December 14, 1964 (AMPAS).
12. *L'Ora della Fantasia* (1944) by Anna Bonacci.
13. Joseph McBride, *Billy Wilder: Dancing on the Edge*, New York: Columbia University Press, 2021.
14. Wilder to Shurlock, January 11, 1965 (AMPAS).
15. Shurlock to Wilder, January 13, 1965 (AMPAS).

Lawrence of Arabia

Columbia Pictures, 1962
Written by Michael Wilson (originally uncredited) and Robert Bolt
Produced by Sam Spiegel
Directed by David Lean
Code seal #20334

Synopsis
Inscrutable British serving officer T.E. Lawrence (Peter O'Toole) inspires a Middle East guerilla campaign in World War I, unifying and then leading Arab tribes against the occupying Turks, yet, with the arrival of peace, his efforts come undone and he withdraws into self-imposed obscurity.

Background
After winning Academy Awards for *The Bridge on the River Kwai* in 1957, director David Lean, producer Sam Spiegel and blacklisted screenwriter Michael Wilson joined forces to explore (and possibly explain) the wartime exploits of Lawrence of Arabia. It took considerable effort to balance the demands of the Lawrence Estate with what the filmmakers felt was the truth within the man. The result was a film which is as complex as its subject and, at times, just as enigmatic.

The Code was not overly concerned about *Lawrence of Arabia*. David Lean's directorial credentials were more than impressive, and producer Sam Spiegel could charm a snake out of the last mouse in the garden. It also did not go un-remarked that, when Spiegel submitted the screenplay to the Shurlock office, it was read in light of the pair's Oscar wins for *The Bridge on the River Kwai*. But it was also read with the same eyes that considered less impressive productions.

Despite Geoffrey Shurlock's predecessor, Joe Breen's sternness as a censor, he also had a hearty sense of humor and a lust for badinage. Jack Vizzard, who worked under him from 1944 until Breen's retirement in 1954, wrote of his boss's glee in sending Columbia Pictures' profane production head Harry Cohn a list of script edits. When Cohn got them, he called Breen and asked, "What's all this shit?" Breen responded, "Mr. Cohn, I take that as a compliment."

"What does that mean?" Cohn challenged.

"My friends inform me," Breen said, "that if there's any expert in this town on shit, it's you. So if I have to be judged, I'm glad it's by professionals."

Breen was also uncorruptible. When a new Cadillac appeared in his driveway one Christmas morning, he called the studio chief who'd hopefully signed the card and told him to take the car back immediately.[1]

Shurlock, on the other hand, arrived at the Code office with a veneer of British sophistication (born in Liverpool, England in 1894) tempered by

European broad-mindedness. That said, he had to enforce the guidelines that Breen established with such zeal, even to the point of nit-picking.

Unless there are lapses in the Academy's Production Code file for *Lawrence of Arabia*, the only reservations Shurlock expressed can be found in Shurlock's one letter to producer Sam Spiegel on March 8, 1962, advising caution on:

> Page 43: In scene 153, we suggest not having the boy raise the camel's tail before prodding it. [ignored]
>
> Page 51: The expression "goddammit" is unacceptable. [heeded]
>
> Page II-46: Lawrence should not kick the bey in the groin. Also, we gather you do not intend in any way to overdo the beating of Lawrence. [The kick is done below frame; the beating is suggested by audio.]
>
> Page II-88-II-96: The acceptability of this scene [the "no prisoners" slaughter of the Turks] will of course depend on how it appears in the finished picture. We urge that it be done as much as possible by suggestion, and not on any too gruesome detail. [The scene is indeed done by suggestion which, of course, makes it seem all the more violent.][2]

On March 21, 1962, Spiegel replied that he hoped Shurlock would find no lapses of either good taste or good judgment in the completed picture, "but thanks all the same for your suggestions." He closed by asking for a personal note as to how he was getting along, "and don't limit yourself to just an official acknowledgment of the script."[3] What is noteworthy about this single exchange is that it took place ten months into what would be a sixteen-month shoot (May 15, 1961-September 21, 1962).

Shurlock took Spiegel up on his request for a personal letter and began by waiving concerns about the length of the *Lawrence* script by saying, "If you and David Lean want it to be that long, then that's the length it should be. After *Kwai* you and he can do no wrong." His other remarks concerned the nearly fifty percent drop-off in script submissions, indicating a production downturn sparked by recent big-budget releases like *Cleopatra* and *Mutiny on the Bounty* using up the film companies' financial resources. And yet, he concluded, "the almost clean sweep of *West Side Story* in Monday's Academy Awards suggests that the big picture will make it every time. All the more reason, therefore, for getting *Lawrence* to us as fast as you can."[4]

The film was awarded its Code seal on December 20, 1962, ten days after its Royal premiere in England and four days after its roadshow engagements began in the U.S.

One of the sensitive topics that the Code did not address, and which has dogged both the man and the film for decades, is the subject of Lawrence's homosexuality and also whether he enjoyed being beaten at the hands of the Turkish bey (José Ferrer). What did happen to Lawrence when he was captured by the Turks, and what broke his spirit and turned him into a bloodthirsty avenger? "The rumor had long been floated," says David Lean's biographer Stephen M. Silverman, "that the whipping scene involving Jose Ferrer and O'Toole was far more graphic as filmed but had to be cut before the film's release. 'Absolute bullshit. Everything that was shot is in the film,' says David, citing the censorship rules of the time. He said that nothing of Lawrence's homosexuality could be mentioned, such was the temper of the times (of which the studio and he were well aware) and that the eye shadow and the mascara they put on O'Toole were the strongest hints they could give about his sex life."[5]

1. Jack Vizzard, *See No Evil: Life Inside a Hollywood Censor*, New York: Simon and Schuster, 1970.
2. Shurlock to Spiegel, March 8, 1961 (AMPAS).
3. Spiegel to Shurlock, March 21, 1962 (AMPAS).
4. Shurlock to Spiegel, April 11, 1962 (AMPAS). Spiegel literally pulled the film out of Lean's and editor Anne V. Coates' hands for the London premiere. It was not restored until 1989.
5. Stephen M. Silverman e-mail interview with author. The author also queried Kate O'Toole, Peter O'Toole's daughter, who responded, "Not sure about the reason for the make-up but I do know he & Lean did the best they could at the time to convey the homosexuality."

The Lost Weekend

Paramount Pictures 1945
Written by Charles Brackett & Billy Wilder, from the novel by Charles R. Jackson
Produced by Charles Brackett
Directed by Billy Wilder
Code seal #10517

Synopsis
A blocked writer (Ray Milland), alone in New York, spends a weekend in an alcoholic haze.

Background
Paramount paid $100,000 for the film rights to the novel only to be told that they would have to scrap the story because the Code prohibited material about alcohol and alcoholism.[1]

So many legends arose about *The Lost Weekend* after it was released that the process of just getting it made has been obscured. Supposedly, director Billy Wilder bought a copy of the book at a Chicago train station and by the time he got back to Los Angeles he knew he would make it as his next film. Supposedly the title is a misprint, that author Charles R. Jackson intended to call it *The Last Weekend*. Supposedly the liquor industry promised Paramount $5 million to burn the negative, and in one version of the story the offer they couldn't refuse was made by gangster Frank Costello. Supposedly temperance groups wanted to stop the picture, fearing it would inspire people to drink. And supposedly Billy Wilder made the picture so he could understand why his previous writing partner, Raymond Chandler (*Double Indemnity*), was an alcoholic. (This last supposition seems to be true.) But the people who really didn't want *The Lost Weekend* made were the Production Code, and it wasn't for any political or idealistic reason, it was simply because the Code flatly prohibited booze on the screen.
    Billy Wilder was not to be dissuaded, and the Production Code Administration files reveal quite an interesting back-and-forth leading up to the film's astonishing success critically, financially, and Oscar-wise. It began with Wilder's oft-mentioned tactic of starting to shoot a film without a complete script, sometimes joking that it kept the studio from firing him. It also meant that it was tough to budget the picture, build sets, or work out a schedule. But Wilder had a way of keeping things going without necessarily explaining what he was up to. For *The Lost Weekend*, this brought him and Paramount's in-house censor, Luigi Luraschi, into conflict with the Code, who remained usure of where the film was going, often until the day before a scene was to be shot.[2] A series of letters between Joseph Breen and Luraschi

between October and November 1944 track Breen's increasing impatience with the pages he was being shown. His chief concern was about a female character, Gloria (Doris Dowling), whom he was afraid was being portrayed as a prostitute.[3]

Sometimes the script's violations were specific, such as including "God" in the dialogue, "Why in the name of…"[4] Others were more indirect, such as cutting Nat the bartender's (Howard DaSilva) dialogue, "One day your guy gets wise to himself' down to 'in a subway under a train' because of its specific reference to methods of committing suicide."[5]

The liquor trade bellied up to the bar on November 15 with a letter to Will Hays. Stanley Baer, executive vice president of Allied Liquor Industries, referenced an alert he had sent to Paramount's vice president Y. Frank Freeman two days earlier. Baer's three-page missive to Hays is a restrained statement of concern that *The Lost Weekend* would undo years of efforts by the liquor industry, as a major employer, to un-demonize their profession. He stops short of making any kind of threat and, as a matter of fact, likens his industry's public relations problems to those facing the film industry, suggesting adding a preamble to the film "which would eliminate all our fears."[6]

Meanwhile the Breen Office was trying to wrangle *The Lost Weekend* within Code by cautioning the filmmakers on moments which, while not specifically prohibited, nevertheless fell within outlawed areas: not showing a hypodermic injection, and not portraying the gruesomeness of the DTs (delirium tremens) involving a bat being killed in a hospital sequence.

There was one very important aspect of Jackson's book that wasn't ever mentioned. In the film, Don Birnam's (Milland) alcoholism is a physiological addiction, an enlightened observation that placed Wilder and Brackett ahead of most mental health professionals of the time. Yet Jackson's book is more explicit in ascribing it to Birnam's residual guilt over a homosexual affair he'd had in college. Jackson himself was either gay or bisexual.[7] This is referenced in the novel and hinted at in the film when a male nurse at Bellevue Hospital makes an approach to Birnam. In 1944, "sex perversion," as homosexuality was known, was not permitted on screen.[8]

By January 1945, all the Production Code Administration hoops had been jumped through but *The Lost Weekend* was still not given its code seal until August. One reason for the delay was a disastrous sneak preview in which the audience laughed at the film, causing both Wilder and Paramount to consider withholding it from release.[9] The matter was corrected when Miklós Rózsa added his musical score, which included a then-new instrument, the Theremin (which he had also used in his score for Alfred Hitchcock's *Spellbound* in 1945), that set the tone of seriousness.

The Code seal was not enough to pacify many of the nation's censors. At that time, per a report from Paramount's Russell Holman, America still had fourteen major censorship boards despite Hollywood's efforts to neutralize them.[10] Each state applied its particular criteria to demand cuts, none of them consistent, and all of them a concern to the studio who, as they had been in the 1920s, resented having to create different edits for separate exhibition venues. A later report from Holman to the company's James J. Donohue, Charles M. Reagan, and Bernard Goodwin revealed that there was nothing in the various censorship statutes that should have prohibited exhibiting the film.[11]

In Great Britain the problem was different. The British censors banned *The Lost Weekend* entirely but, after negotiation with Paramount, admitted that, had the picture been made by a temperance society, they would have no trouble permitting its exhibition. A settlement was reached in which the film would lose two screams uttered during the main character's hospitalization, that it would be subtitled *Diary of a Dipsomaniac*, and that the picture would start with the message:

> *Ladies and Gentlemen*
> As this is a most unusual subject for screen presentation, we have been requested to warn you of the grim and realistic sequences contained in this unique diary carrying such as powerful moral.

As for the noted opposition by the liquor industry, an inside source with the Allied Liquor Industries trade association leaked a confidential report to Paramount, who forwarded it discretely to Breen. It revealed that, at a confab sometime in late October, 1945, the lobbyists agreed to not publicly oppose *The Lost Weekend* lest doing so accord it more publicity, and to request silence about it in their trade publications. Allied acknowledged that everyone connected with the film agreed it was not a screed against taking a drink.[12]

As a precaution, Paramount accorded *The Lost Weekend* limited release in New York and Los Angeles in December 1945. When the reviews were superlative, the studio was emboldened to give it a wider release in January 1946. On an investment of $1.25 million the film earned rentals of $4.3 million[13] as well as Oscars for best picture, best director, best screenplay, and for its star, Ray Milland (who, it turned out, was not a drinker).

---

1. Source: Jimmy Fiddler, Hollywood gossip columnist. IMDb pegs the amount at $50,000.
2. Breen to Luraschi, November 7, 1944: "Again we must urge upon you the necessity of submitting, as soon as possible, the remainder of this script." (AMPAS).
3. Breen to Luraschi, November 3, 1944 (AMPAS).
4. Breen to Luraschi, November 7, 1944 (AMPAS).
5. Breen to Luraschi, November 9, 1944 (AMPAS).
6. Baer to Freeman, November 13, 1944 (AMPAS).
7. Roger Austen, *Playing the Game: The Homosexual Novel in America*, Indianapolis, Indiana: The Bobbs-Merrill Company, 1977.
8. Wilder biographer Joseph McBride notes Wilder's acceptance of homosexuality and suggests that Wilder's writing partner Charles Brackett was a closeted gay, another reason not to mention it in the film.
9. Legend has it that one of the audience comment cards said that it would be a great picture if only they took out all the drinking.

10. They were Georgia (Atlanta), Illinois (Chicago), Kansas, Maryland, Massachusetts, Michigan (Detroit), Missouri (Kansas City), New York, Ohio, Oregon (Portland), Pennsylvania, Tennessee (Memphis), Virginia, and Wisconsin (Milwaukee). Russell Holman (Paramount Home Office), report to Luraschi, September 15, 1945 (AMPAS).
11. Holman to Donohue, Reagan, and Goodwin, September 10, 1945 (AMPAS).
12. Breen to Luraschi, December 5, 1945 (AMPAS). The leaked report is undated. This raises the question of where the supposed $5 million buy-out offer came from. When told of it, Wilder reportedly said that if he'd been promised that much money personally he wouldn't have made the picture.
13. *Variety*, 3 December 1947.

Love Affair

RKO Radio Pictures, 1939
Written by Delmer Daves and Donald Ogden Stewart (uncredited contribution by S.N. Behrman), from a story by Mildred Cram and Leo McCarey
Produced and directed by Leo McCarey
Code seal #4778

Synopsis
Michel (Charles Boyer) and Terry (Irene Dunne) meet aboard a cruise liner and fall in love but, because each is already engaged to someone else, they agree to meet six months hence once they have extricated themselves from their current relationships. He is an artist engaged to a society woman who supports him, she to a banker who helps her live in luxury. Back in New York, he leaves his fiancée and begins a struggle for professional recognition. She leaves her intended and moves into a small room, taking a job to barely survive. On the six-month date (which occurs precisely halfway through the film) Michel shows up on schedule but Terry is hit by a car *en route*. Michel thinks she no longer loves him and goes off. When they meet by chance some time later, she is in the company of her banker whom Michel thinks she has married. He subsequently discovers that she cannot walk and was waiting until she recovered before contacting him. When he learns this, he rushes to her and they live happily ever after.

Background
Easily one of the most romantic movies ever made, its director, Leo McCarey, remade it himself in 1957 (as *An Affair to Remember* with Cary Grant and Deborah Kerr) with more class but less complex characters. The differences between the versions shows how much audiences had changed, not to mention the Code. This essay looks only at the original 1939 version; we'll leave the remake to be watched by Meg Ryan and Tom Hanks in *Sleepless in Seattle* (1993). As for Warren Beatty's 1994 remake, that film was post-Code and rated PG-13.

Originally titled *Memory of Love*, *Love Affair* was rejected in its entirety by the Hays Office when RKO first sent them a treatment in July 1938. Calling it an immoral story about a kept man and a kept woman, Joseph Breen told J.R. McDonough of RKO that it was "a low-toned, sordid story of gross sexual irregularities without even a semblance of what we call 'compensating moral values'" that was "violently in conflict with both the spirit and the letter of our Production Code that it cannot be approved."[1]

The gap between Breen's first appraisal and the film that eventually came out is a testament to Leo McCarey, whose ineffable directing skill has never been equaled, let alone surpassed. Whether directing silent Laurel and Hardy comedies at the beginning of his career or creating cinematic soufflés like *Going My Way* and *The Awful Truth*, taming the Marx Brothers in *Duck Soup* or summoning the skills to make a stone cry (as Orson Welles said[2]) in *Make Way for Tomorrow*, McCarey could seemingly juggle anything and make it work.[3] This is even more of an accomplishment when one considers how many of his actors said he never used a script, yet somehow got it all together.

McCarey had previously scored with *The Awful Truth* (1937), in which a separated husband and wife (Cary Grant and Irene Dunne) continue to see each while waiting for their divorce to become final. Naturally, they end up falling back in love and wind up sharing a bedroom just as the clock chimes out their divorce. In other words, at midnight they become an *unmarried* couple in bed together (albeit offscreen) in violation of Breen's Don't and Be Carefuls. *The Awful Truth* won the Best Picture Oscar in 1938 and nobody at the Code seems to have noticed this little matter of adultery.

Love Affair is McCarey at his peak and the Breen Office at its pique. Breen's main objection was that both Michel and Terry were kept people, Michel by his society patron and Terry by her banker friend, even though no two parties lived together. Terry's opulent apartment, in particular, drew Breen's concern. But what distressed him the most was that neither Michel nor Terry is made to suffer for having an illicit relationship; even Terry's becoming crippled wasn't sufficient to Breen because she wins back Michel after all. Quoting the Code, he declared that "Pictures should not infer that low forms of sex relationships are the accepted, or common, thing" and suggested that the filmmakers "dismiss from your mind any further consideration of it."[4]

After Breen's initial fusillade, a hurried meeting was set among him, Code staffer Iselin Auster, and Pandro S. Berman, head of production at RKO Radio Pictures.[5] More revisions came through after that but Breen kept harping on the lack of sufficient punishment, again, not so much for Michel as for Terry, as though it were all her fault.[6] More than a month later he was still demanding "compensating moral values" despite passionately ending his November 29 letter, "I just want to get into the record, now, that we could not approve anything like the picture we saw this afternoon – despite the fact that it is magnificently done and quite the most charming and delightful screen material we have witnessed in a long, long while."[7]

This highly personal entry, more than any other, exposes the tragic hypocrisy of the censor, though Joseph Breen should not be blamed for personifying it. When an individual sets himself up as the guardian of the morality of others it is the definition of presumptuousness. When an organization is established for the same purpose, however, it goes beyond presumption and enters the realm of totalitarianism.

By December 17, 1938, Breen was still telling McDonough that Terry should not be completely cured of her injury when she and Michel reunite and that this would show that she is still paying the price for her actions. Specifically, he says, "if it can be indicated that there is still some trace of her injury, it will inject some slight flavor of tragedy into the ending and thus serve to emphasize the 'compensating moral values' which are necessary in stories of this kind, under the provisions of the Production Code."[8]

With all the changes made and accepted, *Love Affair* passed the Production Code review on January 30. Two weeks later, Leo McCarey contacted the Code and wanted to restore a cut scene into his film to improve the pace. The scene involved a line spoken to Terry by her maid, "Did you get a better offer?" clearly referring to a richer sugar daddy. Breen and McCarey attended a sneak preview in which the print had the line restored, after which Breen denied its reinsertion.[9] A month later he denied McCarey the chance to restore another line in which Terry laments, "If the punishment fits the crime, I must have been a very bad girl."[10]

Love Affair opened in theatres April 7, 1939 to good reviews and solid business. Given Breen's praise despite his actions, this is one of those films of which one wonders how much better it could have been if both the director and the censor had each been free to do it his way.

---

1. Breen to McDonough, September 15, 1938 (AMPAS).
2. Quoted by Keith Ulich, "Make Way for Tomorrow," *Slant* magazine, July 8, 2004.
3. Exceptions must be made for his rabid anti-Communist tracts *My Son John* (1952) and *Satan Never Sleeps* (1962), where his bile infected his talent.
4. Breen to McDonough, September 14, 1938 (AMPAS).
5. Note to file from L.H., September 19, 1938 (AMPAS).
6. Breen to McDonough, October 11, 1938 (AMPAS).
7. Breen to McDonough, November 29, 1938 (AMPAS).
8. Breen to McDonough, December 17, 1938 (AMPAS).
9. Shurlock memo to the file, February 24, 1939 (AMPAS).
10. Breen to file, March 13, 1939 (AMPAS).

The Maltese Falcon

Warner Bros., 1941
Written by John Huston, from the novel by Dashiell Hammett
Produced by Hal B. Wallis and Henry Blanke
Directed by John Huston
Code seal #7457

Synopsis
After his partner is murdered, private detective Sam Spade (Humphrey Bogart) is lured into a quest for a valuable avian sculpture by an alluring woman, Brigid O'Shaughnessy (Mary Astor), who leads him against men who also desire the bird, Kasper Gutman (Sidney Greenstreet), his partner Joel Cairo (Peter Lorre), and a clumsy gunsel Wilmer Cook (Elisha Cook, Jr.).

Background
Everybody knows that *The Maltese Falcon*, the film that made Humphrey Bogart a star and John Huston a director, had been produced twice before: in 1932, pre-Code, with Ricardo Cortez and Bebe Daniels,[1] and in 1936 as *Satan Met a Lady* with Warren William and Bette Davis. They also know that John Huston didn't really write the script, he just told his secretary to retype the book removing the "he said"s and "she said"s and Warner Bros., thinking it looked like a screenplay, put it right into production. Some people even say that Bogart, who rose to fame playing gangsters, got letters from convicts when he became a detective expressing disappointment that he "went straight."

With the rumors out of the way, it's time to look at how *The Maltese Falcon* had its wings clipped by the Production Code on its flight into immortality. It took off on May 22, 1941 when producer Henry Blanke sent what he called a temporary script to the Breen Office which took 24 hours to return three pages of cuts not to Blanke but to his boss, Jack L. Warner. Of note is that the temporary script ran to at least 164 pages; current scripts are seldom longer than 105, give or take. Among Code prohibitions were:

> While the drinking indicated on Page 93… seems to be necessary in order to prepare for the later scenes where Spade is drugged, we must insist that the actual drinking be kept to an absolute minimum necessary for the development of the plot. It seems that audiences are offended not so much by the presence of liquor but by the actual drinking.
>
> It is essential that Spade should not be characterized as having had a sex affair with Iva (Iva Archer, Spade's partner's wife, played by Gladys George). Accordingly, we request that you cut down the physical contact indicated on this page and elsewhere and

that the following lines be deleted or changed to get away from such inference: "You shouldn't have come here today, darling. It wasn't wise," and Iva's line, "You'll come tonight?" with Spade's reply, "Not tonight."

We cannot approve the characterization of Cairo as a pansy as indicated by the lavender perfume. (They also directed his slap to Brigid be done out of frame.)

There must be no suggestion that Spade and Brigid spend the night together in Spade's apartment.

Reduce the number of times Guttman says "by gad."

Eliminate the shot of the boy (Wilmer) kicking Spade in the face, or do it offscreen.

Spade's speech about the District Attorneys should be rewritten to get away from characterizing most District Attorneys as men who will do anything to further their careers. This is important.

And of course there were the usual orders to remove *hell, damn*, and any curse words implied by three dots (…) in dialogue.[2] Curiously, another letter from Breen to Warner on May 27, after having received and gone over what he referred to as the final script, reiterated his initial prohibitions, plus reactions to the addition of even more sexual innuendos. When Breen rendered his regular status report to Hays at the end of May, he made mention that *The Maltese Falcon*'s script was rejected for "illicit sex and drunkenness."[3]

The Maltese Falcon opened in October 1941. Warner valued Huston so highly as a screenwriter (getting to direct a film was one of his contract renewal demands) that they were prepared to write off *Falcon* as a gift to him should it fail. It did not fail, and the studio discovered that they had a hyphenate on their hands. Did the Production Code know that they were crimping the style of a classic-in-the-making? Of course not. If Warner expected the film to flop, how could the Code, whose people read hundreds of scripts a year, think differently? In filmmaking, nobody knows what, in the end, will work. It's the stuff that nightmares are made of.

---

1. For a time it was renamed *Woman of the World* and then changed again to *Dangerous Female*. Lawrence Grobel, *The Hustons*, New York: Charles Scribner's Sons, 1989.
2. Breen to Warner, May 23, 1941 (AMPAS).
3. Breen to Hays, May 31, 1941 (AMPAS). The six-page, single-spaced report named some two hundred films divided into genres, each of which was being tracked through the production process. Needless to say, this represented an immense amount of work by Code personnel. Most of the films listed in that single report are, today, obscure-to-forgotten.

Mr. Smith Goes to Washington

Columbia Pictures, 1939
Screenplay by Sidney Buchman (uncredited contribution by Myles Connolly), from the story "The Gentleman from Montana" by Lewis Ransom Foster
Produced and directed by Frank Capra
Code seal #5370

Synopsis
An idealistic scoutmaster (James Stewart) from Montana is appointed senator from that state and runs up against corruption and cynicism as he tries to serve his constituents, ending with a filibuster on the floor of Congress.

Background
Mr. Smith had a rougher road getting to the screen than he did going to Washington. The Production Code cautioned the filmmakers against the source material's negative portrayal of politicians. Charges of un-Americanism were leveled against it to such an extent that they frightened its director, Frank Capra, Hollywood's celebrated champion of the "little guy," into becoming a political reactionary.

When Capra wrote in his memoir, *The Name Above the Title*, that he jumped at *Mr. Smith Goes to Washington* when he was handed a two-page synopsis by Columbia Pictures' vice president Joe Sistrom, he either didn't know or wouldn't divulge that he wasn't anybody's first choice to direct it, nor was Columbia the first choice to produce it. Just as they say the two things one must never see being made are sausage and legislation, *Mr. Smith Goes to Washington* should be added to that list.

Lewis R. Foster's "The Gentleman from Montana" was first offered to Metro-Goldwyn-Mayer, whose Al Block submitted it to the Breen Office for comment.[1] Breen's reaction, sent directly to Louis B. Mayer, began, "the novel presents enormous difficulties from the standpoint of industry policy." Keeping in mind that the Code's umbrella organization, the Motion Picture Producers and Distributors of America, was a trade association that had its hand in legislation, Breen's comments were not only pragmatic but prescient:

> The difficulties that we sense in this story fall under the following general heading: The portrayal of the United States Senate as a body of politicians who, if not deliberately crooked, are completely controlled by lobbyists for special interests. The unflattering portrayal of several Senators from various specific states, more particularly the senior Senator from Montana. The generally unflattering portrayal of our system of Government, which might well lead to such a picture being considered, both

here, and more particularly abroad, as a covert attack on the Democratic form of government.²

MGM backed off, but Paramount was still in the running, and that studio's John Hammell got the same opinion from Breen on the same day, suggesting multiple submissions by the agent repping Foster.³ When the Lion and the Mountain passed, that left Columbia Pictures. Columbia, no longer considered "poverty row" thanks to the huge successes that Frank Capra's films had brought the feisty upstart, seemed game for anything that had been passed up by two of its major competitors. The studio's vice president, Joe Sistrom, arranged a confab with the Code's Geoffrey Shurlock, a Code staffer named Lischka, and screenwriters Nat Perrin and Carey Wilson, to discuss the problems adapting the material.⁴ Whether Perrin and Wilson worked on it is unknown, and the project languished at the studio until it was offered to director Rouben Mamoulian, who was confident that the problems could be worked out.⁵ Apparently not, as Mamoulian disappears from the Code correspondence.

Thus, when Capra (who was mourning the loss of his proposed screen biography of Frederic Chopin) was offered a two-page synopsis of the Foster story by Sistrom, he wrote that he immediately saw its possibilities, either not knowing or not noting that the project had been around the block. He then asked for Sidney Buchman to write the script, which was sent to the Code office for evaluation just after January 23, 1939. Breen's response arrived on the desk of Columbia's Harry Cohn on January 30.

Saunders (Jean Arthur), the reporter who befriends Jefferson Smith (Stewart), initially to exploit his naiveté, drew much criticism for using "my God" and for such world-weary laments as, "How could I be decent? How could I have a shred of decency left?" and "perhaps the rottenest political mess I've been caught in to date" and "Congressmen have done antics for the newspapers before." Breen's overall concern, however, remained the script's criticism of the system, and this, he told Cohn, "will be referred to Mr. Hays."⁶ Breen separately suggested to Hays that it might be wise to characterize Senator Fletcher (in the film he becomes Senator Paine, played by Claude Rains) and two others as "the exception that proves the rule" and to showcase the good citizenship of the rest of the Congressmen. Breen told Hays he had discussed this with Sam Briskin and Mendel Silberberg, and wanted Hays' opinion inasmuch as Capra was ready to roll the picture.⁷

Columbia sent the final script to the Association of Motion Picture Producers of America on March 6 accompanied by a checklist of the changes they had made, mostly in dialogue: substituting the word "bad" for "rotten," removing the word "shag" because Australia would cut it, letting Saunders be high but not drunk, and removing from Callahan's (in the film, Taylor, Edward Arnold) dialogue, "That's how these boys got here. I picked them and had them elected. They're doing what I tell them to."⁸ Correspondence continued as page after page was revised through April 21, 1939. The film was finished and prepared for an October 17 premiere in Washington, DC, after which it would hit theaters across America. On September 20, apparently after a work-in-progress screening, Breen sent an urgent letter to Harry Cohn telling him to delete Saunders' line, "Hold your hats, boys, here we go again," saying he believed it to be the tag line of a vulgar joke.[9] After Columbia cut the line down to "Diz, here we go,"[10] Breen was apparently mollified enough to issue a Code seal on September 17, 1939.

Frank Capra was surprised by the negative press reaction to his film – not the critics, who hailed it, but news-side journalists who resented being portrayed as cynics and gadflies. Some even charged Capra with being un-American, an accusation that chilled the Sicilian immigrant to his marrow and began his morphing into a super-patriot, in many ways repudiating the populism that he had infused into his films.

As for the portrayal of politicians as corrupt pawns of lobbyists and special interests, and the reporters who cover them as cynical drunks, it's a good thing that all that has changed over the years and no longer exists.

1. Block to Breen, January 15, 1938 (AMPAS).
2. Breen to Mayer, January 19, 1938 (AMPAS).
3. Breen to Hammell, January 19, 1938 (AMPAS).
4. February 26, 1938 memo to the files from Geoffrey Shurlock (AMPAS).
5. Shurlock to file, June 10, 1938 (AMPAS).
6. Breen to Cohn, January 30, 1939 (AMPAS).
7. Breen to Hays, January 31, 1939. Briskin was head of production at Columbia and Silberberg was Columbia's counsel, a Jewish religious leader, and a liaison among various industry people he represented as lawyer.
8. Columbia to AMPP, March 6, 1939 (AMPAS).
9. Breen to Cohn, September 20, 1939 (AMPAS).
10. Rita Cahoon (illegible), editorial dept. to Breen, September 26, 1939 (AMPAS).

Monsieur Verdoux

United Artists, 1947
Written by Charles Chaplin, based on an idea by Orson Welles
Produced and directed by Charles Chaplin
Code seal #12225

Synopsis
Bigamist Henri Verdoux (Charles Chaplin) supports himself by marrying and murdering wealthy women, at least one of whom, Annabella Bonheur (Martha Raye), poses a comic challenge. When he is ultimately caught, tried, and set for execution, he argues that wars and governments kill more people than he ever did.

Background
Chaplin's black comedy is based on the actual serial killer Henri Desire Landru who plied his trade between 1915 and 1919, was convicted of at least ten murders, and was beheaded in 1922. Chaplin was going through the process of losing a paternity suit brought by Joan Barry (Mary Louise Baker) and thought making a comedy would relieve his gloom.[1]

Monsieur Verdoux, written under the title *A Comedy of Murders*, was Charles Chaplin's first actual contact with the Production Code Administration, but it wasn't his first experience with it. His 1940 film, *The Great Dictator*, had created a scandal involving the German Consul, the British Board of Film Censors, and United States Senator Robert Reynolds over Chaplin's intention to ridicule Adolf Hitler, all of the parties being concerned (in widely differing ways) about making der Führer angry.

Yet when *The Great Dictator* was submitted, in final form, to the Breen Office, who had not seen a page of script in advance, they not only passed it, but they also rebuffed Chaplin's foes by what could only be called malicious compliance, citing arcane protocol and ducking every request for information. Breen's only order to Chaplin was to delete the word *lousy* and added, in personal note, "It is superb screen entertainment and marks Mr. Chaplin, I think, as our greatest artist."[2]

Inasmuch as *The Great Dictator* was settled without Chaplin's involvement, the filmmaker was astonished when the man who had just called him the "greatest artist" rejected *A Comedy of Murders* in its entirety.

"The story contains a false enunciation of moral values, which seems to be in fundamental conflict with the theory of sound ethics as set forth in the Industry's Production Code," Breen protested, "and because of which the story could not be approved by us." In explaining the Code's position, Breen presents an analysis of situational morality worthy of a Jesuit scholar. "[Verdoux's] claim is, effectively, that it is ridiculous to be shocked by the extent of his atrocities, that they are a mere 'comedy of murders' in comparison with the legalized mass murders of war, which are embellished with gold braid by the 'system.'"[3]

The Code office was concerned that their being sent the final shooting script was the first time they had heard from Chaplin about his film, whereas the usual procedure was to be alerted when a story is first proposed so they could clear it early on.

In a helpful (if passive-aggressive) letter, Breen outlined to Chaplin the ritual for future films.[4] In reply, Chaplin sent an equally passive-aggressive apology saying, "As this is the first I have ever submitted, I am naturally not familiar with your [script] markings, whether they mean absolute deletion or revision. As I have worked for over two and a half years on *A Comedy of Murders* I think it only fair that a letter of explanation should follow, clarifying the fact as to what your markings mean."[5]

That same day, Breen wrote Chaplin of his four concerns: 1) his lead had more than one wife; 2) the lead character clouds right and wrong by comparing war and murder; 3) the character of "the girl" is a prostitute and her situation is made profitable; 4) some of the final lines are open to being blasphemous.

Breen insisted that voices of morality should be introduced to condemn Verdoux's bigamy and moral ambiguity, and furthermore posited that "it is pretty well established that mankind in general has agreed down through the centuries, that to kill under certain circumstances – lawful war, for instance – is not a violation of either the moral or human law. On the other hand, to murder – to kill unlawfully – is universally agreed to be a crime against both the moral and the human law." He added a P.S. that the script markings were indications by Code readers for internal use and that the only reason Chaplin saw them was that he had asked for his script copies back.[6]

Chaplin's March 5 answer to Breen is a perfect summary of why so many people chafed under the Code. "To apply rigidly and technically the letter of the Code to certain situations, passages, and phrases in my story," Chaplin wrote, "is an arbitrary procedure because the Code is so elastic that it can construe or interpret whatever it likes, according to its beliefs and prejudices."[7]

The matter was resolved on March 12 in a meeting among Breen, Chaplin, Vizzard, and Lynch settling forty-seven separate items that would be changed or deleted from the proposed film.[8] Breen referred to the meeting as cordial, but Chaplin, in his autobiography, remembered it differently. While his version may be self-serving, it provides a rare look at the in-person negotiating process versus the studied formality of letters. Chaplin refers to "a tall, dour young man" (probably Lynch or Vizzard) who entered the room and asked him, "What have you against the Catholic Church?" The filmmaker had no idea what he was talking about.

> "Here," he said, slamming a copy of my script on the table and turning its pages. "The scene in the condemned cell where the

criminal Verdoux says to the priest, 'What can I do for you, my good man?'"

"Well, isn't he a good man?"

"That's facetious," he said, waving a disparaging hand.

"I find nothing facetious in calling a man 'good,' I answered."

"You don't call a priest 'a good man,' you call him 'Father.'"

Chaplin then describes what he calls "a sort of Shavian dialogue with him" in which he, the filmmaker, had to defend a scene in which Verdoux engages in a discussion of morality with the priest who is preparing to give him absolution before execution. Verdoux doesn't want absolution; he has already made his peace with God in the exchange in which the priest says, "May God have mercy on your soul" and Verdoux replies, "Why not? After all, it belongs to Him." This outraged the Code worker who said, "You impugn society and the whole state." To which Chaplin responded, "Well, after all, the state and society are not simon-pure, and criticism of them is not inadmissible, surely." This teleological reasoning was beyond the dour young man's capabilities, yet Chaplin reported that all he wound up having to do was to not portray "the girl" as a prostitute, after which he was given the go-ahead to make prints and release his film.[9]

Only Pennsylvania is recorded as having ordered cuts in the exhibition prints of *Monsieur Verdoux*, which was the final title for *A Comedy of Murders*. In the following years, Chaplin was to make three more original films – *Limelight*, *A King in New York*, and *A Countess From Hong Kong* – plus re-release his earlier silent classics with original musical scores added. None drew particular Code interest. State Department, yes, but not Production Code.

---

1. Chaplin misremembers the sequence of events inasmuch as letters to and from the Breen Office begin in February 1943 and would have predated shooting anyway. He also calls the Breen Office "a branch of the Legion of Decency," which may be true in theory but not in fact. Charles Chaplin, *My Autobiography*, New York: Simon and Schuster, 1964.
2. Breen to Chaplin Studios general manager Al Reeves, September 6, 1940 (AMPAS).
3. Breen to Chaplin, February 20, 1946 (AMPAS).
4. Breen to Chaplin, February 22, 1946 (AMPAS).
5. Chaplin to Breen, February 28, 1946 (AMPAS).
6. Breen to Chaplin, February 28, 1946 (AMPAS).
7. Chaplin to Breen, March 5, 1946 (AMPAS).
8. Breen to Chaplin, March 15, 1946 (AMPAS).
9. Chaplin, *My Autobiography*. Apparently Chaplin didn't consult his copies of Breen's letters when he wrote his book.

Mutiny on the Bounty

Metro-Goldwyn-Mayer, 1935
Screenplay by Talbot Jennings & Jules Furthman and Carey Wilson (Margaret Booth and John Farrow, uncredited), from the books by Charles Nordhoff and James Norman Hall
Produced by Frank Lloyd and Albert Lewin (Irving Thalberg, uncredited)
Directed by Frank Lloyd
Code seal #1531

Synopsis
In 1789, the crew of H.M.S. Bounty, oppressed by the harshness of Captain William Bligh on a South Seas mission to bring breadfruit back to England, revolts against him and sets sail with mutiny leader first mate Fletcher Christian for a paradise on Pitcairn Island.

Background
It may not be historically accurate – Captain Bligh was nowhere near as sadistic as he is painted, no one died from his cruelty on the voyage, Bligh was not present at the trial of any mutineers, and rather than find paradise on Pitcairn, Christian's men enslaved the islanders – but that didn't matter to audiences as they eagerly consumed the film version of Nordhoff and Hall's *Bounty* trilogy.

There were four film versions of the Bounty story: this one in 1935, a disastrous remake in 1962, a more accurate version called *The Bounty* in 1984,[1] and one in which the story was interpolated into the old west in Howard Hawks' 1948 western, *Red River*. None, however, had the fame of the first, in which Clark Gable faced off against Charles Laughton.

That it raised the Code's eyebrows should not be surprising. The notion of men at sea being beaten by a sadistic captain, then escaping to languish on a tropical island with native women, is practically the definition of an exploitation picture, if not a template for pornography. MGM surely realized this when they sent a close synopsis of the 1932 book to the Breen Office as a precursor to buying the screen rights, and must have been surprised when they heard back that "the material contained in this outline is free from difficulties, both from the standpoint of the Code and of censorship."[2] On that assurance, MGM went ahead and bought the book, proceeded to adapt it for the screen over the next nine months, and sent it to Breen on December 19, 1934.[3] Breen got back to Louis B. Mayer the day after Christmas with a different opinion than the one he had expressed when all he had to go on was the synopsis.

He took issue with three types of scenes: the bawdy atmosphere on the Bounty's deck before sailing, the flogging scenes, and the nudity of the Tahitian men and women. (These were, of course, the film's major selling points.) Breen also called attention to lines such as, "Wot would a brown gal do for that?" Bligh's "and a brown Jill for every Jack," "Try kissing me, snottie!

You'll think the ship has split in 'arf," the last half of Christian's admonition, "If I must kick you off, I'll put you to sleep between your kidneys and your knees," and numerous citations against nudity and suggestive relationships.[4]

The script was tweaked and resubmitted on December 29 and the next day Breen wrote back a virtual repeat of his remarks from the December 26th as if nothing had been changed. By February 27 the disparity seems to have been straightened out because Breen wrote Mayer thanking him for cleaning up the dissolute scenes of brutality on the ship, but again called his attention to the delicate task of cleaning up the scenes of "the aboriginals" with regard to costuming. The one dangling issue was shots of men having been hanged that, Breen warned, would be cut in some foreign countries.[5]

As the film moved through post-production in readiness for its November 1935 premiere, Breen was still on Mayer's case about a scene of Clark Gable and a native girl "lying on the ground embracing. As you know, this horizontal love making has always proved questionable on account of the sex connotations which such scenes inevitably bring to mind, and we have been consistently requesting the deletion of such scenes from pictures." Breen was being more polite than required; in the next paragraph he said that he would hold up issuing a Code seal until the problem was resolved.[6] It was, on October 25, 1935.[7]

Released to wide acclaim (and to predicted censorship in Australia for the violence), *Mutiny on the Bounty* became one of MGM's greatest triumphs, winning the Academy Award for best picture and nominations for Clark Gable, Charles Laughton, Franchot Tone, director Frank Lloyd, the screenplay, music and editing.[8]

When MGM remade the film in 1962 starring Marlon Brando as Christian and Trevor Howard as Bligh it was, to say the least, a troubled production. Shot on location in Tahiti (where Brando found a wife and a new lifestyle), it was begun by director Carol Reed and finished by director Lewis Milestone, who himself was nearly finished by the ordeal.[9]

---

1. Scripted by Robert Bolt, this was to have been directed as two films by David Lean for United Artists and Dino DeLaurentiis in the late 1970s. Lean supervised much of the pre-production before budget issues (primarily how much DeLaurentiis was expected to skim) killed the project. (Kevin Brownlow, *David Lean: A Biography*, New York: St. Martin's Press, 1996).
2. Breen to Mayer, April 9, 1934 (AMPAS).
3. Maurice Renves to Breen, December 19, 1934 (AMPAS).
4. Breen to Mayer, December 26, 1934 (AMPAS).
5. Breen to Mayer, February 27, 1935 (AMPAS).
6. Breen to Mayer, October 15, 1935 (AMPAS).
7. Breen to Mayer, October 25, 1935 (AMPAS).
8. The Internet Movie Database, without explanation, credits Margaret Booth, MGM's chief editor, with uncredited writing contributions to the script.
9. Milestone directed single episodes of two TV series, *The Richard Boone Show* and *Arrest and Trial*, both 1964, before retiring. Carol Reed directed six more features including the musical *Oliver!*, for which he won the Academy Award.

Ninotchka

Metro-Goldwyn-Mayer, 1939
Written by Charles Brackett & Billy Wilder and Walter Reisch, based on the original story by Melchior Lengyel
Produced by Sidney Franklin and Ernst Lubitsch (both uncredited)
Directed by Ernst Lubitsch
Code seal #5494

Synopsis
A Communist emissary (Greta Garbo) sent to Paris to investigate the failure of three earlier comrades (Sig Ruman, Felix Brassart, Alexander Granach) to sell the former Czarina's crown jewels is waylaid by Count Léon d'Algout (Melvyn Douglas) who happily corrupts her with the joys of capitalism and romance.

Background
Billy Wilder, citing his mentor, Ernst Lubitsch, once said that if a man enters a room through the door, you have a scene, but if you have him enter through a window, you have a situation. Lubitsch was all about situations, and *Ninotchka* is wonderfully rife with them – leaving the Code obligated to respond.

Foreword title card
This picture takes place in Paris in those wonderful days when a siren was a brunette and not an alarm, and if a Frenchman turned out the light, it was not for an air raid.

MGM purchased a "Garbo Russian story" from Melchior Lengyel and set the two hottest writers in Hollywood – Ben Hecht and Charles MacArthur – to work developing it for Garbo and Cary Grant.[1] Hecht and MacArthur's fourteen-page synopsis was summarized for the files by Joseph Breen himself after discussing it with his staffers Geoffrey Shurlock and Iselin Auster, and with Bernard Hyman at MGM. Breen's concern was that the story is essentially an affair between "two sympathetic leads."

Hecht, by long distance phone from his home in Nyack, New York, deflected Breen's order to eliminate the affair, saying it was essential. Breen said that the problem was not the affair itself but the way it was portrayed so casually. Hyman offered that, under Communism, sex could be portrayed merely as a biological urge, not romance, to which Breen said that such a notion couldn't even be discussed. The three-hour meeting ended with Hyman indicating that he would find a new writer, someone from England, to revise the story.[2] The American Film Institute catalogue names Jacques Deval (French), S.N. Behrman (American), and Salka Viertel (Austro-Hungarian) as working on drafts, with Gottfried Reinhardt set to direct.[3]

When Lubitsch was signed to a two-picture deal at MGM he chose *Ninotchka* (the second was to be *The Shop Around the Corner*) and borrowed Brackett and Wilder from Paramount. A year later their "temporary incomplete" script dated May 16, 1939, went to the Breen Office. Their two pages of return notes on May 24 included changing Ninotchka's line "from the bottom up," rephrasing Leon's line to his co-conspirator, Swana (Ina Claire), "I assure you no visa will be necessary for my chateau," making sure Leon and Ninotchka are only tipsy, not drunk, and shooting the scene in which Ninotchka refers to sex as "biological" two ways in case the first way is cut by state censors.[4]

By June 8 the script was okayed as meeting the requirements of the Code.[5] On July 18, however, citing rewrites, Breen was back on the horn demanding that Leon's line, "Not so much for Mankind, but for Womankind I can do a lot" be cut, and again insisting on removal of the "biological" definition of sex.[6]

Ninotchka did well at the box office but not well with a handful of censors, notably the Legion of Decency (drinking) and Ontario (portrayal of Russia). On that concern, many territories were caught in an increasing crush between the U.S.S.R. and Hitler: Lithuania, Estonia, Yugoslavia and Bulgaria all deleted jokes about Russia. France deleted the foreword title card and banned the film outright for a short time, then relented. Mexico's censors okayed the film but the country's unions opposed it. Hungary removed most of the opening credits from Lubitsch onward without giving a reason.[7]

Note: *Ninotchka* was advertised as "Garbo laughs!" though, of course, she had laughed in other films. In fact, there has been controversy over whether the laugh is truly hers, that is, whether the laugh when Count Léon d'Algout tumbles off his chair, was dubbed by someone else inasmuch as the sync is supposedly off. In his worshipful biography, Robert Gottlieb says "(a) Garbo could do anything she wanted to for the camera and, besides, she was known as a hearty laugher, and (b) if MGM was clever enough to lip-sync her, they were clever enough to do it right." Gottlieb adds that Billy Wilder said, "There was no need. Her real laugh was wonderful."[8] Lubitsch himself suggested, on September 8, what became the film's famous foreword card, and which the Code had to approve.[9] Breen did – after overturning Lester Thompson of Breen's own Advertising Advisory Council's objection to the line about Frenchmen.[10]

---

1. May 12, 1938 (AMPAS).
2. Breen to file, May 13, 1938 (AMPAS).
3. American Film Institute catalogue.
4. Breen to Mayer, May 24, 1939 (AMPAS).
5. Breen to Mayer, June 8, 1939 (AMPAS).
6. Breen to Mayer, July 18, 1939 (AMPAS).
7. Multiple confidential censorship reports to file (AMPAS).
8. Robert Gottlieb, *Garbo*, New York: Farrar, Straus and Giroux, 2021.
9. Al Block to Breen, September 8, 1939.
10. Thompson to Silas (Si) F. Seadler, September 25, 1939 (AMPAS).

Of Mice and Men

United Artists, 1939
Screenplay by Eugene Solow, from John Steinbeck's play (uncredited) and novel
Produced by Lewis Milestone and Frank Ross
Directed by Lewis Milestone
Code seal #5797

Synopsis
As he did in *East of Eden*, John Steinbeck applies the fable of "my brother's keeper," but twists it to write of two itinerant farmhands, George (Burgess Meredith) and Lenny (Lon Chaney, Jr.). George is the protector of the feeble-minded Lenny, who crushes Curley's (Bob Steele) hand after being taunted, then accidentally kills Curley's wife, Mae (Betty Field). George realizes that it is better to execute Lenny himself than let him fall victim to a lynch mob.

Background
The Code's VGH (V.G. Hart) attended a performance of the play, which Steinbeck himself adapted for the stage, on November 23, 1937 and reported the next day to the Motion Picture Association that it contains "Sex perversion evidenced by the killing of mice and puppies and the strangling to death of a woman; another unpunished murder; suggestion of an incestuous relationship; and much vulgar, obscene, and profane dialogue, including considerable disgusting talk about bawdy houses."[1]

Recognizing the potential that *Of Mice and Men* would be purchased for the screen, the Code's Francis S. Harmon submitted to Will Hays a more elaborate evaluation of the play from the standpoint of the Code. He outlined three areas of concern (paraphrased below):

> a. Profanity, none of which is essential to characterization.

> b. George being taken by a law officer after his mercy killing of Lenny, done to prevent Lenny's certain lynching after he accidentally killed Curley's wife.

> c. Although Lenny is portrayed as feeble-minded, some of his actions could be taken as sex perversion, such as stroking the hair of Curley's wife. There is also the possibility that George and Lenny have a perverted relationship.

Harmon was of the opinion that *Of Mice and Men* could make a good film about "the tragic loneliness of transient agricultural workers" but that it would be unpopular because of "the public distaste for imbeciles" and the lack of glamorous characters.²

The next day he amplified his remarks and extrapolated his interpretation to Hays, saying that Lenny's fascination with small animals raises questions of whether he gets sexual satisfaction from them. He also says that the notoriety of the play would require finding a new title for the film, such as was done with *The Children's Hour* (changed into *These Three*, q.v.).³ His evaluations are more those of a studio reader recommending a script for production than a censor determining acceptability under the Code.⁴ These were essentially the cautions Breen sent to Jack L. Warner when Warner inquired about its suitability for production at his studio.⁵

Breen also sent seven pages of detailed notes to Lewis Milestone on the same day that Milestone submitted a first draft script to him on January 30 of that year. Of particular concern were specifics of how George was to be photographed shooting Lenny (while Lenny was fantasizing about going off to a farm where he could tend the rabbits) and how the sheriff was to take George away for the killing. He closed by further warning Milestone about the pitfalls of this kind of story on the screen and ended with his customary disclaimer that "our final judgment will be based on the finished picture."⁶

The film seems to have gone into hibernation for a year because not until January 1939 do the files reflect tension between Lewis Milestone, who was trying to raise money through lawyer/investor Floyd Odlum (RKO studio and theaters), and other investors to make the film independently. Breen lectured Milestone that while he could make a film that was acceptable to the Code, the Code office could not guarantee that it would be accepted in advance of seeing a script and the resultant film.⁷ By August 10, 1939, producer Hal Roach, best known for making Laurel and Hardy and Our Gang comedies, brought the film to his studio for United Artists release.⁸ The next day, Charles R. Raguse of the Roach Studios sent a final script to Breen advising him that they would start shooting the picture on August 14.⁹ Breen fired back a letter that same day, reiterating most of the prohibitions he had been issuing for more than a year, notably care in showing Lennie's crushing of Curley's hand, Lennie's killing of Mae, and making sure George is led away to justice after shooting Lennie.¹⁰

The title was still an issue with Hays, who took the unusual action of sending a blank copy of the Code seal certificate to Roach to drive home the point that the Production Code Administration must approve not only the film but all advertising materials that support it.¹¹ A formal approval was sent on November 3, 1939 with the qualification that Roach would delete the scene that contained the word "hell."¹²

Of Mice and Men premiered on Christmas eve 1939 for Academy Award consideration and opened wide on January 12, 1940. Reviews called it "outstanding," "adventuresome" and "worthy of considerable comment." One notice, by Robert G. Tucker, even mentioned the difficulty the filmmakers had with the Production Code.¹³ It was nominated for four Academy Awards including best picture, best sound recording (Elmer Raguse) and best musical score (Aaron Copland).

1939, however, was the year of *Gone with the Wind*.

In 2006, New York judge Richard Owen reassigned the copyrights in ten of Steinbeck's work from Penguin Books back to Steinbeck's heirs after deciding that the publisher had taken advantage of the young writer when they acquired his rights in 1938. *Of Mice and Men* could still be held by its publisher until 2012, at which time the rights would revert to the Steinbeck estate.[14]

---

1. Hart to file, November 24, 1937 (AMPAS).
2. Harmon to Hays, December 6, 1937 (AMPAS).
3. The title comes from Robert Burns' poem "To a Mouse" (1785), "The best laid schemes o' Mice an' Men / Gang aft agley/an' lea'e us nought but grief an' pain / For promis'd joy!" Likewise, *The Children's Hour* comes from Henry Wadsworth Longfellow's 1860 poem of the same title.
4. Harmon to Hays, December 7, 1937 (AMPAS).
5. Breen to Warner, January 10, 1938 (AMPAS).
6. Breen to Milestone, January 30, 1938 (AMPAS).
7. Iselin Austen to file, February 7, 1939, and to Milestone, February 8, 1939 (AMPAS).
8. Hays memo to file, August 10, 1939 (AMPAS).
9. Raguse to Breen, August 11, 1939 (AMPAS).
10. Breen to Mat O'Brien of the Roach Studios, August 11, 1939 (AMPAS).
11. Hays to Roach, August 30, 1939 (AMPAS).
12. Code office to Mat O'Brien, November 3, 1939.
13. Tucker's newspaper is not identified in the file.
14. Oliver Burkeman, "After 68 years, Steinbeck's family wins back the rights to his greatest works," *The Guardian*, June 13, 2006.

Pinky

20th Century Fox, 1949
Screenplay by Philip Dunne and Dudley Nichols (Elia Kazan and Jane White uncredited), from the novel *Quality* by Cid Ricketts Sumner
Produced by Darryl F. Zanuck
Directed by Elia Kazan (John Ford uncredited)
Code seal #13731

Synopsis
Patricia "Pinky" Johnson (Jeanne Crain) is a light-skinned black woman who is able to pass for white. When she falls in love with a white doctor (William Lundigan) and is unable to bring herself to tell him, she must confront the meaning of prejudice and privilege. When "Aunt Em" (Ethel Barrymore) leaves Pinky a house and property in her will, the community takes Pinky to court to deny it to her, but she wins and, rather than marry the doctor, stays in town to create a school for her fellow Negroes.

Background
It was the idea of the film, not the film itself, that troubled the industry. Cid Ricketts Sumner's 1946 magazine serial "Quality" was credited as the first book in which an African-American woman appeared as a positive central character, although the ending was criticized for reinforcing the status quo. The overall problem that the Code had to address was whether a story about a Negro could be shown in the South, given that many Southern states banned movies where the races mixed. The Code's code word for this vestige of Jim Crow was "policy."

Pinky became a political football. Everyone who encountered the property at the Code office was of the belief that it could be made into a film, but a flurry of memos and phone calls between February 24 and March 31, 1948, reveals that Colonel Jason S. Joy (the former Code staffer now working in studio relations for 20th Century Fox), Judge Stephen S. Jackson (formerly with the New York State Board of Censors and now with the Code), New York Code staffer Francis Harmon, a staffer named O'Hara, and even MPAA president Eric Johnston himself (whose mother was ill at the time) all got involved.

Not until March 31 did Joy specify, and then only in a memo to the file, not a position letter, the "political" issues. First, that censor boards in the South would block the film because it was about a Negro and a white, and if they didn't, new political censor boards might spring up to do it; the film would be opposed by the DAR (Daughters of the American Revolution), who had already barred black singer Marian Anderson from performing at Washington, DC's DAR-owned Constitution Hall despite Mrs. Roosevelt's intervention; or Fox might want to bypass such venues as might create public friction.[1]

Joseph Breen's carefully worded letter of February 28 to Fox's Colonel Joy laid it out: "From the standpoint of general good and welfare, we strongly urge that you avoid physical contact between Negroes and whites, throughout the picture. This, with the idea of avoiding audience offense in a number of sections of this country." (Of note is that although actress Jeanne Crain is white, her co-stars Ethel Waters, who played her grandmother, Nina Mae McKinney, Kenny Washington, Frederick O'Neal, and many other performers in the film were black.) The only other comments in Breen's letter had to do with a moment where a character raises her dress, the dialogue "having an enema," and the expression, "Lordamussy."[2]

It took Joy nearly a year to get back to Breen reminding him that Fox had run the property past the Code before they bought it, and that not only did no one in the Code express concern about Negroes and whites touching, but that the filmmakers intended to include a great deal of it between Pinky and Dr. Chester (Lundigan). He ended by saying, "Incidentally, you know, of course, that the actress who will play the part of Pinky will in fact be a white girl."[3]

Code staffers brought their own experience to their judgment. Francis Harmon, who hailed from the South, wrote a startling memo to Jason Joy in apparent violation of Breen's edict that all official correspondence go out over his signature. Harmon's letter was hardly official. In it, he passed along his knowledge of southern customs regarding race (summarized here):

> 1. Pinky should be shown to be the daughter of a male relative. "I know case after case where just such situations arose."
>
> 2. Southern white people condone or tolerate "social equality" on the level of vice while shouting to high heaven their opposition to "social equality" on the level of virtue. "A governor of Mississippi, about the beginning of the century, had two families, one by a colored woman and the other by his lawfully wedded wife. One of my best friends, a key man in the Mississippi Legislature in the 1920s and chairman of one of its most important committees, kept a colored mistress, as everybody in his home town knew, yet he and the Legislature of which he was a member lost no opportunity to pass high-sounding resolutions condemning social equality, maintaining the statutory ban against inter-marriage, and even making it a crime in Mississippi to advertise whites and Negroes on the same lyceum program as 'advocacy of social equality.'"
>
> 3. The Mississippi Supreme Court throws out cases where race prejudice appears in the record.

Harmon then offered alternate dialogue (written in dialect) in which the court judge questions Aunt Dicey (Ethel Waters) into revealing Pinky's white heritage. He also suggests dialogue (from his memo) be put into the mouth of Dr. Joe (Griff Barnett) quoting Miss Em (Ethel Barrymore): "'Joe,' she said, 'some of us Southern white people talk high and mighty just to keep up appearances. We act as if we were the Lords of creation when deep inside we know very well that girls like Pinky are the tragic victims of a caste system which tolerates racial equality on the level of vice while opposing it on the level of virtue. Pinky has the blood of my family in her veins. She is going to get the family place. I'll see to that in my will.'"[4]

On March 30, Darryl F. Zanuck himself got into the game, writing Harmon a sensitive response to his entreaty. Among his commendations was: "As you know, we have consulted the Negro representatives of many different Negro points of view, and without exception they have objected to the suggestion of miscegenation, even to the slight phrase which is still in the picture in which Granny says, in effect, upon Pinky's arrival, 'I hope you haven't gotten yourself in trouble as your mother did,' or some such phrase." Zanuck concluded by explaining that they could do more good by sticking to tolerance than by bringing up miscegenation.[5]

The rest of the Code-Fox exchanges have to do with song lyrics and wardrobe suitability, the latter a fixation that seems to be of concern to the Code with this studio.

Pinky opened in U.S. theaters in November 1949 and the only state in which the Code records show censorship was Pennsylvania where there were a few cuts in dialogue and the order that the film would be pulled if there was distress "for any people in the state." None is recorded.

---

1. NAACP papers quoted in the American Film Institute catalogue.
2. Jackson to file, March 31, 1948 (AMPAS).
3. Breen to Joy, March 31, 1948 (AMPAS).
4. Joy to Breen, March 2, 1949 (AMPAS).
5. Harmon to Joy, March 18, 1949 (AMPAS).
6. Zanuck to Harmon, March 30, 1949 (AMPAS).

A Place in the Sun

Paramount Pictures, 1951
Screenplay by Michael Wilson and Harry Brown, from the play by Patrick Kearney, adapted from the novel *An American Tragedy* by Theodore Dreiser
Produced by George Stevens and Ivan Moffat
Directed by George Stevens
Code seal #14461[1]

Synopsis
A poor factory worker (Montgomery Clift) falls in love with the beautiful daughter (Elizabeth Taylor) of a wealthy businessman but their proposed marriage is threatened by his previous affair with a factory worker (Shelley Winters) whom he has made pregnant.

Background
This film was a lawsuit magnet. Paramount had filmed Theodore Dreiser's controversial novel *An American Tragedy* in 1931 (pre-Code), directed by Josef von Sternberg. The story was based on the actual 1906 drowning of Grace Brown by her boyfriend Chester Gillette, who was executed for it.[2] Dreiser sued the studio when they made what he felt was his great American novel into a standard murder mystery (he lost).[3] Grace Brown's family sued Paramount for libel and settled out of court.[4] An additional lawsuit was brought against Paramount by the widow and daughter of playwright Patrick Kearney who held the copyright on the play and argued that the studio no longer held the rights to it. Paramount said that the film was based on the book, not the play. The disposition of the case is unknown.[5] Finally, George Stevens sued Paramount and NBC over their 1965 broadcast of his 1951 film claiming that he had final cut and that time edits and commercials for TV destroyed its artistic integrity. The judge decided that, because the edits were minimal, there was no diminution of artistry, but awarded Stevens one dollar.[6]

The path to making one of cinema's most acclaimed films began quietly on September 26, 1949, when Luigi Luraschi, Paramount's director of censorship, sent two copies of the August 5 first preliminary draft of what was then called *A Modern Story* to the Breen Office. Breen's response four days later was mixed. After assuring Paramount that the script seemed to meet the basic requirements of the Code, he followed with several specific reasons that it did not, among them (paraphrased):

> Do not expose women's bodies, particularly the breasts, in costumes.

> Do not keep the camera on the radio while the two people are talking or it will be suggestive of sex. Keep it on the people so we know it isn't.
>
> Use of the Lord's prayer in this film would be blasphemous.
>
> Don't show George leaving [Alice's (Shelley Winters)] house the next morning as the idea of illicit sex has already been established.
>
> Rewrite Alice's speech, "The first night you came here you said I wouldn't have to worry? Well, it's happened."
>
> No discussion of abortion.
>
> There will be no exposure of Angela (Elizabeth Taylor) while she is changing her clothes.[7]

Subsequent exchanges of revised script pages and reactions alternate between Paramount and the Code from September to December with Breen often repeating previous notes concerning seduction and abortion (specifically the line, "Doctor, you've got to help me"), and warning against passionate, open-mouth kissing. Viewers of the film will recall that the huge close-ups of Taylor and Clift speaking intimately with each other at the party are among the most erotic ever filmed, yet show nothing. Even the lyrics of religious hymns had to be cleared based on the assurance that they would be sung reverently.[8] The last sting came on December 15 when Breen objected to Marlowe's (Raymond Burr) speech, "…gave to him all that a woman can give." That same day, Luraschi conveyed to Breen new dialogue for the scene in which Alice tells George about her pregnancy:

> Alice: George, we're in trouble, real trouble.
> George: How do you mean?
> Alice: Remember the first night you came here? Remember you said if there was any trouble, you'd stand by me?
> George: Yeah?
> Alice: Well, it's happened. Oh, I'm so afraid.

Regional censors had their say when the film was shipped to theaters for its slow, prestigious roll-out in summer 1951. Maryland and Ohio both cut George and Alice dancing in the dark. Pennsylvania and Massachusetts gave it clear sailing. Screen history has since embraced it.

1. The Code certificate carried a P.S.: "This approval is based upon our understanding that the eliminations set forth in Mr. Luraschi's letter of December 15, 1950, will be carried through in all prints put into general distribution."
2. Michelle York, "Century After Murder, American Tragedy Draws Crowd," *The New York Times*, July 11, 2006. Although Gillette was executed, his guilt remains a matter of speculation.
3. Theodore Dreiser v. Paramount Publix Corporation.
4. Brown v. Paramount Publix Corp., 240 A.D. 520, 270 N.Y.S. 544.
5. American Film Institute catalogue. Controlling someone else's film by holding the underlying literary rights is a challenging arena. See Stewart v. Abend, 495 U.S. 207 (1990).
6. American Film Institute catalogue.
7. Breen to Luraschi, September 26, 1949 (AMPAS).
8. Breen to Luraschi, November 14, 1949 (AMPAS).

Psycho

Paramount Pictures, 1960
Screenplay by Joseph Stefano, from the novel by Robert Bloch
Produced (uncredited) and directed by Alfred Hitchcock
Code seal #19564[1]

Synopsis
Norman Bates (Anthony Perkins), who operates a motel in the middle of nowhere, dresses as his dead mother and kills Marion Crane (Janet Leigh), a woman who has just committed robbery and who happens to be staying in one of his rooms.

Background
Perhaps because a Paramount studio reader considered Robert Bloch's 1959 novel *Psycho* "too repulsive for films, and rather shocking even to a hardened reader," it came to Alfred Hitchcock's attention, and he acquired it himself. Hitchcock, basking in a lucrative contract for his new television series, *Alfred Hitchcock Presents*, had become concerned that the rising cost of making theatrical films was cutting his profits. He saw *Psycho* as a chance to reduce these costs and took the risk of being personally responsible for its $810,000 budget (for which he demanded sixty percent of the gross). He kept the budget down by using his television crew to shoot the feature with the same efficiency by which he was producing his TV show. He also shot in black and white, maintaining that color would have been too gory (it was also far cheaper).

Bloch's book was based loosely on the celebrated case of serial killer Ed Gein, who would later serve as the inspiration for *The Texas Chainsaw Massacre* and *The Silence of the Lambs*. It was shot on the back lot of Universal Studios after Paramount denied Hitchcock their facilities. The making of *Psycho* was the subject of Stephen Rebello's 1990 book (q.v.) and, in 2012, became the feature film *Hitchcock*, starring Anthony Hopkins as the Master of Suspense.

Given that *Psycho* has been scaring the bejesus out of audiences since 1960 with its shower murder, stairwell stabbing and themes of mother love and transvestitism, it's a wonder the picture was ever passed by the Code in the first place. To be sure, the Shurlock Office flagged all of those, but they also had a few nits to pick, starting with profanity. Citing complaints they received from general audiences, Shurlock nixed several "damn's," "dammit's," "hell's," and an irreverent use of "God." Marion's nudity in the shower murder scene was also flagged, as was Norman's disposal of her naked body.

The big guns came out for "the very pointed description of an incestuous relationship between Norman and his mother." Among lines in Joseph Stefano's script that were ordered cut or revised were: "their relationship was more that of two adolescent lovers," "fantasy of making love," "lovers," "ever the sweetheart," and "always peeping… and reading those obscene books… and disgusting me with his love."[2]

Hitchcock efficiently filmed *Psycho* and a screening was arranged for Shurlock and his staff on February 19, 1960. It did not go well, as Shurlock's assistant Jack Vizzard wrote for the file (here abbreviated):

> 1. The opening lovemaking scene (Janet Leigh and John Gavin) is too passionate… partially undressed and rolling around the bed together… a quite blatant open-mouthed kiss.
>
> 2. The line "only playground that beats Las Vegas" we objected to at script level.
>
> 3. The shower murder of Janet Leigh. The Peeping Tom scene… stimulates him to the crime which follows. It would seem to be possible to cure this item by cutting so that the inference would be that the most the Peeping Tom sees of the girl is her half-slip and brassiere. [N.B.: This, in fact, was done and the excised footage has recently been restored for home video.] The shower sequence has a number of shots, some impressionistic, some completely realistic, of the girl's nude body. All of these shots are in violation of the Code.

It has been argued over the years that there are neither breasts, groins, nor knife-meeting-body in the shower scene, only the impression of them. Script supervisor Marshall Schlom, however, told Stephen Rebello for his book *Alfred Hitchcock and the Making of Psycho* that "if you stop-frame and magnify it, there are definitely a couple of frames showing bare breast and nipple."[3] Seeing this – or thinking they did – the Shurlock office asked Paramount to confer by phone about solutions.[4] Hitchcock dared to offer them an exchange. According to Schlom, he said, "I will take out the nudity if you will allow me to keep the two people in bed in the opening." When they refused, Hitchcock proposed that if they left the shower sequence as it was, he would reshoot the opening, but he wanted the Code office on the set to tell him, while watching the actors, how they would pass it. According to Schlom, Hitchcock reshot the scene but the Code chaperone never showed up, "and they finally agreed they didn't see the nudity in the shower sequence which, of course, was there all the time."[5]

---

1. The Code certificate, awarded March 3, 1960, carries a P.S. from Geoffrey Shurlock, "The issuance of this certificate is based upon the revised scenes as reviewed in our projection room on March 2, 1960." (AMPAS).
2. Shurlock to Luraschi, November 23, 1959 (AMPAS).
3. Stephen Rebello, *Alfred Hitchcock and the Making of Psycho*, New York: Dembner Books, 1990. These belong to Marli Renfro, Janet Leigh's body double.
4. Vizzard to file, February 22, 1960 (AMPAS).
5. Rebello, op cit. It's true, but it's blurry.

Rebel Without a Cause

Warner Bros., 1955
Written by Stewart Stern, adapted by Irving Schulman, from a story by Nicholas Ray
Produced by David Weisbart
Directed by Nicholas Ray
Code seal #17504

Synopsis
A teenager (James Dean) is torn between the ideals his parents (Jim Backus and Ann Doran) extol him to follow, their inability to live up to them, and peer pressure from his girlfriend Judy (Natalie Wood) and poor lost Plato (Sal Mineo) in a changing society that is tearing him apart.

Background
James Dean became a star in *East of Eden*. With *Rebel Without a Cause* he became an icon. Released barely a month after his death in a car accident, *Rebel* became an anthem of a disaffected postwar generation. It also frightened the Establishment by calling out their hypocrisy and challenging the very ideals that they believed made America what it was. Already a bastion of the status quo, the Production Code found itself judging not just a movie but the lives of the kids they knew would line up to see it.

The five months between the March 9, 1955 release of *East of Eden* and the October 27, 1955 release of *Rebel Without a Cause* included the crucial day of September 30 when the star of both films, James Dean, was killed in an automobile accident near Cholame, California. This hung over the film like a funeral shroud.

Suggested by a book Dr. Robert M. Lindner with the heady title *Rebel Without a Cause: The Hypnoanalysis of a Criminal Psychopath*, it passed through the hands of Jacques Le Mareschal, Theodore Seuss Geisel (that's right, Dr. Seuss), Peter Viertel, Irving Schulman (who gets the nebulous "adaptation" credit) and both H.L. Fishel and Lindner himself before being taken over by director Nicholas Ray (credited with story only, which he originally titled *The Blind Run*) and screenwriter Stewart Stern.[1]

The screenplay was submitted to Geoffrey Shurlock after two conferences with studio executives, and he wrote Jack Warner on March 22, 1955 with four pages of changes headlined with the evaluation, "We are concerned about the emphasis on violence as well as the element of illicit sex now present in the script."[2]

Without a doubt Shurlock had his mind on two recent films – *The Wild One* (1953) and *The Blackboard Jungle* (1955) – that were already raising caution flags about youth rebellion. Wrote Shurlock: "We should not approve stories of underage boys and girls indulging in either murder or illicit sex." To that end, he recommended cutting any stomping and beating, nose-thumbing, eliminating the suggestion that Judy (Wood's first adult role) has been soliciting, shortening the knife fight, removing the suggestion of an incestuous relationship between Judy and her father, not letting the chickie run appear to endanger innocent observers, removing any indication of a homosexual attraction by Plato (Sal Mineo) to Jim (James Dean), avoiding the suggestion of any illicit sex between Jim and Judy, and removing all uses of liquor.

After a rewrite was sent, Shurlock again wrote Warner that "there remain certain minor items" and proceeded to list twelve of them. They included a reminder about Judy not appearing to solicit and not kissing her father on the lips, not making it look as though Judy and Jim have had sex, protecting onlookers in the car race, and downplaying the knife fight. New concerns were girls smoking (tobacco, not marijuana) in the school bathroom, not making it seem as if these high school kids are going in for murder, not showing chains in the chain rumble, and not having Plato fire his gun at Jim, but instead having Jim disarm him and only then the gun goes off.[3] As the revisions kept coming, a watchful Shurlock kept approving them (with the exception of a "good Lord" on May 4 and demands to cut bullies brutalizing Plato on May 16).[4] Inasmuch as the film had begun shooting on March 28 and would continue through May 26, this meant that Stern was revising the script while Ray was shooting it, with every page having to detour via the Shurlock office.

Despite the Code's effort to remove or downplay the very elements that made the film meaningful to its intended audience, *Rebel Without a Cause* still faced censorship in Chicago, Pennsylvania, Australia, and was rated A-2 (for adults) by the Legion of Decency. And yet within a few years the youth audience that had to be "protected" would come to dominate movie attendance and dictate which films got made. They would also be sent off to fight a war infinitely more violent than a movie about juvenile delinquents.

---

1. American Film Institute catalogue.
2. Shurlock to Warner, March 22, 1955 (AMPAS).
3. Shurlock to Warner, March 22, 1955 (AMPAS).
4. Shurlock to Warner, March 31, 1955 (AMPAS).
5. Shurlock to Warner, April 6, 12, 20 and 29, May 4 and 10, 1955 (AMPAS).

Rope

Warner Bros., 1948
Screenplay by Arthur Laurents, from the play by Patrick Hamilton adapted by Hume Cronyn, with uncredited doctoring by Ben Hecht
Produced by Sidney Bernstein and Alfred Hitchcock (neither credited)
Directed by Alfred Hitchcock
Code seal #13027

Synopsis
Two upscale, arrogant college students (John Dall and Farley Granger) murder a young man for the thrill of committing the perfect crime and then invite people, including their professor (James Stewart), to their apartment to gloat at his inability to deduce what's going on – until he does.

Background
Rope is known as Hitchcock's attempt to make a movie without cuts, that is, one continuous shot by constantly moving the camera and hiding the ten-minute reel breaks by having someone walk in front of the lens. Nowadays, of course, this would be a simple task to do on video (viz *Russian Ark*, 2002).

Alfred Hitchcock loved to make films about sex, and the stranger the better: Robert Donat and Madeline Carroll handcuffed together in *The 39 Steps*, Tippi Hedren repressed and raped in *Marnie*; a rapist/necrophile/necktie murderer in *Frenzy*; Ingrid Bergman prostituting herself in *Notorious*; James Stewart as a voyeur in *Rear Window*, not to mention his obsession with Kim Novak in *Vertigo* and the gay subtext between James Mason and Martin Landau in *North by Northwest*. So why not *Rope*, boldly based on the 1924 kidnapping and "thrill murder" of Bobby Franks by homosexual lovers Nathan Leopold and Richard Loeb?

Hitchcock himself sent a copy of Patrick Hamilton's play to Joseph Breen, whom he addressed as "Joe," on September 4, 1946, asking him to "see if it meets all the Code requirements."[1] He should not have been surprised when Breen replied (with the formal vocative "Dear Mr. Hitchcock") five days later that the play was okay but that the screenplay should drop derogatory references to the Ten Commandments, minimize the use of liquor (except for one of the characters who needs to be drunk for the plot), and, even though the villains get their comeuppance, modify their arguments against conventional ethics that are so well written that they might contradict the film's moral lesson.[2]

Nothing else is found in the Code files about *Rope* until the Code's Stephen S. Jackson wrote Transatlantic Pictures (Hitchcock's and Sidney Bernstein's production company at Warner Bros.) reflecting an earlier conference held by several of the men. Jackson was pleased that the filmmakers had agreed to change whatever dialogue might be necessary in order to restrict drinking, reduce the sadistic component of Brandon's character, and to minimize the homosexual content and similarity to Leopold and Loeb.[3]

When Jackson got the revised script just before Christmas, he advised that the opening scene containing the strangulation murder should not be shown in detail (it was) lest it be cut by local censorship boards, that the word "dangerous" should be replaced because it suggested that the boys were sexually turned on by their crime, and that liquor consumption, except for plot purposes, should be de-emphasized.[4] A subsequent exchange between Transatlantic's Victor A. Peers and Jackson reiterated the Code's concern with liquor, both consumed and discussed.[5]

Peers' response to Jackson the next day was a masterful passive-aggressive dismissal of the Code's order. "It has occurred to me that since we are photographing the picture one reel at a time without any cuts, any comments you might have to make when the picture is completed could well be calamitous." Peers mentioned that they would be re-shooting reel 1 again and would appreciate the Code looking at what they have. Otherwise, he explained (but not in so many words), they would take their chances when the picture was finished.

They did, and *Rope* was approved by the Code on March 22, 1948 in time for its August 26 U.S. premiere and September 25 general release. At that stage local boards chimed in. As predicted, the opening murder that sets up the whole film was cut by Maryland, Ohio and Pennsylvania. Holland banned the film in its entirety because on the grounds that it justified killing people of inferior intellect. Coming after Holland's Nazi occupation during World War II, it was an understandable observation.

---

1. Hitchcock to Breen, September 4, 1946 (AMPAS).
2. Breen to Hitchcock, September 9, 1946 (AMPAS).
3. Jackson to Ahern, December 15, 1947 (AMPAS). Anyone familiar with Alfred Hitchcock's films should have realized that dialogue is the last thing he needed to tell a story and that his capitulation to the Code played them for suckers, particularly since both leads, John Dall and Farley Granger, were gay.
4. Jackson to Ahern, December 22, 1947 (AMPAS).
5. Jackson to Peers, January 23, 1948 (AMPAS).

The Searchers

Warner Bros., 1956
Screenplay by Frank S. Nugent, from the novel by Alan LeMay
Produced by Merian C. Cooper and Patrick Ford
Directed by John Ford
Code seal #17787

Synopsis
Civil War veteran Ethan Edwards (John Wayne) spends years searching for his beloved niece Debbie (young: Lana Wood/grown: Natalie Wood) who has been kidnapped by Comanches. As he rides in the company of his adoptive nephew Martin Pawley (Jeffrey Hunter), his hatred of Indians grows to the point where Martin fears that Ethan might do something terrible to Debbie if they find her.

Background
"All recent American cinema derives from John Ford's *The Searchers*," critic Stuart Byron declared in his March 5, 1979 *New York* magazine essay. Citing how the emerging filmmakers of New Hollywood (John Milius, George Lucas, Martin Scorsese and especially Paul Schrader) reference the themes and imagery from the movie, which many of them had seen as youngsters, he points out the conflict between the greatness of the film, the fans' love for it, and the deplorable politics of its star, John Wayne.[1] And yet the same tension fuels the film itself. Here is Ethan Edwards, a virulent racist who hates his adoptive nephew, Martin, for being a "half-breed" (mixed Indian and white); who shoots an already dead Comanche; who scalps his nemesis, Scar, during a final raid on the chief's settlement; and, when he eventually finds Debbie, does so in a cloud of exquisite doubt where neither he, she, nor the audience knows if he is going to kill her or bring her home. The scene is so powerful that none other than Jean-Luc Godard said it filled him with love for a man he despised politically.[2]

Each year during the Code's heyday 1934-48 (before TV), the major and minor studios each churned out roughly one film a week apiece, meaning that the Code staff had to peruse as many as eight hundred films annually. Not all of them were prestige A-pictures like those in this book. Most were routine programmers that sailed in and out of theaters on a split week (Wednesday-Saturday or Sunday-Tuesday) to be forgotten until television discovered them. Of those, a huge number were Westerns, many of them telling tales of cowboys and Indians. Given that the Code specifically prohibited slurs against "patrons of motion pictures in foreign countries," including the terms Chink, Dago, Frog, Greaser, Hunkie, Kike, Nigger, Spic, Wop and Yid, it's noteworthy that nowhere in that document does one find any concern for America's indigenous people.

It was a consistent belief that any "white woman" captured by the Indians would be forced to engage in sex with them and be "ruined," so therefore she either must be killed to prevent being abducted or executed upon being rescued. This racism fuels Ethan throughout his quest: not rescuing Debbie but protecting her from further defiling. What saves her is that, when he looks into her eyes, she reminds him of her mother, Martha (Dorothy Jordan), who is married to Ethan's brother. Ethan and Martha are secretly in love – Ford conveys this several times wordlessly – and this is what drives Ethan to find Debbie and, in the end, to save her. (Some *Searchers* scholars have even suggested that Debbie is Ethan's and Martha's love child.)

None of those elements is remarked upon by the Code. Instead, in a June 20, 1955 letter directly to John Ford, Geoffrey Shurlock urged the director that he "not characterize Sam Clayton (Ward Bond) as a minister of religion in view of the fact that he is a gun-toting member of a quasi-military group" and to change him from a minister to a judge; not have Ethan scalp a dead Comanche; not have Martin taking a bath with Laurie (Vera Miles) in the room; not be vulgar in the treatment of Clayton's wound; and to consult the American Humane Association about the treatment of animals in the film.[3]

Ford's reaction was in keeping with a man who had already made at least half a dozen of the greatest films in cinema history: he simply ignored everything Shurlock said. Sam Clayton is indeed a minister, albeit an atypical one; Ethan does not, in fact, scalp the dead warrior, he more cruelly shoots his eyes out so he cannot enter the spirit world; Ethan does scalp Scar (this is not mentioned by the Code); Laurie stays right in the room with Martin bathing; and Clayton's wound (Patrick Wayne accidentally spears his butt with a sword) stays as it is.

As for the treatment of animals, the letter from Dr. R.A. Young of the American Humane Association regarding two buffalo killed on screen begins: "to date I have no reply…" There is no expressed concern by Young for the many more horses, including those who take falls, only the buffalo. (And they aren't buffalo, they are bison.) No response from Ford is noted.

Arguably, Hollywood's disrespectful treatment of First People was made public when Sacheen Littlefeather respectfully declined Marlon Brando's *Godfather* Oscar in 1973 in protest of how her people were portrayed. Only a handful of films at the time made any effort to positively reflect the widely varied Indian lifestyles (most notably Arthur Penn's *Little Big Man*, 1970).

Apparently Ford's personal attitude toward Indians diverged from that of his films. "Mr. Ford's holy, sorta," Peter Bogdanovich quotes Harry Goulding, who used to own a lodge in Monument Valley, which is Navajo land. "Ev'rytime they've had a rough time, boy, this thing comes outa the blue. They'd been hit pretty hard by the Depression… Well, Mr. Ford came here with *Stagecoach*, and gave a score of jobs to the Navajos and a lot of lives was saved." He did the same with *She Wore a Yellow Ribbon* and *Cheyenne Autumn* and was taken into the Navajo tribe.[4]

The Code is silent on the subject.

Note: For those who think that John Ford simply shot what was handed to him and worked his magic on the set, the screenplay for *The Searchers* has notations throughout citing Ford's comments during production meetings of what he wanted to realize on screen. As to the legend that he once chastised a hectoring producer by ripping un-shot pages out of a script and telling him, "now we're back on schedule," this wonderful story has never been substantiated. But you hope it's true.

---

1. Stuart Byron, "The Searchers: Cult Movie of the New Hollywood," *New York*, March 5, 1979.
2. Referenced by William Bayer, *The Great Movies*, New York: Grossett & Dunlap, 1973. The final production script has Ethan say, "I'm sorry, girl... Shut your eyes" but then tells her "You sure favor your mother" before grasping her to his chest. Those lines are not in the film.
3. Shurlock to Ford, June 20, 1955 (AMPAS).
4. Peter Bogdanovich, *John Ford*, California: University of California Press, 1970.

Some Like It Hot

United Artists, 1959
Written by Billy Wilder and I.A.L. Diamond, suggested by the 1951 German film *Fanfaren der Liebe* written by Robert Thoeren, Heinz Pauck and Michael Logan
Produced by Billy Wilder, I.A.L. Diamond, and Doane Harrison
Directed by Billy Wilder
Code seal #19281

Synopsis
Two male musicians (Jack Lemmon and Tony Curtis) on the run from gangster Spats Colombo (George Raft) after witnessing the St. Valentine's Day Massacre in 1929 Chicago dress in drag to hide in an all-girl band where they both become attracted to the sexy lead singer (Marilyn Monroe).

Background
Billy Wilder said he liked adapting plays and existing films because their authors had already solved structural problems, but he and co-writer I.A.L. ("Izzy") Diamond completely revamped the German original into what is perhaps the finest American sex comedy ever made.

There is no record of any criticism that *Some Like It Hot* received from the Production Code. Everybody liked it except for a handful of local censors, and the Production Code came to the filmmakers' defense. The Catholic Legion of Decency rated it "B" – Morally Objectionable, in Part, for All – because, "though it purports to be a comedy, [it] contains screen material elements that are judged to be seriously offensive to Christian and traditional standards of morality and decency," notably "gross suggestiveness in costuming, dialogue, and situations."[1] Similar thoughts were stated to Eric Johnston, MPAA then-president, by the Episcopal Committee of Motion Pictures, Radio, and Television.[2] The Memphis, Tennessee Board of Censors wanted United Artists to restrict the film to adults only,[3] which UA rejected."[4] Not only did the Code ignore their positions, a list of new films by the Federation of Motion Picture Councils in April 1959 rated *Some Like It Hot* "Excellent acting and direction, plus the nostalgia of the settings of that era, make this wonderful entertainment. Adults & Young People."[5]

This is strange in that most of the film is a drag show with Jerry (Lemmon) camping it up as Geraldine/Daphne and being pursued by Joe E. Brown who, in the end, doesn't care that he's a man; and Joe/Josephine (Curtis) chasing Sugar (Monroe) while he is a man dressed as a woman dressing as a man and, in the end, doffing her/his wig to come out to her. Wilder's biographer Joseph McBride opines that the film gets away with it because it is practically a Restoration comedy whose conventions included men dressed as women, plus it's a period film when all the costumes look odd. This is the rationale that Wilder used for setting *Some Like It Hot* in period (unlike its German and French predecessors), referencing the play *Charley's Aunt*, which is always done in period.[6] The jokes also tempt the code:

> Osgood: You must be quite a girl.
> Daphne: Wanna bet?

> Sugar: I always get the fuzzy end of the lollipop.

> Jerry: Look at that – look how she moves – it's like Jell-O on springs.

> Jerry: Now you've done it.
> Joe: Done what?
> Jerry: Tore off one of my chests.

> Sue: The bass fiddle gets herself pregnant. Bienstock, I oughta fire you.
> Bienstock: Why? I'm the manager of the band, not the night watchman.

And of course:

> Joe: You don't understand. I'm a man.
> Osgood: Well – nobody's perfect.

Even Wilder and Diamond's last descriptive script line tempts the Code: "But that's another story – and we're not quite sure the public is ready for it." FADE OUT.

Perhaps the Code was having too much fun enjoying *Some Like It Hot* to make sure nobody else did.

---

1. Rev. Msgr. Thomas F. Little to Geoffrey Shurlock, March 5, 1959 (AMPAS).
2. Bishop McNulty to Johnston, March 5, 1959 (AMPAS).
3. MPAA's Sidney Schreiber to Shurlock, March 6, 1959 (AMPAS). The author saw the film with his parents at age 11 and joined them laughing ourselves silly – alone in the car in a drive-in, no less.
4. UA Attorney Herbert Glazer to Board of Censors City of Memphis Shelby County, March 3, 1959 (AMPAS).
5. Bulletin of the Federation of Motion Picture Councils, April 1959.
6. Joseph McBride, *Billy Wilder: Dancing on the Edge*, New York: Columbia University Press, 2021.

The Sound of Music

20th Century Fox, 1956
Screenplay by Ernest Lehman, from the stage musical, book by Howard Lindsay and Russell Crouse, the book by Maria von Trapp (uncredited) and with the partial use of ideas by Georg Hurdalek
Produced by Saul Chaplin and Robert Wise
Directed by Robert Wise
Code seal #20734

Synopsis
In the early days of Hitler's rise, a novice nun leaves the convent to become governess for an Austrian sea captain's brood of obstreperous children, tames them, marries the captain, and begins a singing group, eventually escaping into Switzerland when the Nazis encroach.

Background
The true if somewhat romanticized story of the von Trapp family singers, this general audience film was the top-grossing hit of all time for several years and endures as one of Hollywood's most beloved movies.

You'd think that, instead of a Code seal, *The Sound of Music* would come with a prescription for insulin. In fact, there are no objections of any kind noted in the Code files, and the film is included here to show that even movies designed for family entertainment were scrutinized by the Code. Also that class tends to win out.

Stagecoach

United Artists, 1939
Screenplay by Dudley Nichols and Ben Hecht (uncredited), from the short story "Stage to Lordsburg" by Ernest Haycox
Produced and directed by John Ford
Code seal #5029

Synopsis
A stagecoach of widely disparate travelers heads west despite threats of an attack by Geronimo. The group includes a pregnant wife (Louise Platt) rushing to her husband in the cavalry, an alcoholic doctor (Thomas Mitchell) and prostitute (Claire Trevor) expelled from their town, a whiskey salesman (Donald Meek), a thieving banker (Barton Churchill), a gambler (John Carradine), the driver (Andy Devine), his shotgun (George Bancroft) and an escaped convict, the Ringo Kid (John Wayne).

Background
Big budget Westerns were considered dead until producer Walter Wanger and John Ford decided to make this one, which not only revived the genre but made a star out of a young actor who had been going nowhere in B movies.

The very things that the Breen office cited as Code violations are the elements that make *Stagecoach* (originally *Stage Coach*) immortal. His October 28, 1938 letter to producer Walter Wanger alerted the production of four areas of contention (paraphrased):

> 1. The sympathetic female lead (Dallas, played by Claire Trevor) is clearly a prostitute.
>
> 2. A triple revenge shooting of the Plummer boys by the sympathetic male lead is portrayed as justified revenge.
>
> 3. The sheriff condones Ringo's killings and allows him to escape with the prostitute.
>
> 4. Too much display of liquor and drunkenness in connection with the drunken driver [he must mean the doctor].[1]

A meeting was hastily called among Breen, Wanger, director John Ford, and screenwriter Dudley Nichols that resulted in agreements that there would be no specific reference to prostitution but that Dallas will simply be "undesirable," and Ringo gives up the idea of revenge halfway through the film but is attacked by the Plummers and has to defend himself.[2]

By November 9, another draft of the film, now called by the single-word title *Stagecoach*, still hovered on the edge of rejection. First, the pregnant wife was not allowed to faint as this would be cut by some local boards; second, the doctor shouldn't be too drunk; and finally – though only a viewing of the film can explain Breen's vague language – Dallas must forsake becoming a prostitute when she arrives in Lordsburg and, instead, take off with Ringo to start a new life.[3] In the end, the doctor's drunkenness was determined to be necessary to the plot.[4]

The Code files contain numerous reviews, all of them positive, including a rave by Frank S. Nugent. Ford and Nugent later worked together on twelve productions.[5]

---

1. Breen to Wanger, October 28, 1938 (AMPAS).
2. Shurlock to file, October 31, 1938 (AMPAS).
3. Breen to Wanger, November 9, 1938 (AMPAS).
4. Stinnette note to file, January 4, 1939 (AMPAS).
5. Frank S. Nugent, *The New York Times*, March 3, 1939 (AMPAS).

The Story of Temple Drake

Paramount Pictures, 1933
Written by Oliver H.P. Garrett (Maureen Dallas Watkins uncredited), from the novel *Sanctuary* by William Faulkner
Produced by Benjamin Glazer
Directed by Stephen Roberts
Pre-Code

Synopsis
In Faulkner's fictional Yoknapatawpha County, Mississippi, Judge Drake's granddaughter, Temple Drake, is deemed a reckless woman when she refuses to marry respectable lawyer Stephen Benbow and attends a town dance with Toddy Gowan. Temple and Toddy have a car accident and go to a speakeasy run by Lee Goodwin. A gangster at the speakeasy, Trigger, insists that Temple spend the night. Lee's wife, Ruby, prepares a place in the barn where Temple will be safe and assigns young Tommy to watch over her. Come morning, Trigger kills Tommy and rapes Temple, then kidnaps her, forcing her to commit crimes with him. Meanwhile Lee is charged with murdering Tommy and Stephen Benbow is appointed his lawyer. Benbow finds Trigger and Temple at Reba's address, where Temple lies that she went voluntarily with Trigger. After Benbow leaves, Temple tries to escape. Trigger tries to stop her but Temple shoots him with his own gun. Temple returns to town for Lee's trial but doesn't want to testify. Benbow forces her to do so, and she confesses to everything including the rape, Tommy's murder, and her killing Trigger.

Background
The fact that William Faulkner's controversial novel, *Sanctuary*, got made at all is a monument to persistence and patience on both Paramount and the Hays Office. It is also a testament to the inventiveness both of the screenwriters and the negotiators.

This motion picture, more than any other, including *Convention City*, is considered the one that got Will Hays to appoint Joe Breen to enforce the Production Code. The stage was set on June 6, 1932, when Lamar Trotti, in a memorandum to his Code executives, fulminated against any attempt to make a film version of William Faulkner's just-published novel, *Sanctuary*:

> This is the sadistic story of horror – probably the most sickening novel ever written in this country. Important because of its brilliant style, it has had quite a large sale... It is utterly unthinkable as a motion picture.[1]

Of course, this appraisal made it must-read material and set the book on a remarkable odyssey from page to screen. *The Story of Temple Drake*, which is what *Sanctuary* got called on the way to theaters, is the perfect example of how the Code worked. Others will be left to discuss whether it was worth it. Regardless, it took almost a year and a half before *Sanctuary* was again proffered for production, and it was the Code's James Wingate who asked Maurice McKenzie, executive assistant to Will Hays, if an item in the *Hollywood Herald* was true. Had Paramount bought the Faulkner property?[2] While the acquisition was still a rumor, Hays fulminated to Wingate on November 5 about his powerlessness to stop such a sale: "It is an example of the kind of difficulty I have in mind with which I know you are familiar. If we could prevent the purchase of this very objectionable material in the first instance, it would be very much better for the industry."[3] Surely occurrences like this were what prompted Hays to elevate the newly hired MPPDA public relations manager, Joseph I. Breen, to the position of director of the Code two years later.

What continued to infuriate Hays, Wingate and everyone else in the loop was that Paramount seemed to be communicating with the Code by rumor. They went ahead and bought *Sanctuary*, registered the title, and developed a treatment of the story which they insisted was going to be acceptable to the public, but as of mid-November, they hadn't let the Code in on their secret.[4] Not until December 23 did the studio's William H. Wright formally let the Code office know that they were to start shooting *The Story of Temple Drake* on December 27. They did this by sending them two copies of the script which they said not to read as there would be another coming soon.[5] By January 26, 1933, there is a one-line note to file from a Code worker named Fisher that he or she had read it anyway.[6]

Hiding his ire at being excluded from the initial process, Wingate wrote an exceedingly temperate letter to Paramount's Harold Hurley on January 28, noting that it appeared that the studio had removed most of the censorable elements from the story (other than the word "hell") but offered three pages of details that still needed to be corrected. These included omitting references to Miss Reba's house as being a brothel, her as a madam, and her guests being johns (all of which, of course, was what they were).

He concluded perceptively, "We have gone over this in great detail because we have reason to believe that there is already a strong prejudice... against the plan of filming the original book... we recommend the greatest possible care in directing and acting... in order to protect both your investment in this particular picture, as well as public good-will toward the industry in general."[7]

With the picture having rolled as planned on December 27, Will Hays wrote James Wingate in confidence and concern on January 9, 1933 revealing that he had spoken with Adolph Zukor (head of Paramount) about the risks of making the film, and shared with Wingate the urgency of damage control.[8] Wingate tried to mollify Hays by alerting him that he and Geoffrey Shurlock had met with Paramount asking to see the rushes.[9] This was an unusual move. Also unusual was a March 4 letter to Wingate from Hays referencing a conversation Hays had had with the studio's Emmanuel Cohen in which

Cohen said, "If there is anything wrong with *Temple Drake* in Dr. Wingate's opinion, we will remake it." In the letter the film was referred to as *The Shame of Temple Drake*, a title it kept off and on until its release.[10]

Hays continue to impose himself on the process. He heard a rumor that "some shots" had been made involving a corn cob that could never be shown, and he asked that the mogul check into this, not just for the existence of the scurrilous footage but for the disrespectful attitude toward censorship that allowed it to be made.[11]

Joe Breen, not yet head of the Code, chimed in after seeing the picture, congratulating Wingate for turning the film story "into a Sunday school treatise," but echoing Hays' concerns over whether such a film should have been made, period.[12] Nevertheless, on March 21 Hays informed Zukor that the film – once again titled *The Story of Temple Drake* – was screened in workprint (rough) form. Hays held that it did not adhere to the Code and wanted the ending changed.[13] Zukor's executive, Emmanuel Cohen, told Hays, in return, that they would not cut *Temple Drake*'s witness stand confession that she was kept a voluntary prisoner as Wingate had demanded because "it would cause the picture to lose all moral force of the girl's redemption."[14]

The response that followed involved quite literally a list of line-by-line excisions demanded not only by Hays and Wingate but by censors brought in from New York State. A May 8 comment by Wingate to Hays refers to the "phallic symbol" of the corn cob, which was still in the print being screened.[15]

The film entered release on May 6, 1933 and faced severe editing or banning *in toto* in Ohio, Virginia, Massachusetts, Maryland, Alberta, Pennsylvania, Australia, Quebec, India, Holland, New Zealand, Trinidad and Latvia. When Code seals were introduced in 1934, *The Story of Temple Drake* disappeared from sight.

In 2021, somebody posted it on YouTube where anybody could see it.

Times change.

---

1. Trotti to Joy, Milliken, et al, June 6, 1931 (AMPAS).
2. Wingate to McKenzie, November 4, 1932. (AMAPS)
3. Hays to Wingate, November 5, 1932 (AMPAS).
4. Wingate note to the file, November 14, 1932 (AMPAS).
5. Wright to Wingate, December 23, 1932 (AMPAS).
6. Fisher note to file, January 26, 1933 (AMPAS).
7. Wingate to Hurley, January 28, 1933 (AMPAS).
8. Hays to Wingate, February 9, 1933 (AMPAS).
9. Wingate to Hays, February 13, 1933 (AMPAS).
10. Hays to Wingate, March 4, 1933 (AMPAS).
11. Hays to Zukor, March 16, 1933 (AMPAS). Sanctuary includes a rape with a corn cob and the alleged shot was of someone brandishing the cob.
12. Breen to Wingate, March 17, 1933 (AMPAS).
13. Hays to Zukor, Match 21, 1933 (AMPAS).
14. Cohen to Hays, March 24, 1933 (AMPAS).
15. Wingate to Hays, May 8, 1934 (AMPAS).

A Streetcar Named Desire

Warner Bros., 1951
Screenplay by Tennessee Williams from his play, adapted by Oscar Saul
Produced by Charles K. Feldman
Directed by Elia Kazan
Code seal #14871

Synopsis
Blanche DuBois (Vivien Leigh), a fragile Southern belle fallen on hard times, arrives in New Orleans to live with her sister, Stella (Kim Hunter), and Stella's husband, the vulgar Stanley Kowalski (Marlon Brando). Blanche's presence upsets Stanley's life and threatens his marriage, as Blanche, living in an elegant but lost world of her own, tries to draw Stella back there, too. Ultimately Stanley investigates Blanche's sordid past and confronts her with it, driving her over the edge.

Background
An entire book could be written about *A Streetcar Named Desire*'s voyage from Broadway to Hollywood, for not only did the play represent an exciting new direction in American theatre, the film exposed many of the problems that had been keeping movies mired artistically and socially in a bygone era. The country had grown up after World War II. Hollywood hadn't. In a large sense, the Code's efforts to enforce morals that were no longer valid mirrored the drama of Blanche DuBois's inability to let go of the past and move into the future.

Whenever a producer or director would argue that the Code should make allowances for the filming of a play with mature themes, the prevailing wisdom was always: "Sure, those New York playgoers are sophisticated city folk, but the rest of the country won't put up with that kind of material." *A Streetcar Named Desire* is a solid example of how a team of dedicated filmmakers overcame enforced puerility and preserved enough of the original's power to be memorable even decades later.

The Shurlock Office knew what they were wading into when they read Russell Holman's report of the Broadway production after it opened at the Ethel Barrymore Theatre on December 3, 1947. It was routine for the Code to see plays that might be submitted by member film companies, just as it used to be de rigueur for studio story departments to scout new plays and new performers. In addition to extolling the play's virtues, Holman's detailed seven-page report presented the problems that would be faced by whoever bought the screen rights. Summarized:

1. It is an important work that will attract filmmakers.

2. It is impossible to judge the play merely from the script. The direction, acting, and setting are essential.

3. *Streetcar*'s basic story is not dirty. Blanche DuBois represents traditional society facing the rigors of a changing world. Stanley Kowalski's marriage to Blanche's sister Stella represents the infusion of new stock into America.

Holman felt so confident that the censorship problems could be licked that he suggested several solutions. He reasoned that the profanity and crudeness were not essential to the plot, and neither was Stanley's going to bed with Stella early in the play. There would, however, need to be an explanation for Blanche's divorce other than that she had married a gay man. "Discover him in compromising circumstances with another woman rather than another man," Holman advised.

Further, Blanche would not be a nymphomaniac if her marriage had been satisfying. She is living in a dream world, awaiting Prince Charming to whisk her back to the old lost lifestyle. "The audiences' feeling toward Blanche throughout the play," he observed, "is a mixture of fascinated horror and deep sympathy."

Then there is Stanley's rape of Blanche on the night that Stella is having her and Stanley's baby. The rape is not shown in the play, but it is the culmination of Stanley's resentment of Blanche's attempts to draw Stella away from the marriage because of what Stanley represents to her. Holman's assessment was that it makes Stanley unlikable. This could be solved by having Blanche faint, thus bringing on her mental collapse. Lastly, he suggests adding a scene at the end, after hospital attendants take Blanche away muttering about always depending on the kindness of strangers. The new scene would be Stanley explaining to Stella how people like Blanche need to be taken care of, and that is for the best.[1]

The first studio to probe the waters was Paramount, whose stalwart Luigi Luraschi queried Breen on June 22, 1949 and learned with a four-page list of necessary cuts on June 27, 1949 that, if they wanted to film *Streetcar*, the Paramount mountain wasn't the only summit they'd have to scale.[2] At the same time, Breen queried the Code's Margaret Ann Young to determine whether the title *A Streetcar Named Desire* itself was objectionable because of its public association with the play.[3] She let him know that there was nothing wrong with the title itself, and that everything she'd heard about the play was praise.[4]

Breen's rebuff of Paramount reached Irene Mayer Selznick in July. Selznick, one of the play's producers, was also the daughter of MGM head Louis B. Mayer and was married to producer David O. Selznick. She took issue with Breen's list of censorable material and held that it damaged film prospects for the play.[5] Breen wrote Selznick that same day, making the familiar argument that movie audiences were not theater audiences and offered to confer on making *Streetcar* suitable for movies.[6]

In October 1949, Charles K. Feldman bought the screen rights to the play and began setting it up at Warner Bros.[7] When, in a group meeting, Feldman and his associates were made aware by Breen of the problems the film would have with the Code,[8] Feldman later provided them with a rewrite, thanked them for their help, and said he would start shooting the film in mid-August 1950.[9] Breen didn't buy Feldman's bluff and informed him on May 24 that they were not yet out of the woods, that they had dealt with the sex perversion aspect but not with what happens to Blanche and Stanley at the end.[10]

By August 24, about a week into shooting, Breen was still micromanaging the production, enabled by what was apparently an unusually precise screenplay:

Page 11: The word "God" should simply be eliminated.

Page 39: The "whack" should be on the hip, not on the posterior.

Page 53: There should, of course, be no oaths in scene 50.

Page 76: In view of the representations of Mr. Kazan in our most recent conference… there [must] be nothing offensive whatsoever in this scene between her and the young man.[11]

Page 118: We once again direct your attention to the fact that many censor boards will eliminate the business of Blanche smashing the bottle [to fend off Stanley].[12]

Additional remarks[13] from Breen over the next few days repeat the prohibition of oaths, react strongly against mentioning Blanche's ex-husband's homosexuality (referred to as "sex perversion"), and ordering a line change from "even at last *with* a seventeen-year-old boy:" to "even at last *to* a seventeen-year-old-boy." The back-and-forth continued, bringing in Warner's head of operations, Walter McEwen, the Code's Jack Vizzard, and others both on and off the record. Finally, four weeks into production, "Gadge" Kazan himself sent Breen an impassioned handwritten letter citing the feeling he got from Vizzard that there was a "breach of faith" on the filmmakers' part in dwelling on the subject of homosexuality (which Kazan, too, called "perversion") and said that they were changing it to impotence.[14]

Then came the rape.

Despite studio arguments that the scene was necessary on one level to motivate Blanche's departure from reality and, on a deeper level, as the symbolism of modernity encroaching upon tradition, the Code would not yield. Neither would Tennessee Williams who, as Kazan was trying to figure out how to shoot the scene in light of the Code's commands, wrote Breen an extraordinary personal letter. In two pages he noted how the rape had been understood and accepted by the press and public and religious community; how changing it for the film would "arouse widespread attention and indignation," and concluded with nothing less than a direct threat:

> Please remember, also, that we have already made great concessions... no one involved in this screen production has failed in any respect to show you the cooperation, and even deference, that has been called for. But now we are fighting for what we think is the heart of the play, and when we have our backs against the wall – if we are forced into that position – none of us is going to throw in the towel! We will use every legitimate means that any of us has at his or her disposal to protect the things in this film which we think cannot be sacrificed, since we feel that it contains some very important truths about the world we live in.[15]

Breen's response was encouraging, if vague, reading: "Yesterday we had a very satisfactory conference at the Warner Studio with Mr. Elia Kazan, with the result that today we approved the new scene, which he proposes to shoot after his consultation with you, and which will be included in the final reel of the picture."[16]

In the existing version of *A Streetcar Named Desire*, the rape comes after Blanche breaks a bottle and threatens Stanley with the jagged edges. He approaches her tauntingly, smiling, and grabs her. She flings the bottle into a circular wall mirror, which breaks, as he pushes her out of frame. The image in the shattered mirror dissolves quickly into Blanche's head pushed back in what could only be ecstasy. For those sharp enough to notice, it makes the point.

Charles K. Feldman received the Code certificate on December 11, 1950, but that wasn't the end of the story. In early July 1951, Vizzard notified Joe Breen that there were "trouble spots" in the film from the Legion of Decency, chiefly the amount of sex, discussion of sex, the provocative stairwell scene where Stella collapses into Stanley's arms, and lack of moral compensation at the end. Vizzard suggested a meeting with the Legion's Father Masterson and making "Charlie Feldman" sit in on it. He had second thoughts, however, considering that "Charlie's the type of guy who is liable to grab telephones and start calling some of his 'influential friends' to help facilitate things. This would serve no other purpose than to put things in a worse boil than they are in already."[17] In any event, the Legion of Decency completely condemned the picture with Feldman *in absentia*.[18]

Despite having a Code seal, on February 26, 1952, A. Roland Thornton, writing for Eric Johnston, head of the MPAA, asked Breen whether his office had cut *Streetcar* as there had been "oblique attacks" on the Code office because of it.[19] Vizzard replied to Johnston on February 29 that the picture had, in fact, been cut "to make it satisfactory under the Code."[20] By this time the picture had been in release since September 19, 1951.

The cuts were not restored until 1993. Writing about it on his blog, critic Roger Ebert noted, "For years the missing footage – only about five minutes in length, but crucial – was thought lost. But this 1993 restoration splices together Kazan's original cut, and we can see how daring the film really was."[21]

---

1. Holman to file, December 13, 1947 (AMPAS).
2. Luraschi to Breen, June 27, 1949 and Breen to Luraschi, June 29, 1949 (AMPAS).
3. Breen to Young, June 22, 1949 (AMPAS).
4. Young to Breen, July 7, 1949 (AMPAS).
5. Geoffrey Shurlock, July 19, 1949, memo to the files (AMPAS).
6. Breen to Selznick, July 19, 1949.
7. American Film Institute catalogue.
8. Breen to file, April 28, 1950 (AMPAS).
9. Feldman to Breen, Vizzard and Shurlock, May 22, 1950 (AMPAS).
10. Breen to Feldman, May 29, 1950 (AMPAS).
11. Instead, Blanche whispers something into the messenger boy's ear that makes him instantly pull away, making the moment more offensive by throwing the content into the viewer's mind.
12. Breen to Warner, August 24, 1950 (AMPAS).
13. Breen to Warner, August 30, September 8, 12, 13 (AMPAS).
14. Kazan to Breen, received September 14, 21, 25 1950 (AMPAS).
15. Kazan to Breen, October 29, 1950 (AMPAS).
16. Breen to Williams, November 2, 1950 (AMPAS).
17. Vizzard to Breen, July 9, 1951 (AMPAS).
18. Albert S. Howson to Vizzard, July 11, 1951 (AMPAS).
19. Thornton (Johnson) to Breen, February 26, 1952 (AMPAS).
20. Vizzard to Thornton (Johnston), February 19, 1952 (AMPAS). The footage consisted of extra shots in the "Stelllla!" scene where Stanley stands at the base of the stairs and entices Stella down to him. The two embrace sensually and he carries her upstairs, obviously to bed.
21. Roger Ebert, November 12, 1993. RogerEbert.com. The most recognized restored cuts were from Stanley's and Stella's steamy reconciliation on the stairs.

Sunset Boulevard

Paramount Pictures, 1950
Written by Charles Brackett, Billy Wilder and D.M. Marshman, Jr.
Produced by Charles Brackett
Directed by Billy Wilder
Code seal #13955

Synopsis
Down-and-out screenwriter Joe Gillis (William Holden) accidentally meets faded silent screen star Norma Desmond (Gloria Swanson), who believes she can get her script "Salome" filmed by her one-time director Cecil B. DeMille (himself). She becomes obsessed with Joe, endangering his relationship with his girlfriend, Betty (Nancy Olsen), all under the jaded eye of Norma's butler, Max Von Mayerling (Erich von Stroheim), who is also her former husband and director.

Background
Brackett and Wilder originally conceived *Sunset Boulevard* as a comedy about an older actress and a younger man with Mae West and Marlon Brando in mind. It wasn't coming along until they happened to speak with journalist D.M. Marshman, who suggested making the man a young, hungry screenwriter being kept by a faded silent movie star.[1] Mae West declined the role, as did Mary Pickford, but Swanson accepted, and Holden rebuffed his agent's resistance and signed on as well.

Wilder's films appear often in these pages not only because they were provocative at the time but because they have remained so. Of all his films, *Sunset Boulevard* may be the most influential. Not only did it inspire a successful stage musical (although so did *The Apartment* and *Some Like It Hot*), it also contributed a memorable closing line to the American lexicon and stands as a tarnished valentine to a filmmaking era that has become cherished in retrospect.

Several plot elements of *Sunset Boulevard* vexed the Code, but the cougar relationship between Joe and Norma didn't raise their hackles for a very basic reason: Brackett and Wilder hid it from them. As was their habit, the two writers fearlessly wrote their script as filming progressed and sent pages to Breen as they were typed: pages 1-64 on March 22, 1949; page 32 rewrite on March 28; pages 65-86 on April 11; more changed pages on April 26; more changed pages on May 2; and song lyrics for "The Paramount-Don't-Want-Me-Blues" on May 5. Pages sent to the Code office just before they were shot drew perfunctory concerns over "the selection and photographing of costumes for your women," not portraying Norma Desmond as having been married three times, and lines like Gillis' "up the creek and need a job."[2]

The bells went off on May 24 when pages 86-108 came in and Joe Breen finally realized what had been going on. He lost his patience and wrote the embattled Luigi Loraschi that same day: "Inasmuch as we have never read the final sequence for this script, we do not know whether the overall story meets the requirements of the Production Code." He then went on, "The most recent of this material seems to indicate the introduction of a sex affair between Gillis and Norma which was not present in the earlier material. Whether or not this overall story will carry a sex affair, we cannot say. However, it seems to me that at this point there is no indication of a voice for morality by which the sex affair would be condemned nor does there appear to be compensating moral values for the sin. We are quite aware that the story is told in flashback and the leading man is shown to be dead when the story opens."[3] The situation wasn't resolved when E.G. Dougherty wrote a note to the files that he had spoken with Luraschi and that Luraschi "understood our position," from which one can infer that Luraschi didn't have a clue either what Brackett and Wilder were up to.[4]

By July 20, however, Breen seems to have accepted that Gillis' death and Norma's retreat into insanity offered enough compensatory moral value and, along with the other compromises,[5] positioned *Sunset Boulevard* for a Code seal on September 9, 1949.[6] To sharp-eyed viewers with experienced imaginations, everything Wilder and Brackett put in makes more than sense, and they don't have to be ready for a close-up to know what it means.

---

1. Joseph McBride, *Billy Wilder: Dancing on the Edge*, New York: Columbia University Press, 2021.
2. Breen to Luraschi, April 14, 1949 (AMPAS).
3. Breen to Luraschi, May 24, 1949 (AMPAS).
4. Dougherty to file, May 31, 1949 (AMPAS).
5. Breen to Luraschi, July 20, 1949 (AMPAS).
6. Certificate (AMPAS).

The Ten Commandments

Paramount Pictures, 1956
Written by Jesse Lasky, Jr., Aeneas MacKenzie, Jack Gariss and Fredric M. Frank, with work from Dorothy Clarke Wilson, J. H. Ingraham and A.E. Southon.
Produced by Cecil B. DeMille and Henry Wilcoxon
Directed by Cecil B. DeMille
Code seal #18021

Synopsis
With the help of God, Moses leads the children of Israel out of bondage in Egypt.

Background
When he made *The Ten Commandments* as a silent film in 1923, Cecil B. DeMille used the story of Moses and the giving of the law only as a short flashback to a contemporary story of a corrupt construction magnate whose safety compromises cost his mother's life in a building collapse. Persuading Paramount, the company he co-founded, that they could rise from financial turmoil with a remake (and having just won the best picture Oscar for *The Greatest Show on Earth*) he pulled out all the stops on what would become his last, and best-remembered, work.

Contrary to his legend, Cecil B. DeMille made only a handful of the biblical epics for which he is now known. Before he found money in the Bible, he produced and directed a highly successful run of silent sex comedies and trendy dramas. He managed to dodge most of the censors because his films always ended on a moral note, although he ladled copious amounts of sex and naughtiness before getting to the penance part. He wasn't called "the world's greatest showman" for nothing, and his early silent films contained opulence, drama, action and spectacle as well as taste, style and, believe it or not, subtlety. The trouble was that all of those attributes seldom appeared together in the same film.

Mindful of his excesses, the Production Code Administration evaluated his script with the same objectivity as they did those of every other filmmaker. Thus their comment on the first script submitted in August 1954 – remembering that DeMille's screenplays were models of specificity and completeness – were simple: don't show Adam and Eve naked, watch out for diaphanous costumes, don't have anyone on screen cry "Fire!" and beware of showing too much in the orgy scene.[1]

When revised script pages arrived months later, they did not reflect the changes ordered, and Shurlock called this to Luraschi's attention.[2] Apparently they were satisfied because the remainder of the back-and-forth in the Code file on *The Ten Commandments* concerns lyrics for various hymns and other songs, all of which were passed without comment.

Needless to say, the Legion of Decency rated the film A-1 for all audiences, as did international censors with the sole exception of Germany, which ordered to be cut a shot of an Egyptian soldier wiping blood from his sword after killing a Hebrew firstborn, but only if Paramount wanted the film to be seen by juveniles, who would otherwise be barred from attending. (Truth to tell, even today that is one of the most disturbing images in the entire film.)

The Ten Commandments is an example of how the Production Code under Joseph I. Breen accorded no filmmaker any slack, no matter how powerful or credentialed.

---

1. Breen to Luraschi, August 26, 1954 (AMPAS).
2. Shurlock to Luraschi, March 21, 1955 (AMPAS).

These Three

United Artists, 1936
Screenplay by Lillian Hellman (based on her play *The Children's Hour*, which is uncredited)
Produced by Samuel Goldwyn
Directed by William Wyler
Code seal #2003

The Children's Hour

United Artists, 1961)
Screenplay by John Michael Hays from Lillian Hellman's play adapted by Lillian Hellman
Directed by William Wyler
Produced by William Wyler, Robert Wyler and Walter Mirisch
Code seal #20107

Synopsis
Two female teachers who run a girls' school are subjected to a vicious whisper campaign begun by a malicious student. The libel trial that follows ruins not only the school but also the women's friendship, and ends one of the women's lives.

Background
The Children's Hour is an unusual instance in which a director was able to remake one of his earlier films.[1] Lillian Hellman's 1934 play, *The Children's Hour*, starred Katherine Emery as Karen and Ann Revere as Martha under Herman Shumlin's direction. It was Hellman's first produced play and it drew controversy for its theme, as well as job offers for the playwright, who accepted a post from Samuel Goldwyn when he bought the screen rights with no plan in place to get it past the censors. At the time, lesbianism was unacceptable under the Code, which called any form of homosexuality "sex perversion." It took Goldwyn and Hellman nearly two years and many rewrites before the script was acceptable to the Code. Along the way all mention of the title *The Children's Hour* was dropped[2] so Hellman wound up receiving story and screenplay credit on *These Three*, as if her play had never existed. When William Wyler remade his film in 1961 under its original title, he still faced censorship problems.

The perfunctory synopsis above gives only the barest flavor of Lillian Hellman's highly emotional drama but it serves as a baseline to show how it was interpreted in three incarnations: a Broadway play, a film made early in the Code's enforcement, and a remake when pressure to revise the Code was starting to mount. Indeed, the two-year journey from *The Children's*

Hour on the stage to *These Three* on the screen, and then the twenty-five-year journey from *These Three* to *The Children's Hour* is remarkable in that, during that time, America emerged from the Depression, survived a world war, entered the nuclear age, fought the Korean war, saw the invention of television, and witnessed the launching of a satellite into space, and yet the one institution that never budged an inch was the Production Code.

In Hellman's original play, a malicious child, Mary, fabricates that Karen and Martha are in a lesbian relationship, not because she has seen anything, but because she has heard about such things, knows it's trouble, and wants to get even with them for disciplining her. She blackmails fellow students to support her claims, and the one person who can exonerate them at the libel trial that follows, Martha's Aunt Lily, is away. Karen is attracted to a doctor, Joe Cardin, yet Martha secretly loves Karen. When Cardin asks Karen if she and Martha are lovers, Karen says no. But when Martha later asks Karen to move away together, revealing her true feelings, Karen declines and Martha shoots herself.

While the undercurrent of lesbianism gave the play its controversy, Hellman always insisted it was about the power of a lie.[3] That didn't mollify the incoming Breen Office when producer Samuel Goldwyn, one of Hollywood's founding moguls, who prided himself in having good taste, announced that he had purchased the property.[4] The devil, as they say, is in the details, and the details of *The Children's Hour* would bedevil Goldwyn, Hellman and Wyler in 1936 and Wyler, Hellman and producer Walter Mirisch in 1961.

On November 21, 1934, Vincent G. Hart of the Production Code Administration submitted a detailed report to Joseph Breen that he had witnessed the previous evening's opening performance of the play, and wrote, "thematically it is unfit material for the screen." He elaborated by citing the insinuation that "the two girls (women) are degenerates, the sadistic nature of the young student, the confession of the young woman that she had a mental, unnatural affection for her girlfriend, and all profanity."[5] Little was said for the next eight months while Goldwyn and Hellman battled out the changes, and in July 1935 Merritt Hulburd of the Goldwyn Studio submitted a plotline to Shurlock of the Breen Office that turned the film into a love triangle and all "sex situations" had been removed.[6] The solution kept the theme but neutered the plot: Karen is engaged to Joe but Martha secretly loves him, and evil Mary spreads rumors of infidelity between Joe and Martha. In the end, Joe leaves them both but Karen runs off to be with him while a disappointed Martha remains at home, alone but alive.

A revised script dated October 28, 1935 was sent to Breen, who courteously replied the next day that there was nothing censorable in it except the use of the word *damn*.[7] With Miriam Hopkins (Martha), Merle Oberon (Karen), and Joel McCrea (Joe Cardin) cast and ready for William Wyler to say "action," a temporary script was sent to Breen on Saturday, November 9, and three days later he had gone through it and demanded removal of the words *mating* and *lousy*, the latter of which was specifically forbidden by the Code. *These Three* was approved for a Code seal on Valentine's Day, February 14, 1936.

Although there was minor opposition from foreign markets who were concerned about the film's treatment of women, the American film critics wholeheartedly complimented it with nary a longing for what was no longer in it.

Twenty-five years later, a new sheriff, Geoffrey Shurlock, who had cut his teeth under Joe Breen, was head of the Production Code Administration. Now titled *The Infamous* and written by John Michael Hays from Lillian Hellman's play, which Hellman herself adapted,[8] it was rejected *in toto* on May 3, 1961. At the same time, Shurlock said that, while the film itself was unacceptable because of the subject matter, "We found nothing in the treatment of the subject in the script itself that would seem to be offensive." In the spirit of confusion, he proceeded to provide a list of profanity that needed to be deleted "because we have lately been receiving a great many complaints on this score," particularly as to swearing by women.

On May 10, United Artists president Arthur Krim wrote directly to Shurlock's boss, MPAA president Eric Johnston (who had replaced Will Hays), assuring him that in neither *The Infamous* nor in two other films that UA was contemplating, *The Best Man* and *Advise and Consent*, would the sex act itself be shown, only the accusation of it, and the accusations in *The Infamous* would be false. (Frank Capra was to direct Gore Vidal's script for *The Best Man*, later directed by Franklin J. Schaffner [q.v.], and Otto Preminger's *Advise and Consent* would move to Columbia.) Apparently this worked because there was no further word about it and the film was awarded a Code seal (with recommendation for adults only) and was released under Lillian Hellman's original title, *The Children's Hour*.

As if to drive the point home, the Mirisch Company's press release announcing the picture began:

"*The Children's Hour* is the story of a lie – a lie that is believed, with disastrous effects upon two young women, as well as those who are too willing to accept the accusation of evil." In point of fact, it was more than that, and also less. Audrey Hepburn played Karen, Shirley MacLaine was Martha, and James Garner was Dr. Joe Cardin. The spiteful child Mary indirectly plays a more pivotal role because it is only when Karen calls off her engagement to Joe out of embarrassment that she learns of Martha's affection for her. Karen resists, denying the possibility of the two of them continuing together, at which point Martha hangs herself in her room. After Martha's funeral, Joe lets Karen walk off alone.

As was generally the case with any film involving homosexuality, it was incumbent upon the gay character to suffer or die by the end. Martha's death had been in the original 1934 play but not in *These Three* in 1936. While *The Children's Hour* was bring remade, Otto Preminger announced that he would be filming *Advise and Consent*, Alan Drury's novel of political intrigue that had a gay subplot, and dared the Code to stop him. (*In Advise and Consent*, the gay character commits suicide.)

"A debate was effectively begun on the merits of revising the Code to allow the onscreen treatment of sex perversion," wrote Vito Russo in *The Celluloid Closet*. "The proponents of the change pointed out that the taboo against sex perversion was the last of the specific taboos, all the others having been dropped in favor of a Code that considered the taste and treatment of the subject matter of each film."

"But the ball was rolling," Russo continued, citing press statements by Preminger that the Motion Picture Association of America was changing its position on his behalf. "The MPAA hotly denied that such a change had taken place, but on October 3, 1961, it approved the change publicly, 'in keeping with the culture.'"[9]

Of note: Miriam Hopkins, who played Martha in *These Three*, plays Lily Mortar, Martha's aunt, who is a teacher at the school in *The Children's Hour*.

Of note: The title *The Children's Hour* is drawn from a romantic poem of that name written in 1860 by Henry Wadsworth Longfellow and published in the September issue of *The Atlantic Monthly*.

---

1. Frank Capra (*Lady For a Day* and *Pocketful of Miracles*), Alfred Hitchcock (*The Man Who Knew Too Much* twice), and Leo McCarey (*Love Affair* and *An Affair to Remember*) come quickly to mind.
2. Memorandum to file from Will H. Hays, August 5, 1935: "Mr. Goldwyn talked to me on (July 31?). He said that he would not use the title, there would be no reference whatever to the perversion, that there would be no reference in the publicity." (AMPAS.)
3. This explanation had resonance in 1952 when Hellman was summoned before the House Un-American Activities Committee with orders to name names. She took what was called "the diminished Fifth," speaking openly of herself but refusing to discuss others. She might have been charged with Contempt of Congress had a lucky paperwork error not freed her on a technicality.
4. The story, though it is probably apocryphal, is that when Goldwyn was told he couldn't film Radclyffe Hall's 1928 novel *The Well of Loneliness* because it was about lesbians, he said, "So we'll make them Hungarians." The same Goldwynism was recycled when he announced *The Children's Hour*, changing it to, "We'll make them Armenians." Neither story has been authenticated.
5. Memo, Hart to Breen, November 21, 1934 (AMPAS).
6. July 24, 1935 cover letter, Hulburd to Shurlock (AMAPS).
7. George Haight to Breen, October 28, 1935; Breen to Goldwyn, October 29, 1925 (AMPAS).
8. It's unclear whether Hellman actually worked on the script or was contractually credited for her 1935 efforts.
9. Vito Russo, *The Celluloid Closet: Homosexuality in the Movies*, New York: Harper & Row, 1981

Tom Jones

United Artists/Lopert Pictures, 1963
Screenplay by John Osborne, based on the novel by Henry Fielding
Produced by Tony Richardson, Michael Holden, Oscar Lewenstein and Michael Balcon (uncredited)
Directed by Tony Richardson
Code seal #20622

Synopsis
Set in eighteenth-century England, this film is the story of a bastard child, Tom Jones (Albert Finney), whose love for the girl-next-door, Sophie (Susannah York), leads him on merrie adventures ending up with being wrongly accused of murder.

Background
Tom Jones was one of the first pictures to reach American shores and mainstream theaters from Britain's rising cadre of innovative filmmakers. These men (Lindsay Anderson, John Schlesinger, Karel Reisz and Tony Richardson[1]) set their stories in the working class rather than the upper class, and very often dealt with everyday issues such as sport, factory work and sheer survival. Many were written by John Osborne, Kingsley Amis, Alan Sillitoe, John Waine and John Braine, and were celebrated by critic Kenneth Tynan. They were collectively called Angry Young Men (Osborne was the first thus) because of their skill in portraying the frustrations of postwar British life. After first revolutionizing (and democratizing) British theatre, they began making films such as *This Sporting Life* (Anderson), *The Loneliness of the Long Distance Runner* (Richardson) and *Billy Liar* (Schlesinger). Few of their films starred performers who were titled, but many later would be. Their films were usually imported to the States by small distributors and shown in art theaters.

It's a little disappointing to discover that a film that was celebrated for its bawdiness only has twenty-seven pages in its Production Code file, most of which are standard office forms and copies of reviews. And yet, because *Tom Jones* won the Oscar for best picture, it bears asking whether the Code saw past the sizzle and recognized the steak.

Alas, they did not. For that matter, neither did Paramount, where the project was first set up in early May 1962 by Woodfall Films, Tony Richardson's company. For once it wasn't Luigi Luraschi who felt the Code's blowback but Edward Schellhorn who heard from Geoffrey Shurlock, with a letter which, had it been written by a critic, would have been called a money review:

> Granted that this is a classic of English literature, nevertheless, the present script seems to us to utilize an unacceptable amount

of very coarse language, and to be told with altogether too much emphasis on scenes of physical sexual promiscuity. There seems to be an overemphasis on scenes of fornication between Tom and Molly in the first part of the story, and even greater emphasis on the repetition of scenes of physical sex between Tom and Lady Bellaston in the second part. Also, there are two sex scenes in Upton which seem over-emphasized. As to the language used, while it is, of course, acceptable to indicate that Tom is a bastard, the expression is used continuously and repetitiously throughout the whole script to the point where it seems to become offensive. Also, the use of such expressions as "whore," "whoremaster," "son-of-a-bitch," "son-of-a-whore," fart," "arse," etc. seem unacceptably coarse, even in a period picture.

They also objected to a plot point in the film where Tom believes he has slept with his mother.[2]

Paramount dropped *Tom Jones* as fast as Tom's parents had dropped him, and on May 21, 1962, he landed at United Artists, where a fast-rising junior executive, David Picker, became what's known in the trade as the film's rabbi. After first being rejected by Bud Ornstein, UA's head of European production, the script was sent by Picker along with its $1,259,000 budget to his New York executives with a note telling them the project was "ribald, bawdy, Hogarthian; it jumps from bed to bed, from adventure to misadventure – it could be great fun… Made by these picture makers, I see this as a potentially important worldwide grosser." Picker got the green light but, to cover themselves, UA released it through their subsidiary Lopert (as they would the next year's controversial *Kiss Me, Stupid*).[3] Four Oscars and several million dollars' profit later, *Tom Jones* not only made Albert Finney a star, it extended the studio's remarkable run: winning five of the decade's ten Best Picture Oscars.

The Code's giving United Artists a Code seal on October 17, 1963 was made without further comment.

---

1. Richard Lester is sometimes mistakenly added to this list, but he was born in America, although he shared their influences and contributed massively to British and world cinema.
2. Shurlock to Schellhorn, May 16, 1962 (AMPAS).
3. Tino Balio, *United Artists: The Company That Changed the Film Industry* (Volume 2: 1951-1978), Wisconsin: University of Wisconsin Press, 1987, 2009.

Touch of Evil

Universal-International Pictures, 1958
Screenplay by Orson Welles, from the novel *Badge of Evil* by Whit Masterson.
Reshoots written by (uncredited) Franklin Cohen and Paul Monash
Produced by Albert Zugsmith
Directed by Orson Welles
Code seal #18506

Synopsis
In the Mexican-American border town of Los Robles, Mike Vargas (Charlton Heston), a special investigator for the Mexican government, runs up against a corrupt police detective, Hank Quinlan (Orson Welles) who always gets his man because he plants evidence to assure conviction. When Vargas thinks that Quinlan has framed a Mexican boy, Sanchez (Victor Millan), for a double murder, he tries to persuade Quinlan's admiring sergeant, Menzies (Joseph Calleia), to entrap his boss. At the same time, the crime lord Grandi (Akim Tamiroff) joins forces with Quinlan to stop Vargas by kidnapping Vargas's new wife, Susan (Janet Leigh). Quinlan ups the ante by strangling Grandi, having Susan drugged, and making it look as though she is a party girl. At last, seeing how corrupt Quinlan is, Menzies helps Vargas bring him down.

Background
Charlton Heston, on learning that Orson Welles was hired to star opposite him in *Badge of Evil*, suggested that Welles be hired to direct it, too. This Welles did, plus rewrite it, plus create a masterful film, only to have the studio fire him and recut it for unknown reasons. Restored in 1998 by Rick Schmidlin, Walter Murch, Bob O'Neil, Jim Waters and Bill Varney, based on a fifty-eight-page memo written by Welles, *Touch of Evil* now exists as close as possible to what Welles wanted – twenty-seven years after his death. How much of what Welles wanted was prohibited by the Code?

Those who have seen the reconstituted Welles cut of *Touch of Evil*, or even the version that Universal-International originally released, will notice, from the warnings issued by the Code, that Welles paid the Shurlock office very little heed and made the film he wanted to make. Had he followed the Code's notes it would, in effect, have removed much of what now distinguishes the film. What emerged in 1958 was not recognized by contemporary reviewers, who were largely indifferent or dismissive.

On January 30, 1957, Geoffrey Shurlock wrote William Gordon of Universal-International a three-page letter with seventeen specific Code infractions that needed to be corrected. Overall, these were designed to sand off the edges of an admittedly seedy story in seedy settings with seedy people doing seedy things. In other words, Shurlock seemed bent on turning a film noir into *The Thin Man* or a similar glossy mystery. Among the dictates (paraphrased here):

> Please bear in mind that we cannot approve of any of the bump and grind types of gyrations throughout the dance numbers staged in the honky-tonk. Also reduce the number of references to "strippers." [The movie calls them "strip teasers" instead.]
>
> The repeated beating of Risto's (Lalo Rios) head against the wall is unacceptably brutal.
>
> Pages 47 and 49: The brutalizing by Quinlan on these pages seems excessive and we ask that it be considerably minimized. [It was reduced to one slap on the kid's face, but hard.]
>
> Avoid any undue mention of marijuana cigarettes or reefer throughout this production. Also it would be well to eliminate the line, "The hypo – who has that?" [The only remnant is Dennis Weaver, as a motel attendant, sniffing a roach in panic. Earlier, the female gang leader, Mercedes McCambridge, handles an ampule and what is unrecognizable as a syringe.]
>
> The following dialogue is unacceptable inasmuch as it deals with the methods of taking drugs in detail: "Somebody who takes heroin by needle, isn't it?" and "Not the muscle, honey, you take it in the vein."
>
> The scenes showing the boys overpowering Susan seem to suggest some sort of group rape. This is completely unacceptable and we ask that this scene be eliminated. In addition, the following line is unacceptable and could not be approved: "Lemme stay Sal – I'll do it – I wanna watch." [Instead, the men lick their lips and say, "Hold her legs"; McCambridge, the female gang leader who is dressed as a man, says, "Lemme stay; I wanna watch."]

Other cuts had to do with showing or suggesting Susan's nakedness, more drug talk, more brutality, and uses of the word "hell."[1]

After receiving more revised pages, on February 13 it was necessary for Shurlock to send another letter repeating practically everything from his January 30 letter, ending, as his and Breen's letters always did, with the disclaimer, "You understand, of course, that our final judgment will be based on the finished picture."[2]

No further communications passed between the parties, or at least none that were saved. Sometime after February 27 (the final exchange), *Badge of Evil* was changed to *Touch of Evil* and on December 20 it received Code approval and opened a "limited" run on March 30, which is to say barely at all. The saga of the film is well recorded in any number of Welles biographies, all of which mention that it was his last studio film made in Hollywood.

---

1. Shurlock to Gordon, January 20, 1957 (AMPAS).
2. Shurlock to Gordon, February 13, 1957 (AMPAS).

Trouble in Paradise

Paramount Pictures, 1932
Screenplay by Samson Rafaelson, adapted by Grover Jones from the play by Alazar Laszlo
Produced and directed by Ernst Lubitsch
Pre-Code

Synopsis
Two polished thieves in Venice, Gaston (Herbert Marshall) and Lily (Miriam Hopkins) meet, expose each other, and then fall in love. Complications arise when their plot to bilk wealthy widow Mariette (Kay Francis) of a fortune is foiled by actual love.

Background
Begun under the less provocative title *The Honest Finder*, *Trouble in Paradise* was at various times called *Thieves and Lovers* and *The Golden Widow*.[1]

When sent to the Breen office in July 1932 in incomplete form, *The Honest Finder* drew rare praise from the Code's Colonel Jason S. Joy, who noted that he read it "with pleasure and amusement." He also noted its negative portrayal of Venice, Italy and suggested that romantic moments be added to offset any Italian being offended. He thought that the police should be portrayed as less bumbling for the same reason. On the whole, however, Joy praised "the light Lubitsch touch [which] is rather the all-governing factor insofar as domestic censorship is concerned."[2] Joy later assured Will Hays that "the new Lubitsch story, *The Honest Finder*, has many of the Lubitsch touches, but he handles his situations so delicately that there is nothing to worry about there."[3] Since the film was to go into production on August 25, speed was becoming important.

Joy was still singing Lubitsch's praises when he received the last of the script pages, nevertheless advising Paramount's Harold Hurley to think about the Major's remark, "I like to take my fun and leave it," Lily's question, "What has she got that I haven't got?" and Marianne's line, "But I don't want to be a lady."[4]

By September 29, the film was rolling and a song titled "Trouble in Paradise" by Leo Robin was being added to it. Code rules specified that its lyrics needed to be cleared, which they were the next day.[5]

When the finished film – by then called *Trouble in Paradise* – was reviewed by Code staff on October 8, Joy's sole complaint to Hurley was the portrayal of the Italian police detectives, something that had also rubbed them the wrong way with an earlier film *This is the Night* (Frank Tuttle, 1932),[6] a gripe he repeated to John Hammell, the difference being that Hurley was in Hollywood and Hammell was in New York. Neither of them responded.

The Italians may not have complained, but several American censorship boards did. New York ordered the line "And we'll celebrate the second anniversary of the day *we didn't get married*" (cuts in italics); Maryland nixed "I'm not the marrying type; *I like to take my fun and leave it*" (cuts in italics); British Columbia cut lines referring to bedrooms; Chicago caught and cut the line "But I don't want to be a lady" that Lubitsch had kept in; Ohio removed mirror shots of Gaston and Mariette reflected in bed; Alberta, Pennsylvania and Australia asked for assorted cuts; and the film was rejected *in toto* in Latvia, Finland and Batavia.

When Paramount applied for a Code seal for a 1935 reissue, the newly empowered Breen office refused to approve it. In 1943, intending to turn it into a musical, Paramount again sent the material to the Code asking what changes would have to be made for them to proceed. Permission was denied again and the matter was dropped.[7]

---

1. American Film Institute catalogue.
2. Joy to Harold Hurley, Paramount-Publix Corp., July 21, 1932 (AMPAS).
3. Joy to Hays, July 24, 1932 (AMPAS).
4. Joy to Hurley, July 26, 1932 (AMPAS).
5. Tom Baily to Joy, September 29, 1932, and Joy to Hurley, September 30, 1932 (AMPAS).
6. Joy to Hurley, October 8, 1932; Joy to John Hammell, October 12, 1932 (AMPAS).
7. American Film Institute catalogue.

Vertigo

Paramount Pictures, 1958
Screenplay by Alec Coppel & Samuel A. Taylor, based on the novel *D'entre Les Morts* by Pierre Boileau and Thomas Narcejac, with Maxwell Anderson (uncredited contributing writer)
Produced by Alfred Hitchcock and Herbert Coleman
Directed by Alfred Hitchcock
Code seal #18867

Synopsis
After his acrophobia (technically it wasn't vertigo) prevents him from saving the life of Madeline (Kim Novak), whom he was following for a friend and with whom he had become obsessed, detective Scotty Ferguson (James Stewart) discovers her lookalike, Judy (Kim Novak), and molds her into his lost, obsessive love, not realizing that she is, in fact, Madeline, who did not die, but decoyed him while another woman was murdered.

Background
Sight and Sound in 2012 may have named Alfred Hitchcock's *Vertigo* the best film of all time, but the Production Code didn't know that when they issued their censorship orders in 1957. By forcing Hitchcock to use his mastery of nuance and juxtaposition instead of dialogue, the Code arguably made *Vertigo* even more sexy, personal and disturbing.

At first titled *From Among the Dead*, the film was evaluated, undoubtedly via a minutely detailed Hitchcock screenplay, after which Geoffrey Shurlock wrote Paramount's Luigi Luraschi that the basic story conformed to the Code but that certain elements of it did not, such as:

> The dialogue about the brassiere and Midge's (Barbara Bel Geddes) love life should be eliminated.
>
> We recommend the elimination of the line, "Oh dammit, dammit."
>
> If the present indication is to be approved that Scottie has completely undressed Madeline and put her to bed, the evidence of embarrassment on her part, on pages 48, 39 and 52 will have to be played way down. Also, on page 60, Scottie's broken line, "I enjoyed – talking to you," should be read without the break and also without any show of embarrassment.
>
> Please observe proper care with the dissolve to avoid any inference of an illicit sex affair.

You will have in mind, of course, the Code prohibition against open-mouth kissing.[1]

A September 18 letter repeated earlier protestations of August 5 of anything indicating an illicit sex affair between Scottie and Madeline and then with Judy.[2]

By September 12, the title of *From Among the Dead* had been changed to *Vertigo*[3] and a Code seal document was issued on January 30, 1958 for the film's May 28 national opening. Typically, the reviews were either condescending or mixed or both. It would be years and a re-release before the childhood memories of a new generation of critics would venerate Hitchcock's achievement. As Donald Spoto[4] and others have written, Hitchcock was a man riddled with neuroses, almost all of them having to do with sex or police. James Stewart's remaking of Kim Novak into a woman he thinks is dead is not merely an exercise in sexual obsession, it is practically necrophilia, something either the Code observers missed or simply couldn't bring themselves to imagine.

---

1. Shurlock to Loraschi, August 1, 1957 (AMPAS)
2. Shurlock to Loraschi, September 18, 1957 (AMPAS).
3. Final white script synopsis (AMPAS).
4. Donald Spoto, *The Life of Alfred Hitchcock: The Dark Side of Genius*, New York, HarperCollins, 1983.

Who's Afraid of Virginia Woolf?

Warner Bros., 1966
Screenplay by Ernest Lehman, from the play by Edward Albee
Produced by Ernest Lehman
Directed by Mike Nichols
Code seal #21074

Synopsis
Weak college professor George (Richard Burton) and his domineering wife Martha (Elizabeth Taylor) invite newly hired professor Nick (George Segal) and his frail wife Honey (Sandy Dennis) to an after-party at their house, where the drinking continues and the painful but exorcising truth comes out.

Background
Mike Nichols and his improv partner Elaine May opened in *An Evening with Mike Nichols and Elaine May* at the Golden Theatre on Broadway in 1960. The Golden's stage door lets out onto the same alley as the Majestic Theatre, where Richard Burton was starring in the musical *Camelot*. Both shows had intermissions at the same time, and Nichols and Burton made friends catching smokes together in the alley between the two houses. Later, when Burton's not-yet-wife, Elizabeth Taylor, and he were shooting *Cleopatra* in London, Burton invited Nichols to visit them. Over the course of the visit, Nichols and Taylor became friends, and when the world's most famous movie stars were signed to make *Virginia Woolf*, Nichols jokingly asked if he could direct it. To his astonishment, Taylor, Burton and Jack L. Warner said yes. "So you might say," Nichols once explained with his dry humor, "I got my first job through connections."[1]

When Jack Valenti replaced Eric Johnston as president of the Motion Picture Association of America in 1966 at the urging of Universal Pictures' head Lew Wasserman and Valenti's former boss, President Lyndon Johnson, Geoffrey Shurlock, then 70, continued to run the MPAA's Production Code.[2] Among Valenti's first duties was updating the Code. His first act was to introduce the label SMA (Suggested for Mature Audiences) to meet exhibitors' and filmmakers' demands to address public tastes, which had changed significantly since 1934. (It would be two years before Valenti introduced what is now known as the movie rating system.) One of the first pictures to be scrutinized under this new system was *Who's Afraid of Virginia Woolf?*

In March 1964,[3] Jack L. Warner had paid $500,000 plus a percentage of the anticipated gross[4] for Edward Albee's landmark 1962 stage play, knowing it would be tough to get it past the Shurlock office. Indeed, Shurlock's initial response to Warner's sending him the play was stern but pragmatic:

As discussed over the telephone, in order to bring this material within Code requirements, it would be necessary to remove all the profanity and the very blunt sexual dialogue. This of course would considerably reduce the impact of this very highly regarded play. We regret having to report unfavorably on this material but under the circumstances it is the only judgment we can render.[5]

Unfazed, Warner hired Ernest Lehman to write the film (Albee's contract cut him out of the production, although he offered to supervise it) which Fred Zinnemann was to direct. Lehman, after watching staged productions in America and England, decided to cut the play's three-hour running time down to two hours and introduce additional characters to the celebrated four-hander (only a single roadhouse attendant survived that unwise choice).[6] In December 1964, Mike Nichols, making his filmmaking debut, replaced Zinnemann as director.[7]

Meanwhile the evisceration of Albee's script progressed. Shurlock's initial five-page letter to Warner listing mandatory Code deletions read like the transcription of a street fight: nineteen *goddams*, seventeen variations on *Jesus Christ*, four *screws*, three *buggers*, and assorted *friggings*, *hump the hostess*, *melons*, *balls* and other inventive profanities. Shurlock ended his missive with a sarcastic and challenging, "should you care to discuss this material any further, we will place ourselves at your disposal."[8]

Apparently, Warner did not, and proceeded to make the movie he and Nichols and Lehman wanted to make. With the film in production, Warner sent the final shooting script to the Code office in early October 1965. It was rejected on October 9, 1965.[9]

Curiously, the file is silent between that declaration and the time at which the finished film was screened for the MPAA on May 3, 1966. Shurlock's letter confirming a denial of a Code seal arrived four weeks before the film's scheduled June 21 premiere.[10] By that time, Shurlock was out of power and Warner Bros. took no time advising Valenti that the studio intended to appeal, saying so in a hand-delivered declaration to Valenti's New York office.[11] The appeal took place June 10 at New York's St. Regis hotel.[12] Valenti and MPAA counsel Louis Nizer announced that they still supported the Code but would abide by the appeal board's decision.[13]

The afternoon following the screening, the MPAA issued a press release with their decision, which was no doubt influenced by Jack Warner's conciliatory move (announced in May 1966) that all exhibition contracts for *Who's Afraid of Virginia Woolf?* would include an "adults only" clause that restricted admission to persons under age eighteen unless accompanied by an adult.[14] Warner discovered that he had a surprising ally in the Legion of Decency, which approved the film based on its artistic merits while overlooking the profanity and shocking situations. The MPAA appeals board agreed, declaring in their decision overturning the Shurlock ban that the content, while vivid, "was not designed to be prurient" and reflected the "tragic realism of life."[15]

A Code seal was issued on June 13, 1966,[16] but that wasn't the end of *Virginia Woolf*'s travails. In September 1966, a print of the film was seized by police in Nashville, Tennessee, on grounds of obscenity. The MPAA went to bat for Warner Bros., offering to share the $1,500 municipal fee involved in getting the print returned. It seems that a provision of the film companies' agreement with the MPAA was that the organization would help them in legal matters when they were defending their films that had received Code seals.

Who's Afraid of Virginia Woolf? not only won Academy Awards for Elizabeth Taylor, Sandy Dennis, Mike Nichols, Haskell Wexler (B&W cinematography), Irene Sharaf (B&W costume design), and Richard Sylbert and George James Hopkins (B&W art direction/set decoration), it moved the movies into the realm of real life.

---

1. Jordan Riefe, *The Hollywood Reporter*, February 22, 2016. The quote comes from an unsourced TV interview.
2. Shurlock remained as advisor until his retirement in 1974. He died in 1976.
3. *The New York Times*, March 5, 1964.
4. *The New York Times*, July 12, 1964.
5. Shurlock to Warner, March 20, 1963 (AMPAS).
6. American Film Institute catalogue.
7. *The New York Times*, December 12, 1964.
8. Shurlock to Warner, March 26, 1963 (AMPAS).
9. Shurlock to Warner, October 9, 1965 (AMPAS).
10. Shurlock to Warner, May 27, 1966 (AMPAS).
11. Warner Bros. to Valenti, June 3, 1966 (AMPAS).
12. Notices were sent by MPAA's Sidney Schreiber to Shurlock, Ralph D. Hetzel, Kenneth W. Clark, Stanley R. Weber, Taylor Mills, and Mrs. Anna Rosenberg Hoffman (AMPAS).
13. *Daily Variety*, June 5, 1966.
14. *Los Angeles Times*, May 16, 1966.
15. MPAA press release, June 10, 1966 (AMPAS).
16. Code certificate (AMPAS).

Afterword

By the time the Motion Picture Producers and Distributors of America imposed the Production Code, America had already survived one sweeping attempt to legislate morality: Prohibition. Passed in 1919, implemented in 1920, and repealed in 1933, the failure of "the great experiment" to force people to change their ways should have been a lesson to Hollywood moralists. But while the U.S. Constitution didn't permit bootlegging, which was a direct outgrowth of Prohibition, it very much encouraged freedom of speech, and stemming it would be a matter of coercion rather than legislation. This is where Hollywood took up Uncle Sam's cudgel and privatized something which would not have withstood judicial review.

As was stated earlier, censorship by the government is forbidden, but private censorship is fair game, and that's what fueled the Production Code. It might be said that the only reason Hollywood tied its own hands is because thousands of theaters around the country were afraid of local interference from any number of third parties: churches, politicians, civic groups, the press, crusading individuals, and, of course, police.

Will H. Hays became president of the Motion Picture Producers and Distributors of America on March 6, 1922, shortly after the trade association was founded. His annual salary was $100,000 at a time when the President of the United States earned $75,000 and the average worker brought home $1,367 a year if he was lucky enough to have a job in Depression-ravaged America.[1] As a former postmaster general, Hays was often addressed by his former title "General." After implementing the list of "Don'ts and Be Carefuls" in 1930, he used the new medium of talking pictures to address the public. "The Code sets up high standards of performance for motion picture producers," he barked from the screen. "It states the considerations which good taste and community value make necessary in this universal form of entertainment. Respect for law. Respect for every religion. Respect for every race and respect for every nation."

When this promise wasn't kept in what are now called "pre-Code films," Hays hired journalist Joseph I. Breen in January 1932 to oversee public relations for the MPPDA at an annual salary of $60,000. Breen's announcement to the newsreel audience was more dynamic than Hays': "Our job as I see it is quite simple. Nobody expects us to, when polled among the public, [make] motion pictures which are lacking in vitality and vigor. No intelligent person would argue that we are to make pictures that are only for children. We must have stories with power and punch and backbone. At the same time, we must be on the lookout for scenes or action or dialogue that are likely to give offense… The vulgar, the cheap, and the tawdry is out. There is no room on the screen at any time for pictures which offend against common decency. And these the industry will not allow."[2]

Blustering aside, Hays, Breen, Shurlock, Johnston and their successors Jack Valenti, Dan Glickman, Chris Dodd, and Charles Rivkin knew that they were walking a tightrope. After all, their salaries – indeed, the budget of the MPPDA (later MPAA and currently the MPA) – were paid by the member film companies who were charged for Code seals in addition to their membership fees in the trade organization. In a very real sense, it was employees giving orders to their bosses, which may explain the obsequiousness in official Code correspondence. The few "notes to the file" of phone conversations and in-person meetings are also carefully objective. This is helpful for history but not for journalism. Were it not for Jack Vizzard's wonderful memoir *See No Evil: Life Inside a Hollywood Censor,* scholars would be forced to think of the Code staff as near-sighted bluenoses picking over everything but the commas in each page they were handed to vet.

What mitigates their legitimacy – and disqualifies all censors, actually – is the innate arrogance of believing that they need to protect people who are too sensitive, naïve or ignorant to handle the film content presented to them. Imagine if the tenets of the Code could have been applied to daily newspapers. There would simply be no news published if it disturbed or expanded the horizons of readers. However –

There is an important asterisk. What about protecting children? The days have passed when all motion pictures were made for family viewing. Perhaps some children, brought by their parents to see *Of Mice and Men* in 1939 or *Casablanca* in 1941, might not have understood the films, but they would not, thanks to the Code, have been offended by them or exposed to ideas they were not prepared to handle. Beginning in the 1950s, however, Hollywood began serving an audience that had lived through World War II and was ready for mature films such as *The Best Years of Our Lives* and *Crossfire*. Sanitizing those films for young audiences deprived grown-ups of material they would have appreciated. The Code had to change.

Jack Valenti was aware of this when he instituted the Movie Ratings in 1968. When confronted with people who objected to the self-censorship his system commanded, Valenti argued that there were some films that children should not be allowed to see. "You've got to set yourself down and think about it in another milieu, that is to say, as a parent," he said. "If I went in to see this film, how would I feel about having my ten-year-old daughter or nine-year-old son with me? That's the thing you want to think about. Now, to me, the freest, wildest left-wing liberals in the world wouldn't quarrel with that because freedom of expression is obviously embedded in the whole ethos of the American spirit. But a child is not quite ready. That's how we judge a new film. So when you see the ratings, it's not on intellectual content or lack of intellectual content. It's based on common sense. It's based on common sense, a kind of gut-level instinctual feeling of how parents would feel about that particular film."[3]

Yet even with Valenti (heir to LBJ's mastery of congressional manipulation) running the MPAA, he still shared Will Hays' concern about federal censorship, despite prevalent case law. "We're fighting federal censorship with all the fervor we can summon," he continued. "I think it's wrong, it is philosophically, morally wrong and, most of all it, is as pragmatically wrong as it is constitutionally wrong. The rating system is a weapon to show that this industry can do for itself what an enterprise or a family or a business or a group or an organization rather than the government can intrude with the bludgeon of the law. The rating system is the greatest shield of freedom that a filmmaker could ever have, that a critic could ever want. Because if you pass a law the right to judge [a director's] film to a political bias then you are embarking on the slipperiest and most torturous path a society can take, in my judgment, because not only is it going to constrain and constrict him in every way, but where do you draw the line?"[4]

Ultimately, good taste is a matter of public consensus, not law, and when it becomes enforced, it is no longer up to the individual, it is the sign of a corrupt State. Congress realized this when they repealed Prohibition in 1933, and it can be argued that Jack Valenti used the same reasoning when he revised the Code in 1968. As this book is being written, so-called "cancel culture" is rife in America and has become enshrined in law. Despite what its groomers claim, a simple reading of these laws shows that their purpose is not to protect children, but to force a belief system upon all people regardless of age. As Clarence Darrow said in defending freedom of speech in the Monkey Trial of 1925 against this same mindset, "Ignorance and fanaticism are ever busy and need feeding. Always it is feeding and gloating for more."

Yet when legislatures and other elected officials venture into setting public taste, such as by banning books, ending college courses, denying or lying about history, or restricting pronoun usage, it is not only un-American, it is contrary to the human gift of thought. As has been said many times, nowhere in history have people who ban books been regarded as heroes. Shakespeare got it right five hundred years ago in his play about the dangers of dictatorship: "Men at some time are masters of their fates. The fault, dear Brutus, is not in our stars but in ourselves."

---

1. https://www.archives.gov/publications/prologue/2012/spring/1940.html
2. Universal Pictures newsreel, 1934
3. Interview with the author, February 11, 1969.
4. Interview with the author, February 11, 1969.

Appendix 1: Production Code Administration Employees

According to Jack Vizzard's memoir, when he entered the Production Code Administration building (then located at 5504 Hollywood Boulevard)[1] after being hired in 1944, "the first impression of the Code offices themselves was of worn-out carpets. The reception room was smothered in a sickly green flooring, which looked as though a hustle and bustle of traffic had passed over it until the burlap backing was beginning to show through. Buried in one wall was an alcove with an antique switchboard. I had the feeling that the oak woodwork needed to be sanded and varnished."[2]

There is no readily available record of who worked there over the years, but by listing all those mentioned in Vizzard's memoir and named in PCA correspondence, it's possible to construct a reasonable roster.

No matter who viewed a film or read a script, once Joseph I. Breen became director in 1934 the policy became that all cautionary correspondence should go out under his signature. Geoffrey Shurlock also followed that dictate until his retirement. Internal memos, however, reveal staff names.

As stated earlier, the work of the Code Administration was crushing. Staffers had to read not just every screenplay and every rewrite, but every treatment, novel, and short story published in magazines, and see every play that was submitted by a member film company or that might be considered for submission. These were the days when each studio could turn out fifty films a year, and there were eight studios (five majors and three minors). In effect, the Code functioned like a studio story department (which, in those golden days, would actively search for new material rather than hope an agent would submit it to them).

Breen, and later Shurlock, had to trust their staff to deliver accurate assessments with remarkable speed, often turning around reports in 24 hours because a studio had held up production waiting for the okay on rewritten pages. This was before faxes and certainly before e-mail, and correspondence is rife with notations of "hand delivery" and "delivery by special car."

Here is the "who's who" of those who enforced the "don'ts and be carefuls" and their job titles, where known:

Auster, Iselin: Breen's assistant
Breen, Joseph I.: PCA public relations, then director of the PCA
DeBra, Arthur: MPAA staffer
Dougherty, E. G. "Doc": censor
Durland, Addison: censor, expert on Latin America
EEB: New York office, name unreported
Fisher (no first name given): Code staff
Harmon, Francis S.: censor, New York office
Hart, Vincent G.: censor
Hays, Will H.: President of the MPPDA

Hoderfield, Milt: secretary to Will Hays, later a censor
Houghton, Arthur: censor
Jackson, Judge Steve: censor
Joy, Jason S.: first Code manager, later director of studio relations for Fox
LaRue, Emily: secretary-receptionist
Linden, Michael: Code's advertising office
Lischka (no first name available): censor
Lynch, Al: censor
McKenzie, Maurice: executive assistant to Will H. Hays
Metzger, Charles: censor
Murphy, Morris: censor
Reid, Peter: Code literary
Schreiber, Sidney: administrator
Shurlock, Geoffrey M.: censor, then director of the PCA
Stinnette, F.: Code film reviewer
Van Schmus, Albert A.: censor
Vizzard, Jack: censor
Wilson, J.V.: reader
Wilstach, Fred J.: advertising censor
White, Gordon S.: MPAA staff
Wingate, Dr. James: censor, formerly with NY State Censor Bureau
Young, Margaret Ann: title researcher
Zehner, Harry: censor specializing in serials

Those wishing to know how today's rating system works may wish to see *This Film Is Not Yet Rated* (2006), a documentary directed by Kirby Dick and written by Dick, Eddie Schmidt and Matt Patterson. Unable to learn anything from the Motion Picture Association about who sat on their ratings board and how they reached their decisions, Dick and his crew followed people as they left the MPAA offices to uncover their identities and how they plied their trade. Needless to say, the film is not rated. The year after it was released, however, the MPAA ratings board began to be more open about its workings.

---

1. Later moving to 8480 Beverly Boulevard, Los Angeles.
2. Jack Vizzard, *See No Evil: Life Inside a Hollywood Censor*, New York: Simon and Schuster, 1970.

Appendix 2: The Production Code

MPAA – The Motion Picture Production Code
The 36 Don'ts and Be Carefuls

> *Published in October 1927 by the Motion Picture Producers and Distributors of America (MPPDA)*

Resolved: That those things which are included in the following list shall not appear in pictures produced by the members of this Association, irrespective of the manner in which they are treated:

1. Pointed profanity – by either title or lip – this includes the words "God," "Lord," "Jesus," "Christ" (unless they be used reverently in connection with proper religious ceremonies), "hell," "damn," "Gawd," and every other profane and vulgar expression however it may be spelled;
2. Any licentious or suggestive nudity – in fact or in silhouette; and any lecherous or licentious notice thereof by other characters in the picture;
3. The illegal traffic in drugs;
4. Any inference of sex perversion;
5. White slavery;
6. Miscegenation (sex relationship between the white and black races);
7. Sex hygiene and venereal diseases;
8. Scenes of actual childbirth – in fact or in silhouette;
9. Children's sex organs;
10. Ridicule of the clergy;
11. Willful offence to any nation, race or creed;

And it be further *Resolved:* That special care be exercised in the manner in which the following subjects are treated, to the end that vulgarity and suggestiveness may be eliminated and that good taste may be emphasized:

1. The use of the flag;
2. International relations (avoiding picturizing in an unfavorable light another country's religion, history, institutions, prominent people and citizenry);
3. Arson;
4. The use of firearms;
5. Theft, robbery, safe-cracking, and dynamiting of trains, mines, buildings, etc. (having in mind the effect which a too-detailed description of these may have upon the moron);
6. Brutality and possible gruesomeness;
7. Technique of committing murder by whatever method;
8. Methods of smuggling;
9. Third-degree methods;
10. Actual hangings or electrocutions as legal punishment for crime;

11. Sympathy for criminals;
12. Attitude toward public characters and institutions;
13. Sedition;
14. Apparent cruelty to children and animals;
15. Branding of people or animals;
16. The sale of women, or of a woman selling her virtue;
17. Rape or attempted rape;
18. First-night scenes;
19. Man and woman in bed together;
20. Deliberate seduction of girls;
21. The institution of marriage;
22. Surgical operations;
23. The use of drugs;
24. Titles or scenes having to do with law enforcement or law-enforcing officers;
25. Excessive or lustful kissing, particularly when one character or the other is a "heavy."

A Code to Govern the Making of Talking, Synchronized and Silent Motion Pictures. Formulated and formally adopted by The Association of Motion Picture Producers, Inc. and The Motion Picture Producers and Distributors of America, Inc. in March 1930.

Motion picture producers recognize the high trust and confidence which have been placed in them by the people of the world and which have made motion pictures a universal form of entertainment.

They recognize their responsibility to the public because of this trust and because entertainment and art are important influences in the life of a nation.

Hence, though regarding motion pictures primarily as entertainment without any explicit purpose of teaching or propaganda, they know that the motion picture within its own field of entertainment may be directly responsible for spiritual or moral progress, for higher types of social life, and for much correct thinking.

During the rapid transition from silent to talking pictures they have realized the necessity and the opportunity of subscribing to a Code to govern the production of talking pictures and of re-acknowledging this responsibility.

On their part, they ask from the public and from public leaders a sympathetic understanding of their purposes and problems and a spirit of cooperation that will allow them the freedom and opportunity necessary to bring the motion picture to a still higher level of wholesome entertainment for all the people.

General Principles

1. No picture shall be produced that will lower the moral standards of those who see it. Hence the sympathy of the audience should never be thrown to the side of crime, wrongdoing, evil or sin.
2. Correct standards of life, subject only to the requirements of drama and entertainment, shall be presented.
3. Law, natural or human, shall not be ridiculed, nor shall sympathy be created for its violation.

Particular Applications

I. Crimes Against the Law
These shall never be presented in such a way as to throw sympathy with the crime as against law and justice or to inspire others with a desire for imitation.

1. Murder
    a. The technique of murder must be presented in a way that will not inspire imitation.
    b. Brutal killings are not to be presented in detail.
    c. Revenge in modern times shall not be justified.
2. Methods of Crime should not be explicitly presented.
    a. Theft, robbery, safe-cracking, and dynamiting of trains, mines, buildings, etc., should not be detailed in method.
    b. Arson must be subject to the same safeguards.
    c. The use of firearms should be restricted to the essentials.
    d. Methods of smuggling should not be presented.
3. Illegal drug traffic must never be presented.
4. The use of liquor in American life, when not required by the plot or for proper characterization, will not be shown.

II. Sex
The sanctity of the institution of marriage and the home shall be upheld. Pictures shall not infer that low forms of sex relationship are the accepted or common thing.

1. Adultery, sometimes necessary plot material, must not be explicitly treated, or justified, or presented attractively.
2. Scenes of Passion
    a. They should not be introduced when not essential to the plot.
    b. Excessive and lustful kissing, lustful embraces, suggestive postures and gestures, are not to be shown.
    c. In general passion should so be treated that these scenes do not stimulate the lower and baser element.

3. Seduction or Rape
   a. They should never be more than suggested, and only when essential for the plot, and even then never shown by explicit method.
   b. They are never the proper subject for comedy.
4. Sex perversion or any inference to it is forbidden.
5. White slavery shall not be treated.
6. Miscegenation (sex relationships between the white and black races) is forbidden.
7. Sex hygiene and venereal diseases are not subjects for motion pictures.
8. Scenes of actual childbirth, in fact or in silhouette, are never to be presented.
9. Children's sex organs are never to be exposed.

III. Vulgarity
The treatment of low, disgusting, unpleasant, though not necessarily evil, subjects should always be subject to the dictates of good taste and a regard for the sensibilities of the audience.

IV. Obscenity
Obscenity in word, gesture, reference, song, joke, or by suggestion (even when likely to be understood only by part of the audience) is forbidden.

V. Profanity
Pointed profanity (this includes the words, God, Lord, Jesus, Christ – unless used reverently – Hell, S.O.B., damn, Gawd), or every other profane or vulgar expression however used, is forbidden.

VI. Costume
1. Complete nudity is never permitted. This includes nudity in fact or in silhouette, or any lecherous or licentious notice thereof by other characters in the picture.
2. Undressing scenes should be avoided, and never used save where essential to the plot.
3. Indecent or undue exposure is forbidden.
4. Dancing or costumes intended to permit undue exposure or indecent movements in the dance are forbidden.

VII. Dances
1. Dances suggesting or representing sexual actions or indecent passions are forbidden.
2. Dances which emphasize indecent movements are to be regarded as obscene.

VIII. Religion
1. No film or episode may throw ridicule on any religious faith.

2. Ministers of religion in their character as ministers of religion should not be used as comic characters or as villains.
3. Ceremonies of any definite religion should be carefully and respectfully handled.

IX. Locations
The treatment of bedrooms must be governed by good taste and delicacy.

X. National Feelings
1. The use of the Flag shall be consistently respectful.
2. The history, institutions, prominent people and citizenry of other nations shall be represented fairly.

XI. Titles
Salacious, indecent, or obscene titles shall not be used.

XII. Repellent Subjects
The following subjects must be treated within the careful limits of good taste:
1. Actual hangings or electrocutions as legal punishments for crime.
2. Third degree methods.
3. Brutality and possible gruesomeness.
4. Branding of people or animals.
5. Apparent cruelty to children or animals.
6. The sale of women, or a woman selling her virtue.
7. Surgical operations.

Reasons Supporting the Preamble of the Code

I. Theatrical motion pictures, that is, pictures intended for the theatre as distinct from pictures intended for churches, schools, lecture halls, educational movements, social reform movements, etc., are primarily to be regarded as ENTERTAINMENT.

Mankind has always recognized the importance of entertainment and its value in rebuilding the bodies and souls of human beings.

But it has always recognized that entertainment can be a character either HELPFUL or HARMFUL to the human race, and in consequence has clearly distinguished between:

a. Entertainment which tends to improve the race, or at least to re-create and rebuild human beings exhausted with the realities of life; and

b. Entertainment which tends to degrade human beings, or to lower their standards of life and living.

Hence the MORAL IMPORTANCE of entertainment is something which has been universally recognized. It enters intimately into the lives of men and women and affects them closely; it occupies their minds and affections during leisure hours; and ultimately touches the whole of their lives. A man may be judged by his standard of entertainment as easily as by the standard of his work.

So correct entertainment raises the whole standard of a nation.

Wrong entertainment lowers the whole living conditions and moral ideals of a race.

Note, for example, the healthy reactions to healthful sports, like baseball, golf; the unhealthy reactions to sports like cockfighting, bullfighting, bear baiting, etc.

Note, too, the effect on ancient nations of gladiatorial combats, the obscene plays of Roman times, etc.

II. Motion pictures are very important as ART.

Though a new art, possibly a combination art, it has the same object as the other arts, the presentation of human thought, emotion, and experience, in terms of an appeal to the soul through the senses.

Here, as in entertainment, Art enters intimately into the lives of human beings.

Art can be morally good, lifting men to higher levels. This has been done through good music, great painting, authentic fiction, poetry, drama. Art can be morally evil it its effects. This is the case clearly enough with unclean art, indecent books, suggestive drama. The effect on the lives of men and women are obvious.

Note: It has often been argued that art itself is unmoral, neither good nor bad. This is true of the THING which is music, painting, poetry, etc. But the THING is the PRODUCT of some person's mind, and the intention of that mind was either good or bad morally when it produced the thing. Besides, the thing has its EFFECT upon those who come into contact with it. In both these ways, that is, as a product of a mind and as the cause of definite effects, it has a deep moral significance and unmistakable moral quality.

Hence: The motion pictures, which are the most popular of modern arts for the masses, have their moral quality from the intention of the minds which produce them and from their effects on the moral lives and reactions of their audiences. This gives them a most important morality.

1. They reproduce the morality of the men who use the pictures as a medium for the expression of their ideas and ideals.

2. They affect the moral standards of those who, through the screen, take in these ideas and ideals. In the case of motion pictures, the effect may be particularly emphasized because no art has so quick and so widespread an appeal to the masses. It has become in an incredibly short period the art of the multitudes.

III. The motion picture, because of its importance as entertainment and because of the trust placed in it by the peoples of the world, has special MORAL OBLIGATIONS:

A. Most arts appeal to the mature. This art appeals at once to every class, mature, immature, developed, undeveloped, law abiding, criminal. Music has its grades for different classes; so has literature and drama. This art of the motion picture, combining as it does the two fundamental appeals of looking at a picture and listening to a story, at once reaches every class of society.

B. By reason of the mobility of film and the ease of picture distribution, and because of the possibility of duplicating positives in large quantities, this art reaches places unpenetrated by other forms of art.

C. Because of these two facts, it is difficult to produce films intended for only certain classes of people. The exhibitors' theatres are built for the masses, for the cultivated and the rude, the mature and the immature, the self-respecting and the criminal. Films, unlike books and music, can with difficulty be confined to certain selected groups.

D. The latitude given to film material cannot, in consequence, be as wide as the latitude given to book material. In addition:

a. A book describes; a film vividly presents. One presents on a cold page; the other by apparently living people.

b. A book reaches the mind through words merely; a film reaches the eyes and ears through the reproduction of actual events.

c. The reaction of a reader to a book depends largely on the keenness of the reader's imagination; the reaction to a film depends on the vividness of presentation.

Hence many things which might be described or suggested in a book could not possibly be presented in a film.

E. This is also true when comparing the film with the newspaper.

a. Newspapers present by description, films by actual presentation.

b. Newspapers are after the fact and present things as having taken place; the film gives the events in the process of enactment and with apparent reality of life.

F. Everything possible in a play is not possible in a film:

a. Because of the larger audience of the film, and its consequential mixed character. Psychologically, the larger the audience, the lower the moral mass resistance to suggestion.

b. Because through light, enlargement of character, presentation, scenic emphasis, etc., the screen story is brought closer to the audience than the play.

c. The enthusiasm for and interest in the film actors and actresses, developed beyond anything of the sort in history, makes the audience largely sympathetic toward the characters they portray and the stories in which they figure. Hence the audience is more ready to confuse actor and actress and the characters they portray, and it is most receptive of the emotions and ideals presented by the favorite stars.

G. Small communities, remote from sophistication and from the hardening process which often takes place in the ethical and moral standards of larger cities, are easily and readily reached by any sort of film.

H. The grandeur of mass settings, large action, spectacular features, etc., affects and arouses more intensely the emotional side of the audience. In general, the mobility, popularity, accessibility, emotional appeal, vividness, straightforward presentation of fact in the film make for more intimate contact with a larger audience and for greater emotional appeal.

Hence the larger moral responsibilities of the motion pictures.

Reasons Underlying the General Principles

I. No picture shall be produced which will lower the moral standards of those who see it. Hence the sympathy of the audience should never be thrown to the side of crime, wrong-doing, evil or sin. This is done:

1. When evil is made to appear attractive and alluring, and good is made to appear unattractive.

2. When the sympathy of the audience is thrown on the side of crime, wrongdoing, evil, sin. The same is true of a film that would throw sympathy against goodness, honor, innocence, purity or honesty.

Note: Sympathy with a person who sins is not the same as sympathy with the sin or crime of which he is guilty. We may feel sorry for the plight of the murderer or even understand the circumstances which led him to his crime: we may not feel sympathy with the wrong which he has done. The presentation of evil is often essential for art or fiction or drama. This in itself is not wrong provided:

a. That evil is not presented alluringly. Even if later in the film the evil is condemned or punished, it must not be allowed to appear so attractive that the audience's emotions are drawn to desire or approve so strongly that later the condemnation is forgotten and only the apparent joy of sin is remembered.

b. That throughout, the audience feels sure that evil is wrong and good is right.

II. Correct standards of life shall, as far as possible, be presented.

A wide knowledge of life and of living is made possible through the film. When right standards are consistently presented, the motion picture exercises the most powerful influences. It builds character, develops right ideals, inculcates correct principles, and all this in attractive story form. If motion pictures consistently hold up for admiration high types of characters and present stories that will affect lives for the better, they can become the most powerful force for the improvement of mankind.

III. Law, natural or human, shall not be ridiculed, nor shall sympathy be created for its violation. By natural law is understood the law which is written in the hearts of all mankind, the greater underlying principles of right and justice dictated by conscience.

By human law is understood the law written by civilized nations.

1. The presentation of crimes against the law is often necessary for the carrying out of the plot. But the presentation must not throw sympathy with the crime as against the law nor with the criminal as against those who punish him.

2. The courts of the land should not be presented as unjust. This does not mean that a single court may not be presented as unjust, much less that a single court official must not be presented this way. But the court system of the country must not suffer as a result of this presentation.

Reasons Underlying the Particular Applications

I. Sin and evil enter into the story of human beings and hence in themselves are valid dramatic material.

II. In the use of this material, it must be distinguished between sin which repels by its very nature, and sins which often attract.

    a. In the first class come murder, most theft, many legal crimes, lying, hypocrisy, cruelty, etc.

    b. In the second class come sex sins, sins and crimes of apparent heroism, such as banditry, daring thefts, leadership in evil, organized crime, revenge, etc. The first class needs less care in treatment, as sins and crimes of this class are naturally unattractive. The audience instinctively condemns all such and is repelled.

Hence the important objective must be to avoid the hardening of the audience, especially of those who are young and impressionable, to the thought and fact of crime. People can become accustomed even to murder, cruelty, brutality, and repellent crimes, if these are too frequently repeated. The second class needs great care in handling, as the response of human nature to their appeal is obvious. This is treated more fully below.

III. A careful distinction can be made between films intended for general distribution, and films intended for use in theatres restricted to a limited audience. Themes and plots quite appropriate for the latter would be altogether out of place and dangerous in the former.

Note: The practice of using a general theatre and limiting its patronage to "Adults Only" is not completely satisfactory and is only partially effective.

However, maturer minds may easily understand and accept without harm subject matter in plots which do younger people positive harm.

Hence: If there should be created a special type of theatre, catering exclusively to an adult audience, for plays of this character (plays with problem themes, difficult discussions and maturer treatment) it would seem to afford an outlet, which does not now exist, for pictures unsuitable for general distribution but permissible for exhibitions to a restricted audience.

I. Crimes Against the Law
The treatment of crimes against the law must not:
1. Teach methods of crime.
2. Inspire potential criminals with a desire for imitation.
3. Make criminals seem heroic and justified.

Revenge in modern times shall not be justified. In lands and ages of less developed civilization and moral principles, revenge may sometimes be presented. This would be the case especially in places where no law exists to cover the crime because of which revenge is committed.

Because of its evil consequences, the drug traffic should not be presented in any form. The existence of the trade should not be brought to the attention of audiences.

The use of liquor should never be excessively presented. In scenes from American life, the necessities of plot and proper characterization alone justify its use. And in this case, it should be shown with moderation.

II. Sex
Out of a regard for the sanctity of marriage and the home, the triangle, that is, the love of a third party for one already married, needs careful handling. The treatment should not throw sympathy against marriage as an institution.

Scenes of passion must be treated with an honest acknowledgement of human nature and its normal reactions. Many scenes cannot be presented without arousing dangerous emotions on the part of the immature, the young or the criminal classes.

Even within the limits of pure love, certain facts have been universally regarded by lawmakers as outside the limits of safe presentation.

In the case of impure love, the love which society has always regarded as wrong and which has been banned by divine law, the following are important:
1. Impure love must not be presented as attractive and beautiful.
2. It must not be the subject of comedy or farce, or treated as material for laughter.
3. It must not be presented in such a way as to arouse passion or morbid curiosity on the part of the audience.
4. It must not be made to seem right and permissible.
5. It general, it must not be detailed in method and manner.

III. Vulgarity; IV. Obscenity; V. Profanity; hardly need further explanation than is contained in the Code.

VI. Costume
General Principles:
1. The effect of nudity or semi-nudity upon the normal man or woman, and much more upon the young and upon immature persons, has been honestly recognized by all lawmakers and moralists.

2. Hence the fact that the nude or semi-nude body may be beautiful does not make its use in the films moral [sic]. For, in addition to its beauty, the effect of the nude or semi-nude body on the normal individual must be taken into consideration.

3. Nudity or semi-nudity used simply to put a "punch" into a picture comes under the head of immoral actions. It is immoral in its effect on the average audience.

4. Nudity can never be permitted as being necessary for the plot. Semi-nudity must not result in undue or indecent exposures.

5. Transparent or translucent materials and silhouette are frequently more suggestive than actual exposure.

VII. Dances
Dancing in general is recognized as an art and as a beautiful form of expressing human emotions.

But dances which suggest or represent sexual actions, whether performed solo or with two or more; dances intended to excite the emotional reaction of an audience; dances with movement of the breasts, excessive body movements while the feet are stationary, violate decency and are wrong.

VIII. Religion
The reason why ministers of religion may not be comic characters or villains is simply because the attitude taken toward them may easily become the attitude taken toward religion in general. Religion is lowered in the minds of the audience because of the lowering of the audience's respect for a minister.

IX. Locations
Certain places are so closely and thoroughly associated with sexual life or with sexual sin that their use must be carefully limited.

X. National Feelings
The just rights, history, and feelings of any nation are entitled to most careful consideration and respectful treatment.

XI. Titles
As the title of a picture is the brand on that particular type of goods, it must conform to the ethical practices of all such honest business.

XII. Repellent Subjects
Such subjects are occasionally necessary for the plot. Their treatment must never offend good taste nor injure the sensibilities of an audience.

Advertising Code

These additions and modifications are attributed to the ascension of Joseph I. Breen to head the Production Code in 1934:

1. We subscribe to the Code of Business Ethics of the International Advertising Association, based on "truth, honesty, and integrity."
2. Good taste shall be the guiding rule.
3. Illustration and text in advertising shall faithfully represent the pictures themselves.
4. No false or misleading statement shall be used directly or implied.
5. No text or illustration shall ridicule or tend to ridicule any religion or religious faith.
6. The history, institution and nationalities of all countries shall be represented with all fairness.
7. Profanity and vulgarity shall be avoided.
8. Pictorial and copy treatment of officers of the law shall not be of such a nature as to undermine authority.
9. Specific details of crime, inciting imitation, shall not be used.
10. Motion picture advertisers shall bear in mind the provision of the Production Code that use of liquor in American life be restricted to the necessities of characterization and plot.
11. Nudity with meretricious purpose, and salacious postures, shall not be used.

Modifications and expansions of The Production Code of Ethics:

I-3. The illegal drug traffic must not be portrayed in such a way as to stimulate curiosity concerning the use of, or traffic in, such drugs; nor shall scenes be approved which show the use of, or the effects of illegal drugs in detail.

V. No approval by the Production Code Administration shall be given to the use of words and phrases in motion pictures including, but not limited to, the following:
Alley-cat (applied to a woman)
Bat (applied to a woman)
Broad (applied to a woman)
"Bronx Cheer" (the sound)
Chippie
Cocotte
Cripes
Fanny
Fairy (in a vulgar sense)
Fire – cries of
Gawd

God, Lord, Jesus, Christ (unless used reverently)
Goose (in a vulgar sense)
"Hold your Hat" (or "hats")
Hot (applied to a woman)
"in your hat"
Louse
Lousy
Madam (relating to prostitution)
Nance
Nerts
Nuts (except when meaning crazy)
Pansy
Razzberry (the sound)
Slut (applied to a woman)
S.O.B.
Son-of-a
Tart
Toilet gags
Tom-cat (applied to a man)
Traveling salesman and Farmer's daughter jokes
Whore
Damn, Hell (excepting where the use of said last two words shall be essential and required for portrayal, in proper historical context, of any scene or dialogue based upon historical fact or folklore, or for the presentation in proper literary context of a Biblical, or other religious, quotation, or a quotation from a literary work, provided that no such use be permitted which is intrinsically objectionable or offense good taste).

In the administration of Section V of the Production Code, the Production Code Administration may take cognizance of the fact that the following words and phrases are obviously offensive to the patrons of motion pictures, in the United States, and more particularly to patrons of motion pictures in foreign countries: Chink, Dago, Frog, Greaser, Hunkie, Kike, Nigger, Spic, Wop, Yid.

Bibliography

Balio, Tino, *United Artists: The Company That Changed the Film Industry* (Volume 2: 1951-1978), Wisconsin: University of Wisconsin Press, 1987, 2009.

Behlmer, Rudy, *Memo from David O. Selznick*, New York: The Viking Press, 1972.

Berg, A. Scott, *Goldwyn: A Biography*, New York: Alfred A. Knopf, 1989.

Bogdanovich, Peter, *John Ford*, Los Angeles, California: University of California Press, 1968, reprinted 1970.

Brownlow, Kevin, *David Lean: A Biography*, New York: St. Martin's Press, 1996.

Capra, Frank, *The Name Above the Title*, New York: MacMillan and Company, 1971.

Gardner, Gerald, *The Censorship Papers: Movie Censorship Letters from the Hays Office 1934 to 1968*, New York: Dodd, Mead & Company, 1987.

Grobel, Lawrence, *The Hustons*, New York: Charles Scribner's Sons, 1989.

Haver, Ronald, *David O. Selznick's Hollywood*, New York: Alfred A. Knopf, 1980.

Mankiewicz, Joseph L. and Gary Carey, *More About All About Eve, a Colloquy with Gary Carey*, New York: Random House, 1972.

McBride, Joseph, *Billy Wilder: Dancing on the Edge*, New York: Columbia University Press, 2021

McBride, Joseph, *Frank Capra: The Catastrophe of Success*, New York: Simon and Schuster, 1992

Moley, Raymond, *The Hays Office*, New York: Bobbs-Merrill, 1945.

Paul, William, *Ernst Lubitsch's American Comedy*, New York: Columbia University Press, 1983.

Rebello, Stephen, *Alfred Hitchcock and the Making of Psycho*, New York: Dembner Books, 1990.

Russo, Vito, *The Celluloid Closet: Homosexuality in the Movies*, New York: Harper & Row, 1981.

Sikov, Ed, *On Sunset Boulevard: The Life and Times of Billy Wilder*, New York: Hyperion, 1998

Silverman, Stephen M., *David Lean*, New York: Harry N. Abrams Publishers, 1989, 1992.

Silverman, Stephen M., *The Fox That Got Away*, Secaucus, New Jersey: Lyle Stuart, Inc., 1988.

Vizzard, Jack, *See No Evil: Life Inside a Hollywood Censor*, New York: Simon and Schuster, 1970.

Author biography

Nat Segaloff is a writer-producer-journalist. He covered the film industry for the *Boston Herald* and CBS radio but has also variously been a studio publicist and film critic (not at the same time), college teacher and TV producer. His previous books include *Hurricane Billy: The Stormy Life and Films of William Friedkin*, *Arthur Penn: American Director*, and *Final Cuts: The Last Films of 50 Great Directors*, in addition to career monographs on Stirling Silliphant, Walon Green, Paul Mazursky and John Milius, and documentaries on Stan Lee, John Belushi, Larry King, and Shari Lewis and Lamb Chop.

Other books include *A Lit Fuse: The Provocative Life of Harlan Ellison*, nominated for Hugo and Locus awards, *More Fire! The Building of The Towering Inferno*, *The Exorcist Legacy: 50 Years of Fear* and *Say Hello to My Little Friend: A Century of Scarface*.

Nat lives in Los Angeles with his Italian greyhound, Louie, waiting for their phone calls to be returned.

Personnel Index

Academy of Motion Picture Arts and
  Sciences, 5, 17, 21, 32, 39, 51, 82, 101,
  115, 116, 138, 142, 199
Aitken, H.E., 35
Akoum, Gaston, 7
Albee, Edward, 197, 198
Alexander, Will W., 35, 36, 37, 139
Allen, E.H., 8, 10
Allison, Joan, 59
Anderson, Milo, 13, 145, 187, 195
Andrews, Dana, 31–33
Arbuckle, Roscoe "Fatty," 8
Arnold, Edward, 130
Ashby, Hal, 104
Astaire, Fred, 55, 77
Astor, Mary, 127
Auster, Iselin, 79, 86, 90, 124, 139, 205

Bacharach, Burt, 22
Backus, Jim, 155
Baer, Stanley, 120, 121
Baker, Mary Louise (a.k.a. Joan Barry), 133
Balcon, Michael, 187
Balio, Tino, 188, 221
Bancroft, George, 167
Bel Geddes, Barbara, 195
Bloch, Robert, 153
Blondell, Joan, 55, 56
Bloom, Sol, 7
Blore, Eric, 61
Bogart, Humphrey, 6, 45, 49, 51, 127
Bonacci, Anna, 111, 113
Bond, Edward, 39, 63, 160

Booth, Margaret, 137, 138
Botsford, A.M., 64–66
Boulle, Pierre, 43, 45, 46
Brackett, Charles, 119, 120, 139, 140, 179, 180
Brady, Alice, 77
Braine, John, 187
Brando, Marlon, 138, 160, 173, 179
Brassart, Felix, 139
Breen, Joseph I., 8, 9, 11, 13–15, 17–19, 21,
  23–26, 28, 31–33, 36, 37, 46–51, 55–61,
  66–69, 72–75, 78–83, 86–90, 92, 93,
  96–98, 109, 110, 115, 116, 119–25,
  127–31, 133–35, 137–40, 142, 143, 146,
  147, 149–51, 157, 158, 167–71, 174–77,
  179, 180, 182, 184–86, 193, 194, 201, 202,
  205, 218
Brent, George, 25
Briskin, Sam, 48, 97, 130, 131
Brooks, Richard, 59
Brown, Grace, 149
Brynner, Yul, 80
Buchman, Sidney, 129, 130
Burnett, Murray, 49
Burstyn, Joseph, 11
Burton, Richard, 197
Byron, Stuart, 159, 161

Calleia, Joseph, 189
Canfield, Mark (Darryl F. Zanuck), 23
Canutt, Yakima, 89
Capra, Frank, 27, 28, 30, 129–31, 185, 186,
  221
Carmichael, Hoagy, 32

226 The Naughty Bits

Carradine, John, 91, 167
Carroll, Madeline, 157
Cassell, Duncan, 43, 46
Chaney, Lon Jr., 141
Chaplin, Charles, 133–35
Chaplin, Saul, 165
Chatkin, Rose, 74, 75
Coburn, Charles, 6
Cohn, Harry, 44, 96–98, 115, 130, 131
Connolly, Myles, 28, 129
Cooper, Gary, 66
Cooper, Melville, 13
Cooper, Merrian C., 159
Copland, Aaron, 143
Coppel, Alec, 195
Costello, Frank, 119
Cragg, Adolf, 24
Cronin, Paul, 10
Cronyn, Hume, 157
Crouse, Russell, 165
Cukor, George, 85, 86, 88, 89
Cummings, Sidney S., 72
Cummins, Samuel, 71–73, 75
Curtis, George, 66
Curtis, Tony, 63, 163
Curtiz, Michael, 13, 14, 49

Dall, John, 157, 158
Daniels, Bebe, 127
Darrow, Clarence, 203
Darwell, Jane, 91, 93
Da Silva, Howard, 120
Davalos, Richard, 67
Daves, Delmer, 123
Davis, Davis, 17, 90, 109, 110, 127
Dean, James, 67, 69, 103, 111, 155, 156
DeHavilland, Olivia, 13
DeLaurentiis, Dino, 138
DeMille, Cecil B., 179, 181
DePalma, Brian, 39
Deval, Jacques, 139
Devine, Andy, 167
DeWilde, Brandon, 99
Dixon, Rev. Thomas W., 35
Dmytryk, Edward, 59, 61
Dodd, Chris, 202
Donat, Robert, 157
Donohue, James J., 121, 122
Doran, Ann, 155
Dougherty, E.G., 180, 205
Dowling, Doris, 120
Dreiser, Theodore, 149, 151
Drury, Alan, 185
Duggan, Pat, 31–33
Dunne, Irene, 123
Dunne, Philip, 145
Durland, Addison, 50, 205

Ebert, Roger, 177
Edelman, Louis F., 109
Edison, Thomas A., 7
Eisenhower, Dwight D., 27
Emery, Katherine, 183
Epstein, Julius and Philip, 49
Everson, William K., 53

Fairbanks, Douglas, 13
Farr, Felicia, 111
Farrow, John, 137
Fatima, 6
Faulkner, William, 169, 170
Feldman, Charles, 173, 175–77
Ferrer, José, 117
Fiddler, Jimmie, 73, 121
Fielding, Henry, 187
Finkel, Abem, 109
Fishel, H.L., 155
Fleming, Victor, 85, 89
Fonda, Henry, 27, 91, 93, 109
Ford, John, 9, 91-93, 145, 159–61, 167, 168, 221
Foreman, Carl, 43, 45, 46
Foster, Lewis Ransom, 129, 130
Franklin, Sidney, 85
Friedhofer, Hugo, 32
Friedkin, William, 223
Furthman, Jules, 137

Gable, Clark, 85, 137, 138
Gadge (Elia Kazan), 175
Gallagher, Bishop Michael J., 65
Garbo, 139, 140
Gariss, Jack, 181
Garner, James, 185
Garrett, Oliver H.P., 85, 169
Gaudio, Tony, 13
Gavin, John, 154
Gein, Ed, 153
Geisel, Ted (Dr. Seuss), 155
Glickman, Dan, 202
Godard, Jean-Luc, 159
Goetz, William, 81
Goldwyn, Samuel, 31–33, 104, 183, 184, 186, 221
Gordon, William, 59, 61, 74, 78, 90, 189, 191, 206
Gottlieb, Robert, 140
Goulding, Harry, 160
Grable, Betty, 78
Grant, Cary, 47, 53, 95, 123, 124, 139
Griffith, David Wark (D.W.), 1, 3, 23, 35, 37
Grunhut, Morris, 71
Gullan, Campbell, 63

Hackman, Gene, 39
Hale, Alan, 13
Hamill, John, 66
Hamilton, Patrick, 157
Hammell, John, 130, 131, 193, 194
Hammett, Dashiell, 127
Hanemann, H.W., 77
Hanks, Tom, 123
Hansen, Edmund H., 93
Harmon, Francis F., 36, 37, 72–75, 89, 90, 93, 141, 143, 145–47, 205
Harmon, Teresa, 24
Harris, Julie, 63
Harris, Frank, 100
Harrison, Doane, 105, 111, 163
Harvey, Paul, 112, 113
Havoc, June, 82
Hawkins, Jack, 43, 45
Hawks, Howard, 47, 48, 95, 96, 137
Hayakawa, Sessue, 43
Haycox, Ernest, 167
Hays, Will H., 8, 9, 11, 23–26, 35–37, 46, 65, 66, 72, 74, 75, 78–80, 82, 89, 90, 92, 93, 96–98, 109-110, 120, 123, 128, 130, 131, 141–43, 169–71, 183, 185, 186, 193, 194, 201, 202, 206, 221
Hellman, Lillian, 183–86
Hemmings, David, 39, 41
Henreid, Paul, 49
Hepburn, Katharine, 47, 48, 185
Herczig, Gaston, 73
Heston, Charlton, 189
Hitchcock, Alfred, 153, 154, 157, 158, 186, 195, 196, 221
Hobson, Laura Z., 81, 82
Hoderfield, Milt, 206
Hoffenstein, Samuel, 63, 77
Holden, William, 43–45, 77, 179, 187
Holm, Celeste, 17, 82
Holman, Russell, 120–22, 174, 177
Hoover, J. Edgar, 9
Hopkins, Arthur, 153
Hopkins, Miriam, 63, 184, 186
Horne, Geoffrey, 43
Horton, Arthur, 61, 63, 77, 78
Hughes, Howard, 95, 98
Hulburd, Merritt, 184, 186
Hurdalek, George, 165
Hurley, Harold, 170, 171, 193, 194
Huston, John, 35, 109, 127, 128, 221
Hyman, Bernard, 139

Ince, Thomas, 8
Ingraham, J.H., 181

Jackson, Charles R., 119, 120
Jennings, Talbot, 137

Jewison, Norman, 103, 104
Johnson, Lyndon B., 195
Johnson, Minnie, 89
Johnson, Nunnally, 91, 93
Johnston, Eric, 36, 37, 82, 90, 103, 106, 112, 145, 163, 164, 176, 177, 185, 197, 202
Jones, David D., 36
Jones, Christopher, 44
Jones, Grover, 193

Kantor, MacKinlay, 31
Kaufman, Edward, 77
Kaye, Danny, 111
Kazan, Elia (Gadge), 67–69, 81, 82, 145, 173, 175–77
Kearney, Patrick, 149
Keighley, William, 13, 14
Kennedy, Bobby, 27, 29, 112
Kerr, Deborah, 123
Kibbee, Guy, 53
Kiesler, Hedy (Lamar), 71, 72, 75
Koch, Howard, 49
Koenig, William, 24, 31
Koerpel, 71
Korngold, Erich Wiolfgang, 13
Kram, Stanley, 74
Krim, Arthur, 185

Lamar, Hedy, 71, 72, 74
Landau, Martin, 157
Landru, Henri Desire, 133
Lange, Dorothea, 91
Lardner, Ring, Jr., 61
LaRue, Emily, 206
Lasky, Jesse L., 35, 181
Laszlo, Alazar, 193
Laughton, Charles, 137, 138
Laurents, Arthur, 117, 157
Lean, David, 7, 43–46, 115–17, 138, 221, 222
Lebeau, Madeline, 50, 51
Lederer, Charles, 95
Lehman, Ernest, 165, 197, 198
Leigh, Janet, 153, 188
Leigh, Rowland V., 13
Leigh, Vivien, 109, 173
LeMay, Alan, 159
Lemmon, Jack, 21, 105, 106, 163
Lengyel, Melchior, 139
Lewenstein, Oscar, 187
Lewin, Albert, 137
Lewton, Val, 88, 90
Licht, Martin, 73, 75
Linden, Michael, 40–42, 104, 206
Lindner, Dr. Robert H., 155
Littlefeather, Sasheen, 160
Lloyd, Frank, 137
Lopert, Ilya, 111, 113, 187, 188

Lord, Father Daniel H., 10, 112
Lord, Robert, 53
Lubitsch, Ernst, 63–66, 112, 139, 140, 193, 194, 221
Lucas, George, 159
Lundigan, William, 145, 146
Lunt, Alfred, 63
Luraschi, Luigi, 66, 105, 107, 119–22, 149–51, 154, 174, 177, 180, 181, 182, 187, 195, 196

MacArthur, Charles, 95, 139
MacEwen, Walter, 14, 15, 68, 175
Machaty, Gustav, 71, 73, 74
MacKenzie, Aeneas, 181
MacLaine, Shirley, 21, 105, 106, 185
MacMurray, Fred, 21
Mamoulian, Rouben, 130
Mandell, David, 32
Mandl, Frederick, 71, 75
Mankiewicz, Joseph L., 17–19, 221
March, Fredric, 31, 32, 63
Mareschal, Jacques, 155
Marion, Francis, 77, 82, 153
Markey, Gene, 23
Marlowe, Hugh, 17
Marshall, Herbert, 193
Marshall, Martin, 82
Marshman, D.M., 179
Mason, James, 157
Massey, Raymond, 67
Masterson, Father William Francis, 176, 189
Mayer, Louis, 36, 37, 61, 72, 129, 131, 137, 138, 140, 174
Mayo, Archie, 32, 53
Mazursky, Paul, 223
McBride, Joseph, 28, 30, 112, 113, 121, 163, 164, 180, 221
McCambridge, Mercedes, 190
McCarey, Leo, 123–25, 186
McCarthy, Joseph R., 29
McCrea, Joel, 184
McDermid, Finlay, 67–69
McDonough, J.R., 123–25
McKenzie, 170, 171, 206
McKinney, Mae, 146
McMurtry, Larry, 99
McNicholas, Archbishop John T., 66, 112
Melniker, Ben, 40
Melnicker, Harold, 59
Menjou, Adolphe, 53, 98
Merrill, Gary, 17
Metzger, Charles R., 72, 75, 206
Milestone, Lewis, 95, 98, 138
Millan, Victor, 189
Milland, Ray, 119–21
Millar, Stuart, 27–29

Miller, Seton I., 13, 106
Milliken, Carl E., 72, 78–80, 171
Milne, Peter, 53
Mineo, Sal, 155, 156
Mirisch, Walter, 103, 104, 112, 183–85
Mitchell, Thomas, 167
Murch, Walter, 189
Murphy, Morris, 206

Narcejac, Thomas, 195
Newman, Paul, 91, 99, 101
Nichols, Dudley, 47, 145, 167
Nichols, Mike, 197–99
Nizer, Louis, 198
Novak, Kim, 111, 157, 195, 196
Nugent, Frank S., 159, 168

Oates, Warren, 103
Oberon, Merle, 184
Odlum, Floyd, 142
Olsen, Nancy, 179
Orry-Kelly, 111
Osborn, Paul, 67–69
Osborne, John, 187
Osmond, Cliff, 111
O'Connor, Una, 13
O'Neal, Frederick, 146
O'Neil, Bob, 189
O'Toole, Peter, 115, 117

Pallette, Eugene, 13
Pangborn, Franklin, 61, 66
Pasternak, Joseph, 105
Patterson, Matt, 206
Paxton, John, 59
Peck, Gregory, 81
Penn, Arthur, 39, 160
Perkins, Tony, 153
Perrin, Nat, 130
Phillips, Rutherford T., 100
Pickford, Mary, 179
Plunkett, Walter, 63
Poitier, Sidney, 103, 104
Ponti, Carlo, 39, 40
Powell, Michael, 56
Preminger, Otto, 10, 106, 185, 186

Qualen, John, 95
Quigley, Martin, 10, 112

Rackin, Marty, 99, 100
Rafaelson, Samson, 193
Raguse, Charles A., 142, 143
Raine, Norman Reilly, 13
Rains, Claude, 13, 49, 51, 130
Randall, Tony, 111
Rathbone, Basil, 13

Ravetch, Irving, 99, 100
Raye, Martha, 133
Reagan, Charles M., 121
Rebello, Stephen, 153, 154, 221
Redgrave, Vanessa, 40
Reid, Cliff, 47
Reid, Peter, 67, 206
Reid, Wallace, 8
Reisch, Walter, 139
Reisz, Karel, 187
Rhodes, Eric, 77, 79
Richardson, Tony, 187
Ripley, Clements, 109
Ritt, Martin, 99
Ritter, Thelma, 17
Rivkin, Charles, 202
Roach, Hal, 83, 142
Roberts, Stephen, 169
Robertson, Cliff, 27, 29, 30
Robinson, Casey, 49
Robson, Mark, 47
Rogers, Ginger, 77
Rogoz, Zvonimir, 71, 74
Ross, Frank, 141
Rózsa, Miklos, 120
Ryskind, Morrie, 95

Sandrich, Mark, 77
Saunders, George, 17, 130, 131
Schaffner, Franklin J., 27, 185
Schellhorn, Edward, 99, 100,101, 187, 188
Schenck, Joseph , 81
Schlesinger, John, 187
Schlom, Marshall, 154
Schmidlin, Rick, 189
Schmidt, Eddie, 206
Schmus, Herbern van, 206
Schrader, Paul, 159
Schreiber, Sidney, 40, 42, 74, 75, 164, 199, 206
Schulman, Irving, 155
Scola, Katherine, 23
Scorsese, Martin, 159
Scott, Adrian, 59, 61
Seitz, John, 39
Sellers, Peter, 111
Selznick, David O., 85, 86, 88–90, 109, 177, 221
Selznick, Irene, 124
Dr. Seuss (Theodore Geisel), 155
Shakespeare, William, 2, 3, 203
Sharaf, Irene, 199
Sherwood, Robert E., 31, 32
Shumlin, Herman, 183
Shurlock, Geoffrey, 11, 24, 28, 29, 40–44, 46, 59, 64, 65, 68, 73, 77, 79, 82, 89, 99–101, 103–7, 111, 113, 115–17, 125, 130, 131, 139, 153–56, 160, 161, 164, 168, 170, 173, 177, 181, 182, 184–91, 195–99, 202, 205, 206
Silliphant, Stirling, 103, 104, 223
Sillitoe, Alan, 187
Silverman, Stephen M., 44, 46, 83, 117, 222
Simon, Neil, 22
Sistrom, Joe, 129, 130
Sobel, Lee, 10
Solow, Eugene, 141
Southon, A.E., 181
Spiegel, Sam, 43, 45, 46, 115–17
Stanwick, Barbara, 23, 24
Stefano, Joseph, 153
Steiger, Rod, 103, 104
Steinbeck, John, 67, 68, 91, 92, 141, 143
Sterling, Donald J., 97
Stern, Stewart, 155, 156
Sternberg, Josef von, 149
Stevens, George, 149
Stevenson, Adlai, 27
Stewart, James, 129, 130, 157, 195, 196
Stroheim, Erich von, 57, 179
Swanson H.N. "Swanie," 77
Sylbert, Richard, 199

Tamiroff, Akim, 189
Taylor, Dwight, 77
Taylor, Elizabeth, 149, 150, 197, 199
Taylor, Samuel A., 195
Taylor, William Desmond, 8
Terrell, Don S., 40, 42
Thalberg, Irving, 8, 10, 137
Thompson, Lester, 140
Thornton, A. Roland, 176, 177
Trauner, Alexandre, 105
Trilling, Steve, 68, 69
Truman, Harry S, 27, 145
Trumbo, Dalton, 61
Tucker, Robert, 142
Turman, Lawrence, 27, 28

Valenti, Jack, 41, 42, 103, 112, 197–99, 202, 203
Varney, Bill, 189
Vidal, Gore, 27–30, 185
Vizzard, Jack, 37, 41, 68, 69, 115, 117, 134, 154, 175–77, 202, 205, 206, 222
Vogel, Robert, 40–42

Waine, John, 187
Wallace, George C., 8, 27
Waller, Arthur O., 89, 90
Wallis, Hal, 13, 24, 49–51, 53, 106, 107, 109, 127
Walston, Ray, 111
Warner, Harry, 24

Warner, Jack L., 13–15, 23–26, 49–51, 68, 128, 142, 155–57, 198
Wasserman, Lew, 42, 197
Watkins, Maureen Dallas, 169
Wayne, John, 159, 167
Webb, Kenneth S., 77
Weisbart, David, 155
Welles, Orson, 57, 124, 133, 189, 191
Wexler, Haskell, 199
White, James H., 7
White, Gordon S., 74
White, Jane, 145
Wilcoxon, Henry, 181
Wilde, Hagar, 47
Wilder, Billy, 21, 39, 57, 64, 66, 105, 106, 111–13, 119–22, 139, 140, 163, 164, 179, 180, 221, 222
Wilkerson, W. R., 86
Williams, Joy, 74
Williams, Tennessee, 173-175
Wilson, Michael, 43, 45, 46, 115, 149
Wilson, Carey, 130, 137
Wilson, Dorothy Claude, 181
Wilstatch, Frederick, 206
Wingate, James, 23–26, 53, 54, 57, 58, 64–66, 77, 79, 80, 170, 171, 206
Winters, Shelley, 149, 150
Wright, Teresa, 32
Wurtzel, Sol, 8, 10
Wyatt, Jane, 82
Wyler, William (Willy), 31, 32, 109, 183, 184

Yost, Dorothy, 77
Youngstein, Max, 28, 30

Zanuck, Darryl F. (Mark Canfield), 17, 19, 23, 24, 26, 81–83, 91, 92, 93, 145, 147
Zinnemann, Fred, 198
Zugsmith, Albert, 189
Zukor, Adolf, 170, 171

www.ingramcontent.com/pod-product-compliance
Lightning Source LLC
Chambersburg PA
CBHW070134080526
44586CB00015B/1683